Gender, Planning and the Policy Process

Policy, Planning and Critical Theory

Series Editor: **Paul Cloke**
University of Bristol, UK

This major new series focuses on the relevance of critical social theory to important contemporary processes and practices in planning and policy-making. It demonstrates the need to incorporate state and governmental activities within these new theoretical approaches, and focuses on current trends in governmental policy in Western states, with particular reference to the relationship between the centre and the locality, the provision of services, and the formulation of government policy.

Titles published in the series include

Policy and Change in Thatcher's Britain
Paul Cloke

The Global Region: Production, State Policies and Uneven Development
David Sadler

Selling Places: The City as Cultural Capital, Past and Present
C Philo and G Kearns

Globalized Agriculture: Political Choice
Richard Le Heron

Forthcoming titles in the series

The Power of Apartheid: Territoriality and Government in South African Cities
Jennifer Robinson

Uneven Reproduction: Industry, Space and Society
Andrew Pratt

Gender, Planning and the Policy Process

Jo Little

University of the West of England, Bristol, UK

PERGAMON

UK	Elsevier Science Ltd, The Boulevard, Langford Lane, Kidlington, Oxford OX5 1GB, England
USA	Elsevier Science Inc., 660 White Plains Road, Tarrytown, New York 10591-5153, USA
JAPAN	Elsevier Science (Japan), Tsunashima Building Annex, 3-20-12 Yushima, Bunkyo-ku, Tokyo 113, Japan

First edition 1994

Library of Congress Cataloging in Publication Data
Little Jo.
Gender, planning, and the policy process/Jo Little.—
1st ed.
p. cm.—(Policy, planning, and critical theory)
Includes bibliographical references and index.
1. Women—Government policy.   2. Social
planning.   3. Women—Social conditions.
4. Women—Economic conditions.   5. Sex role.
I. Title.   II. Series.
HQ1236 L58 1994
305. 42—dc20   93-49389

ISBN 0 08 040481 2 (Hardcover)
ISBN 0 08 040480 4 (Flexicover)

Printed in Great Britain by Galliard (Printers) Ltd, Great Yarmouth

Contents

Acknowledgements

Many people have helped in the preparation of this book. I should like to express my thanks to them all. I am especially grateful to those planners who took time to complete the questionnaire—particularly those who provided the extra information or comments which proved so valuable in writing the book. I am indebted to the women of Birmingham Cities for People, for providing me with insights on the experiences of women outside the formal planning process, and to the women of Bristol City Council's Women's Unit and to Andy May for their helpful comments. This book would never have been written without much support from students and colleagues at the University of the West of England, Bristol. I am grateful to the postgraduate students who elected to take the 'Social Inequality' course and who provided many useful and stimulating comments on their experiences as Local Authority planners. I should also like to thank Helen Price for her patient librarian services, Tessa Coombes for invaluable word processing advice and Ron Griffiths for early comments on the proposal and for providing much support in shared teaching.

Outside the University I have been supported and encouraged by friends and family who will no doubt be as pleased as I am to see the completion of this book. Thanks to Paul Cloke, in his capacity as editor and friend, for giving me the confidence to begin. Sarah Whatmore, Jan Penrose, Peter Jackson, Andrew Harrison and Lindy Gibbon, deserve special mention. The feline distraction provided by Charlie has also helped to keep me sane (muddy paw prints and an uncanny ability to stand on the 'delete' key notwithstanding). Finally, special thanks to Dougal for 'professional advice and comments', for practical help and most of all for his care and support especially during the final stages of writing.

Jo Little, Bristol, 1994.

1

Introduction

Background

During the 1970s and 1980s the development of feminist perspectives emerged as a legitimate (if not widely adopted) area of work in academic disciplines such as sociology, geography, anthropology and political science. Challenging the invisibility of women (within these disciplines) and demonstrating the androcentricity or male-centred nature of existing approaches, feminist perspectives provided a new way of looking at the world and of redefining social, political and economic relations. An initial and exclusive focus on women's lives and women's roles gave way to a broader recognition of the importance of gender relations in the understanding of social processes and outcomes. Into the early 1990s feminist perspectives continue to highlight and explain gender inequality and women's subordination. Moreover, they have begun to contribute directly to other mainstream theoretical discussions within the different disciplines (see, for example, recent contributions by feminist geographers to debates on postmodernism—Bondi, 1990; McDowell, 1991).

Despite these major gains, it must be acknowledged that progress towards a general acceptance of feminist perspectives and their contribution to knowledge remains patchy. Large areas of work within and across disciplines still remain closed to the recognition of feminist approaches and even hostile to any discussion of gender inequality. It is also true that links between theory and practice have not been substantially developed. It is generally accepted that feminist approaches in academia evolve from the raising of political consciousness inspired by the feminist movement. Notwithstanding this fundamental relationship, it is fair to argue that more recent developments in feminist theory in academia have apparently contributed little to policy initiatives.

These main characteristics, the uneven development of feminist perspectives and the poor links between theory and practice, have provided important inspirations for this book. Planning, as an academic subject, may be counted amongst those disciplines that have been slow to adopt feminist approaches—both in terms of the recognition of women's inequality and gender divisions *and* the development of feminist theory. Despite close links between planning and geography, planning has been very reluctant to take up the sorts of debates that have increasingly characterised geography over the past ten years. Yet planning is ideally placed to initiate, encourage and reinforce links between theory and practice. With a direct input into the policy process, planning has the potential to ensure that the development of feminism as an academic discipline stands not only to learn from but also to contribute to policy formation and implementation.

Clearly feminism and a broad based concern for improving women's lives has been a motivating factor in some areas of planning practice and many examples of policies that have been inspired by women's needs spring readily to mind. These examples have been drawn on by those working in planning education and research as demonstrations of 'good practice' (albeit in a largely *ad hoc* fashion) and are discussed in this book. But what has been missing from both the practice and study of planning has been a sustained and integrated commitment to the development of wider feminist perspectives. Thus individual policies have not been able to draw on, or indeed inform, debates on the nature and causes of women's inequality and the absence of such debates has perpetuated the current emphases and priorities within contemporary planning, and helped obscure their male bias. In addition, the lack of an identifiable and coherent feminist approach (or set of approaches) within planning has meant that those initiatives that *have* been attempted have been developed largely in isolation. It has been difficult for individual policies to be seen within the framework of wider strategies for addressing inequality or pursuing equal opportunity.

This book, then, seeks to provide a feminist perspective on the planning process and on specific areas of planning policy. In doing so it will incorporate theoretical debates on gender divisions and gender inequality, discussions from academic literature on women's needs and the planning system, and practical examples of policies that have recognised and/or reinforced women's disadvantage. In applying an understanding or interpretation of gender inequality to the planning system and to the everyday formation and implementation of policy, this book hopes to make an important contribution. It is argued throughout that women's subordination within the built environment is a consequence of the operation of gender relations in society as a whole and that, therefore, attempts to understand the implications of planning *per se* on women's inequality must acknowledge the way planning reinforces and is shaped by broader gender relations. In short, it is only possible to comprehend the role of planning in addressing women's inequality from a starting point that recognises the underlying causes of that inequality. This book maintains that such an understanding itself can only be achieved through an explicitly feminist approach that focuses on gender relations.

The absence of texts on gender or women and planning makes it quite tempting (and in some ways justifiable) to produce a book that simply documents past and present examples of planning initiatives aimed at 'women's needs'. There is no doubt that such a book would fill a gap. This approach would, however, be to ignore the over-riding aim of *this* book; the development of a feminist perspective on planning involving the interpretation of the policy process and its outcome in the context of a system of gender relations. This dialogue between theory and practice is essential if we are ever to do more that just record planning's positive contribution to alleviating women's inequality. If we are to really explain not only how planning can and does affect positive changes in women's experiences within the built and natural environment but also how it reinforces existing inequality (and creates new divisions) then we need to ground our observations of planning's practical role in feminist theory. This, as described below, involves more than simply producing a check-list of planning policies for women. It demands that we recognise (or at least start to explore) the basic causes of women's inequality and how they are expressed within society and within the planning process.

It is important at the outset to provide a number of definitions and in doing so to establish the boundaries of the book. To this end the first task is to clarify what exactly is meant by a feminist perspective. Chapter 2 will look in detail at certain issues and concepts that have characterised debates *within* feminism and that are pertinent to the problem of definition—in effect exploring different feminisms. The purpose here is to describe in a wide ranging fashion the key ways in which feminist approaches differ from non-feminist approaches. Some of the principle objectives inherent in a feminist perspective will be briefly outlined and while it is recognised that there is not one but several feminist perspectives, discussion will concentrate on the 'unity of purpose' that these differing perspectives incorporate (Little *et al.*, 1988). In introducing debates around what constitutes a feminist approach, the following section will draw quite heavily on recent work in geography.

What is a Feminist Perspective?

Feminist perspectives involve a specific focus on the lives and experiences of women—not as 'insignificant others' or as somehow non-conformists to a male norm—but as 'equal' members of society with legitimate ways of perceiving the world. Feminist perspectives challenge the automatic assumption for women's actions and problems to be judged against male preferences and expectations. They reject many of the divisions that a male production of knowledge has pre-supposed—divisions, for example, between subjective and objective reality that determine which (or rather whose) experiences are seen as important in terms of the organisation of society.

Feminist perspectives incorporate a strong commitment to change and to a re-evaluation of our priorities which would emerge from an appreciation of the legitimacy and meaning of women's lives. Feminism is seen, crucially, not simply as a theoretical position or approach but as a political strategy aimed at improving and validating women's experiences. Central to the evolution of both theory and practice within feminism is a recognition of the importance of male power in society. Implicit within the commitment to change which lies at the heart of feminist perspectives is an attack on the basis and expression of such power.

In trying to be more specific than this as to the nature of feminist perspectives one quickly runs into areas of potential division between feminisms. The basis for such divisions is, as Snitow (1990) believes, the inevitable inconsistency within feminism. This 'inconsistency' manifests itself in the "common divide" between the need to

> "build the identity of 'woman' and give it solid political meaning and the need to tear down the very category 'woman' and dismantle its all-too-solid history" (Snitow, 1990, p. 9).

Chapter 2 takes up this debate and demonstrates its relevance not only to the development of feminist theory but also to the direction and emphasis of feminist political activity. It is sufficient here to recognise the existence of diversity within feminist perspectives and to note that such diversity has an important role within the policy process.

Thus far, in describing the purpose of the book and in outlining some of the unifying aspects of feminist approaches, discussion has centred on the problems, needs and activities of **women**. In the thematic chapters that follow the focus is on the relationship between **women's** experiences and on the implications of specific planning policies for the quality and content of **women's** lives. Yet the title of this book is *Gender*, Planning and the Policy Process. This apparent anomaly reflects another key issue in the development of feminist theory and the evolution of feminist perspectives in academic debate. It is an issue which is clearly demonstrated in the history of the adoption of feminist approaches in geography.

Early feminist research and writing within geography was concerned primarily with the invisibility of women—their virtual absence from what were seen as legitimate areas/subjects of study. Thus work by geographers such as Tivers (1978), Palm and Pred (1974), Hanson and Hanson (1976) and the Women and Geography Study Group (1984) sought to 'put women on the map' by describing the reality of their experiences and demonstrating how many of the issues studied as 'geography' often had very different meanings for the lives of women than they had for the lives of men. Such work provided much valuable information on the characteristics of women's roles and while it can undoubtedly be criticised for ignoring important differences *between* women, it marked a major first step towards a feminist geography.

The major limitation of early feminist analysis of women's roles was that they failed to provide *reasons* for women's inequality. Gender roles moreover, were interpreted as somehow given and as operating within fixed parameters. There was thus no basis on which to challenge women's subordination since little progress had been made towards establishing the underlying causes.

During the early 1980s feminist geographers began to argue the need to look beyond the identification and description of women's roles towards some sort of explanation of their inequality. To do so, they asserted, it was essential to move away from focusing entirely on women and to begin to look at gender. In other words women's inequality should be theorised not in isolation but in the context of the operation of gender relations and of male power over women. Patriarchy, the term used to describe male control over women, was seen as fundamental to the explanation of women's position in society. At the same time it was also recognised that gender relations themselves were cross-cut by other social divisions within society, primarily those of class and race.

Debates concerning the relative importance of different forms of social division developed and feminist geographers were divided over the relationship between, in particular, patriarchy and class. Despite these differences (which, again, are elaborated on in Chapter 2) there was a general agreement on the importance of patriarchy to the lives and experiences of women and of its key role in shaping gender relations. Agreement has also been widespread as to the need to explore gender relations in order to explain women's inequality — in short to examine the relationship between men and women as the basis for women's subordination.

It was noted earlier that planning as an academic discipline has been slow to incorporate a specific emphasis on women or to apply feminist approaches. Consequently progress in the development of feminist analysis has been very limited — what attempts that have been made to focus on women have mainly followed the approach taken in earlier geographical work (and by no means redundant today), namely a descriptive approach which aims to identify the problems faced by women in relation to the roles they perform. Planning has, of course, been particularly interested in the reproduction of these problems within the built and 'planned' environments.

By including 'gender' within the title of this book and by focusing throughout on gender relations, I hope to underline the importance of the sort of debates that have accompanied the evolution of feminist perspectives in geography (and elsewhere) to planning. Attempts to understand women's relationship with planning; the effects of policy decisions on women's lives, the inequality that results from certain emphases and priorities within planning and the role of the planning system in *improving* women's experiences in the built environment, must recognise the importance of gender relations both within and outside the planning system. An important tool in this recognition, as feminist geographers have argued, is an awareness of the importance of patriarchy.

Perhaps an initial glance at the content of this book would appear to contradict this argument, with chapters on Women and Employment, Women's Accessibility etc. Despite the importance of explaining women's inequality in the context of gender relations, there is still a need, particularly with respect to planning, to identify the problems women face and the steps that have and could be taken to address them. The book, therefore, highlights what are seen to be the main issues for women within defined policy areas. It also looks at existing and potential policy responses. Emphasis is placed, however, on explaining issues—on locating the problems experienced by women in the built environment within a discussion of wider causes and manifestations of their inequality. Consequently, the treatment of women's safety, for example, not only identifies the extent and nature of women's fear but also attempts to ground that fear within an appreciation of the underlying exertion of male power over women from which it originates. Any attempts to identify a planning response to women's fear, it is contested, is dependent on an understanding of these fundamental 'causes'.

Defining Planning

Although perhaps less contestable than 'feminist approach', the term 'planning' as used in this book also requires some explanation. Defining the boundaries of planning and the limits of planners' influence is a long standing problem. It is a problem, moreover, of particular relevance today in the context of the major changes in the balance of power between central and local government with the so-called rolling back of the state. Planning as a local state function has in many senses seen a considerable weakening of its influence over the past eight to ten years as legislative, administrative and ideological constraints have been placed on its operation (see Cloke and Little, 1990 and Thornley, 1991 for a discussion). This weakening of power is evident, as will be argued later, in planning's ability to respond to women's needs.

Defining the scope of planning by reference simply to its statutory functions such as the production of structure and local plans and the control of development is straight forward enough (see Rydin, 1993). Identifying planning's exact influence within these processes is a harder task. Equally problematic is deciding where the lack of action by planners (where action is possible) has been influential. It is sometimes argued that planning has little scope for positive action within the built environment, and that it is a reactive as opposed to a proactive force. Thus planners can rarely initiate development but must 'carry the can' for its consequences. This perception of planning's power has been reinforced by recent central government moves to 'free up' the development system and empower the private developer (see, for example, the formation of Development Corporations) and by the reduction in money available for public services at the level of the local state (see Colenutt, 1990).

Others argue somewhat less pessimistically that despite the constraints imposed by 'new right thinking' and the free market, planning can do much to maintain the public interest. Thornley (1991) in his review of planning under Thatcherism, suggests that planning can act positively by, for example

> "repealing unwanted Circulars, ensuring that all bodies are democratic, increasing public involvement, giving greater importance to social and economic criteria and extending joint venture, partnership and planning gain approaches" (Thornley, 1991, p. 226).

Above all, planning can exist to provide an alternative to the free market even if its alternative is not always or wholly acted upon.

The opportunity still exists in, for example, the writing of a local plan, for planners to provide a broad vision for shaping our urban and rural areas. Despite long standing and continued attempts by some to restrict planning to a technical activity concerned entirely with land use, there remains a broad concensus that planning should concern itself with protecting the *public* interest (against that of the developer) and addressing issues of social equity. Just how far it should go down this path is sometimes questioned—especially in the context of what are frequently portrayed as 'minority interests' such as gay and women's issues. This does not negate the essential legitimacy of planning's stake in addressing social goals. The belief here is that, albeit within firmly defined parameters, planning does retain a potency in at least working towards greater equality in society.

This is not, however, to argue that the lack of equity or the neglect of the public interest is necessarily the fault of planners or of the planning system. While planners may have the ability to create a vision and to work towards that vision, in actually advancing it they are largely dependent on the co-operation of 'other interests'. Money available to local government planners has been systematically reduced under the Conservative government and consequently social goals are increasingly reliant on 'planning gain'—the attaching of non- or negative profit making requirements (from rented/

low cost housing to crèch facilities or children's play space) to development schemes as a condition of approval.

Finally, it must be remembered that 'planning' is more than simply a statutory function. The comments so far have been directed largely at the local government planner—partly because this is the particular area of planning of concern to this book. We cannot ignore the fact, however, that land-use planning is something done by an increasingly wide group of people in public and private agencies and businesses. Companies with very different interests—from Tesco to British Rail and from housing associations to leisure developers—are involved in land development and consequently employ planners to work in their interests. It would be wrong to assume that all 'planners' share common goals and interests and that all 'planning' is working in the same direction. Frequently planners are working in opposing ways to secure very different aims.

In terms of the scope of planning anticipated within this book, quite a heavy emphasis is placed on written documentation. Local plans and, in particular, the new unitary development plans are used to identify the extent to which planners have incorporated either a direct or an indirect emphasis on women's needs within their policy statements. This examination is undertaken over a range of policy areas within such documents rather than focusing simply on 'women's sections' where they exist. One of the central concerns of this book is to identify the extent to which planning, almost by default, can act against women's interests and in doing so help maintain the unequal distribution of power between women and men. This clearly involves looking beyond the explicit recognition of gender issues and equal opportunities within planning policies in a more general examination of the priorities and principles that characterise past and contemporary directions.

The original research included here is not simply in the form of the analysis of written documentation. Interviews were undertaken with a number of local government planners and councillors. Their views form an important input to the discussions.

This book is concerned with more than just the recognition (or lack of it) of women's needs in planning policies. It is interested in women's wider relationship with the decision-making process. This stems, again, from the desire to *explain* women's inequality within the built environment. It is asserted throughout the book—and especially in Chapter 4—that the general reluctance of planning to recognise the gender implications of problems and decisions and women's needs in particular is in part a function of the actual process of policy making and not simply its content. Women's exclusion from decision making positions, especially at the higher levels, means that their problems often go unrecognised and consequently their demands are not legitimised. There are many obstacles to women's participation in the policy process and at their root lies the powerlessness of women that results from patriachical gender relations. These obstacles, and their cause, must be recognised if planning is to strive for and achieve greater equality for women in the planned enviroment.

Chapter Contents

From the description provided so far it is quite clear that the scope of the book is potentially vast. The approach that has been advocated necessitates the inclusion of both theoretical debates on the nature of feminist approaches *and* practical examples of legislation, policy and practice in planning. Moreover, the commitment to explaining women's inequality involves looking, as noted in the previous section of this introduction, beyond 'policies for women' as formulated and implemented by planning departments, to incorporate a more comprehensive analysis of planning's responsibilities. Obviously there is a need to be selective both in terms of the theoretical material included *and* the discussion of 'planning' initiatives. This is reflected in the structure of the book and the decision to include a mixture of more thematic chapters on feminist theory, power and basic location and land use together with a number of issue-based chapters which go into more specific detail on a variety of topic areas (namely employment, transport and housing).

Before going on to outline the content of the individual chapters it is important to say something about the sources of information used in the course of writing this book. The discussion of feminist theory obviously relies heavily on literature from other academic disciplines—partly because of the scarcity, already referred to, of work in this area from a planning background, and partly because of the irrelevance of disciplinary boundaries in understanding the concepts involved. Particular use has been made here, as noted, of feminist work within geography. The evolution of feminist approaches in geography has incorporated a strong emphasis on womens use of space and their relationship with the built environment. These debates are of immense importance in developing a feminist approach within planning. The relationship between the two areas of work is especially evident in Chapter 3 in the discussion of women's experience of suburban development, new towns and the changing urban form. The more general debates on feminism and women's access to power and decision making, Chapters 2 and 4, rely more heavily on literature from a range of subject areas such as sociology, politics and anthropology.

The topic-based chapters, while making reference to the available literature and academic research that is relevant, draw to a much larger extent on policy documentation and original sources of material. The review of planning policies in the specific sectors is based partly on published plans and other documentation and also on the views and beliefs of planners themselves. As was implied earlier, in understanding the perception and treatment of equality issues we need to look beyond written documentation. Simply relying on policy statements potentially obscures important conflicts between officers in the recognition of inequality, for example conflict that may fundamentally influence a planning authority's approach and their own interpretation of policy. So, as well as identifying initiatives aimed at women's needs, research was undertaken to explore more thoroughly local authorities' commitment to gender equality through, for example, the promotion of training and awareness amongst staff, the appointment of women and the support of women's units, committees etc.

This information was obtained through a questionnaire survey of all county, metropolitan and district planning authorities in England. The questionnaire generated a good response (64% of all authorities, 66% of districts, 58% of metropolitan councils, 73% of London boroughs and 79% of counties) and provided a great deal of important information—in addition to the standard answers many respondents included extra comments which proved invaluable in identifying the extent to which 'gender issues' were recognised and, indeed, where differing views existed *within* the authority or department as to the role or value of a separate focus on women. As well as from the questionnaire, information was also obtained from interviews with policy makers *outside* planning departments. Included here were representatives from women's units and community groups and also councillors.

The major part of the original data is used in the later chapters of the book in discussions on women's access to decision making and on specific policy areas. Chapters 2 and 3 on the other hand, are devoted to establishing the broader theoretical and contextual background within which a feminist analysis of planning can take place. Chapter 2 therefore explores a number of theoretical issues in the context of defining more clearly the nature of women's subordination and identifying the contribution of feminist approaches to the understanding of gender inequality. The concept of patriarchy is introduced and its essential role in shaping and maintaining gender relations and as a tool of feminist analysis examined. In discussing the notion of patriarchy, Chapter 2 looks in some depth at the underlying power relations that exist between women and men and attempts to identify their origins. This chapter reinforces the importance of debates on the evolution and operation of gender relations for our understanding of women's relationship to and treatment by the planning system.

Chapter 3 goes on to look more directly at women's use of space within the built environment. Initially concentrating on broad land use issues, the chapter considers the gender implications of the development of the industrial and post-industrial city together with the growth of suburban living. With reference to the theoretical debates incorporated in Chapter 2, this chapter explores the way in which urban growth, particularly residential growth, has been strongly influenced by, and in turn has reproduced a set of, gender stereotypes. These stereotypes have incorporated assumptions about the appropriate roles for men and women reflecting the dominence of patriarchal gender relations. The chapter argues that the development of the built environment, and planning's role within it have reinforced the importance of the family and of the gender division of labour. Women's activities within the planned environment have been constrained as a result of the expectations that have both contributed to and grown from the social and physical organisation of the domestic household.

In this context, Chapter 3 places considerable emphasis on the planning of suburban residential development and on new towns in Britain. Both are seen as highly influential in contributing to the creation and maintenance of the domestic 'idyll' and to a particular organisation of family life. The chapter briefly mentions the attempts that have been made by women to reject conventional ideas concerning the organisation of space — and in particular residential environments within the city. Relevant here are 'experiments' in the design of new communities in which domestic roles and consequently the use of space in and around the home were organised along non-conventional lines. Also pertinent to this debate is the issue of gentrification and the extent to which this largely recent trend represents both a shift in the traditional organisation of the domestic household and a change in the gendered use of space.

In Chapter 4 attention turns to the planning process itself and to women's access to power within that process. Women's role in decision making is considered on a number of levels from national politics to local community groups. The purpose of the chapter is to demonstrate the extent to which women are excluded from the formal channels of planning and decision making in this country and to explore how this exclusion has resulted in the under representation of women's views. After looking at the participation of women in formal politics the chapter goes on to focus on the planning system. The representation of women as planners working within the decision-making process, as members of the community and as recipients of planning decisions is discussed. Particular attention is paid to the operation and effectiveness of formal channels for addressing women's needs (women's units and committees) and their relationship with the planning process. The main argument here is that women are denied access to decision making, especially at the more senior levels. In the light of the discussions in Chapters 2 and 3, it is maintained that this exclusion from decision making is a function of the lack of power experienced by women. Women's powerlessness is demonstrated not only in the absence of women from high level posts in planning but also in the low priority that is attached to supporting and maintaining women's committees and units as formal channels for representing women's needs.

Chapters 5, 6 and 7 follow broadly the same format. Each focuses on a particular sector of planning and explores the nature of gender inequality and the characteristics of women's needs within that sector. The contribution of policy to the problems experienced by women is examined and the potential role of planning in addressing these problems is outlined. Emphasis is placed within each of these chapters on establishing the links between gender inequalities and the resulting problems for women and the identification of practical planning responses. Accordingly, the chapters draw on a combination of theoretical/conceptual literature, existing policy analyses and original survey work.

The first of these topic-based chapters examines employment. Initially the chapter outlines the major trends in women's involvement in the labour market, identifying in particular the recent increases in the numbers of married women in paid work. The chapter then goes on to critique the various theoretical approaches that have been used to account for the involvement of women in the labour force. The inadequacies of existing, largely economic, explanations are outlined in arguing that women's role in paid work must be explained in the context of the operation of gender relations and of the balance of power between women and men. The influence of patriarchy in terms of both the entry of women into paid work *and* their experiences within the labour market is discussed with reference to various case studies.

The chapter then moves to a consideration of the contribution of policy initiatives to women's employment participation. National legislation affecting women's employment opportunities is reviewed, in particular legislation concerning equal pay and sex discrimination, and the broad direction of employment policy in Britain assessed. In the second part of this policy analysis the contribution of planning is discussed. As is recognised in the chapter, we must avoid unrealistic expectations of either planning's real or its potential role in addressing employment issues. The chapter, very importantly, establishes those areas of employment provision where planning is empowered to stimulate or direct real change. It subsequently examines the ways in which that change has affected the nature of women's employment provision.

Planning's influence over women's accessibility, the subject of Chapter 6, is perhaps more easily identifiable. Two major issues emerge in this chapter; firstly, the provision of transport and, secondly, the production of safe environments. Women's accessibility is seen as fundamentally related to these key planning related responsibilities. Both are areas in which existing work has acknowledged important gender implications. Attention is drawn, in the chapter, for example, to previous work on women's mobility and travel (see Pickup, 1988; Greico *et al.*, 1989) and on the constraints placed on women's accessibility by the threat and actuality of sexual violence (see Valentine, 1992; Trench and Jones, 1991). In planning and policy analysis too mobility/transport is one area where the particular nature of women's needs has been recognised.

This chapter builds on existing work in the area by providing a wide-ranging assessment of existing local authority policy. It demonstrates not only what initiatives are available to planners but also which are currently being supported and by whom. The chapter develops important links back to theoretical discussions around women's use of space and the constraints (particularly safety issues) on their mobility. Previous studies have either made no attempt to explain the constraints on women's accessibility or have seen them purely as a 'planning problem'. While not denying the improvements that can be offered through the planning system, it is important that these are not used to obscure the underlying causes of women's low levels of mobility. An understanding of the constraints on women's accessibility and the efficacy of responses to it must derive from an appreciation of the nature and causes of women's wider subordination.

The final topic-based chapter focuses on the issue of housing. Again, there is a growing body of research and literature on women and housing (see, for example, Austerberry and Watson, 1985; Watson, 1990; Matrix, 1984; Munro and Smith, 1989 and Roberts, 1990) including work on homelessness, access to housing, gentrification and design. While some of this work is descriptive in the 'women and' genre, some provides a very important feminist perspective on women's experience of housing that not only documents their inequality but also attempts to explain it. Existing work has established important links between women's experience of housing and planning policy. It has done so, however, in either an historic or a very generalised way (exceptions include Roberts, 1990) and there have been few attempts to examine the problems encountered by women in the housing market in the context of the operation of national and, in particular, local planning policies, or to suggest ways in which planning may help to alleviate some of the inequalities experienced by women.

As with the other topic based chapters, the discussion of housing reviews some of the most relevant established research. In doing so it recognises the importance of identifying historical trends in both women's experience and in housing policy. Two key areas emerge from the discussion of women's continuing inequality which are then taken up in depth in the remaining part of the chapter; firstly, women's *access* to housing and, secondly, housing *design*. Both areas have very clear-cut and immediate links into the planning process—although both are clearly influenced considerably by forces *beyond* planning.

Chapter 7 examines in detail the nature of women's disadvantage in terms of access to housing—incorporating here the problem of homelessness—and the layout and design of 'conventional' housing. Links are made, particularly in relation to design and the use of space, to Chapter 3 in an attempt to identify elements of the physical layout and construction of housing that reinforce women's disadvantage. Again the point is stressed that we need to look beyond these physical manifestations of women's inequality in order to understand their real causes and to appreciate planning's role.

The final chapter attempts to draw together some of the important conclusions of the book, reinforcing in doing so the essential aim of applying a feminist perspective to the study of planning and the policy process. It is easy, in dealing with what is such a potentially huge area of work, to get pre-occupied with the details of women's experiences and inequality. The conclusion recognises this problem and attempts to stand back from the detail of women's everyday lives in demonstrating what a feminist analysis can achieve in terms of our understanding and the possible reform of the planning system. Comments by planners (either from the questionnaire survey or from informal discussions) are used to identify the differing perceptions of individuals concerning the continuing inequality experienced by women and the role of planning in attempting to alleviate it. Such comments provide a broad indication of changing levels of awareness amongst planners of gender issues and of the commitment to future change (or not!).

The conclusions of the book, indeed its main messages, are both optimistic and pessimistic. In documenting the extent and nature of women's inequality in the planned environment one can not help but feel disheartened. Similarly, an understanding of the underlying causes of women's subordination together with an appreciation of the limited (and declining?) power of planning can encourage little but a sense of helplessness. But while the planning *system* itself may be ill-equipped to address women's overall disadvantage, it is clear that individuals, groups and organisations within it do retain a commitment to challenging the existing status quo. The way forward, as we shall see in the following chapters, may be through very piecemeal action—particularly from those working in 'conventional' planning posts. While this may be contributing little, on the face of it, to a reassessment of the balance of power within planning, it may result in a real improvement in the quality of life for some individuals.

In the course of teaching 'Social Inequality' to planners at The University of the West of England, Bristol, discussion returns time and time again to debates around the value of small-scale change versus the need for more fundamental shifts in social, in particular gender, relations. A final answer on the role and direction of planning within this debate is never found but agreement is generally reached on the importance of taking action, however small-scale. Hopefully the energy and strength of those working within planning will be sufficient to continue to fight for such action and to ensure that it fuels a growing appreciation of the need for change and at the same time helps to alleviate elements of women's disadvantage.

Whatever our assessment of the role of planning it is clear from the observations of this book that planning's contribution cannot be detached from wider changes in society. The extent to which planning can really influence gender equality is bound up in prevailing social attitudes and the struggle between the forces of capitalism and patriarchy. This highlights again the importance of developing feminist perspectives and through these perspectives recognising the interaction between planning and the wider forces of social and economic change.

2

Male Power and Women's Inequality

Introduction

In the introduction to her book, *Is the Future Female?*, Lynne Segal (1987) writes that:

> "After two decades of feminist research it is now easier to see that men globally have greater wealth, power and privilege than women....Everywhere... women remain considerably poorer and less educated than men, and are largely absent from positions of power in *all* political, economic and judicial institutions" (my emphasis) (Segal, 1987, pp. 2–3).

As this quote would suggest and as parts of the following chapters demonstrate, the need to 'prove' the existence of male power *per se* over women has receded. While we may argue over the extent and exact implications of male power, few would deny its existence. The emphasis of academic debate, as explained in Chapter 1, has shifted to looking at ways of explaining women's subordination and, in particular, identifying the basis of unequal power relations.

An extensive literature has recently emerged on the nature of male power and its key role within gender relations. The roots of this power together with its reproduction in past and contemporary society have been at the heart of wide-ranging theoretical discussions—many of which have considerable relevance here. The application of feminist perspectives to the study of planning and the policy process must incorporate, as was asserted in Chapter 1, an understanding of the underlying causes of women's inequality. This understanding must itself derive from an examination of male power and of the theoretical debates which surround its conceptualisation.

The purpose of this chapter, then, is to review various theoretical debates on the basis of women's relative powerlessness. The chapter aims, through this review, to identify the underlying roots of male power and to demonstrate how such power has been used to maintain women's subordination. There is clearly not time here to undertake an exhaustive review of all literature on the subject and the intention is simply to highlight key areas of debate in an attempt to demonstrate the range of arguments that have characterised the development and application of theory in this area.

Having examined different theoretical perspectives on the origins and expressions of male power over women, the chapter will go on to consider women's struggle for greater equality. The discussion will again explore theoretical debate but will also examine the practical expression of women's struggle for power in the evolution of feminism and the feminist movement. In identifying the characteristics of women's fight against male domination, it becomes clear that there are important divisions *within* feminism and between feminists. These 'internal' divisions represent differences not only in the emphasis and methods of political activity, but also in beliefs about the essential basis of women's subordination. The discussion of differences leads inevitably to a re-assessment of power relations between men and women and to a re-evaluation of theoretical perspectives.

In examining the issue of male power over women there are a number of themes that need to be explored—firstly, the conceptualisation of gender and the different frameworks that have been used in the social analysis of gender. How do gender divisions arise and how are they reinforced? Secondly, the translation of gender categories into gender relations— different theoretical positions on the way in which power relations are incorporated into and reproduced by gender divisions. And thirdly, the concept of patriarchy and how its use has cross-cut a range of different theoretical positions. This latter will include discussions around issues such as male violence and the control of women's sexuality.

In debating these themes the intention is not to produce a definitive answer on the question of women's subordination—indeed many of the discussions may appear inconclusive and open ended. The purpose is rather to move towards an appreciation of the main strengths and weaknesses of different theoretical frameworks within which gender relations have been unpacked/located. This is not to say that a view of the relative merits of different positions will not be expressed—it is clear that in terms of the arguments raised in this book, certain theoretical positions offer much more than others. It is, however, impossible in the space of just one chapter to provide a comprehensive review of relevant theory which would permit its conclusive acceptance or rejection. The driving force behind this chapter is the wish to demonstrate how much richer a feminist analysis of planning can be if part of that analysis incorporates theoretical debate of male power and control.

Theoretical Frameworks for the Analysis of Gender Divisions

The range of different theoretical perspectives for the study of gender relations put forward by feminist (and non-feminist) writers is often difficult to reconcile. Classifications tend to cross-cut one another in a confusing and at times apparently illogical way. Divisions are made in one 'set' of perspectives that are then reconstituted in another leaving considerable uncertainty as to what the key differences between theories actually are. A frequently used distinction in feminist theory is that between radical (or cultural as it is termed in the United States) and socialist perspectives—this distinction has proved particularly useful to those wishing to draw out the relationship between feminist theory and practice. Again, however, useful as it is, the radical/socialist divide obscures what some authors see as important theoretical distinctions and demonstrates that divisions constituted as a framework for the analysis of political activity may be very different from those arising from the construction of social theory.

Ultimately, of course, it is the need to convey certain ideas, not the building of elaborate classifications that is important. The key issue is how different theoretical perspectives have attempted to conceptualise gender relations (both internally and in relation to other variables) and what are seen as the main determinants of women's inequality. The following section puts forward a variety of different theoretical perspectives including biological determinism, Marxist theories and dual systems theory. In discussing the relative merits of different theoretical approaches reference is made to the work of Connell (1983, 1987) and to his notion of intrinsic and extrinsic theories of gender inequality. The divisions that Connell draws are particularly helpful here since they incorporate explicit references to the recognition and conceptualisation of male power over women. At the most simple level what Connell is seeking to do is to separate those theories which see the "direct power relations between men and women as the main determinant of women's oppression " (Connell, 1987, p. 41) (intrinsic theories) and those that see oppression as based *outside* patriarchal gender relations (extrinsic).

Biological determinism

Biological determinism, or biologism, as a school of thought derives from the belief that male and female are distinct, definable and separable biological categories which arise from a specific form of sexual reproduction. Biological determinism has been applied to the analysis of gender divisions with varying degrees of rigour and sophistication. While all proponents of the idea would subscribe to the biologically determined basis of gender and to the essential biological roots of male/female characteristics (aggressive males, submissive, gentle females and so on), there is some variation in opinion in relation to the extent to which biological categories may be mediated by social practice. On the one hand are those who believe that 'natural difference' or biology *determines* gender (Connell, 1987) and on the other those who argue that while biology establishes the *primary* difference between men and women, this difference is then built upon and reinforced by social practice.

The American feminist, Shulamith Firestone, argued strongly during the 1970s that women's oppression is grounded in the biological separation of men and women. Biological differences mean that women are dependent on men in the process of reproduction and child-rearing. Emotional bonds that develop between men and women increase women's vulnerability since they are the product of this unequal dependency relationship. The only possible departure from this state of affairs, Firestone argued, is the development of technologies that will fundamentally change the mode of reproduction (Firestone, 1979).

It is not necessary here to dwell on the principles of biological determinism. Some elements of, in particular, Firestone's arguments will be introduced again in discussions surrounding radical feminism. Before moving on, however, it is worth summarising the main weaknesses of the concept as this will help in the evaluation of alternative theories.

The main criticisms of biologistic theories is that they are reductionist — that is they reduce the differences between men and women to a single cause subsuming

"complex socially and historically constructed phenomena under the simple category of biological difference" (Barrett, 1980, p. 12).

As such, biological determinism plays little regard to history and can not accommodate within it the idea of change in the relationship between men and women. As well as being static, biologistic arguments remove the possibility of progress or resistance. In a sense they encourage passivity and acceptance since they present a fixed 'reality' which cannot (except through Firestone's changing technology) be broken down. What feminism and women's struggle against oppression are seeking to achieve is to this way of thinking unachievable since women's (and men's) position is fixed by their biology.

It is perhaps necessary to stress that in criticising biological reductionism the importance of biological difference in gender analysis is not being rejected. There is clearly a very strong relation between social practice and biology. The abuse of women's bodies and men's control over women's sexuality are, as is argued at some length later in the chapter, fundamental to the existence of male power and to women's subordination. The belief, however, that biology is the basis of gender relations is untenable.

Biological determinism serves largely to obscure the social construction of gender relations by seeing women's bodies not as the objective of male domination but as its source.

Sex role theory

Sex role theory rejects the idea that the basis of gender inequality rests on some form of 'natural difference' as advocated by biological determinism but claims rather that men and women are socialised into different roles. Individuals, groups and organisations all hold expectations as to the behaviour of men, women, boys and girls. At a very early age we are taught to conform to the prescribed roles and consequently socialised into the 'female' or 'male' role. Role theory as Connell writes:

> "offers a simple framework for describing the insertion of individuals into social relations. The basic idea is that this occurs by 'role learning', 'socialization' or 'internalization'. Thus feminine character is produced by socialization into the female role, masculine character by socialization into the male role—and deviants by some kind of failure in socialization" (Connell, 1987, p. 49).

While latterly discredited, role theory did, during the 1960s and 1970s, command considerable support and inspire a substantial literature. A particular focus of research concerned the translation of ideas about masculinity and femininity to children and the 'rewards' introduced to sustain stereotypes—the praising of boys for being tough and aggressive and of girls for being neat and tidy etc. Early feminist work on gender inequality gave a boost to the whole notion of role theory since, as noted in Chapter 1, much of the work did little more than articulate the differences between male and female roles. This being the case, however, it must be said that such work aimed very often simply to provide empirical information on men and women's lives rather than to explain the observed inequalities through the use of role (or any other) theory.

There are several major problems with role theory that make it unacceptable as a social theory for the explanation of gender inequality. First it is essentially a static theory which pays little attention to (and indeed cannot entertain) the empirical diversity in male and female roles over time and space. Linked to this is the failure of role theory to recognise lesbianism, male homosexuality, prostitution and male violence except as deviance from accepted roles. Secondly, role theory, when analysed in depth, dissolves inevitably into voluntarism. In other words the idea of rewarding conformity to roles and thus the process of socialisation rests on the question of individual will. The fact that socialisation happens in a particular way assumes that individuals wish to conform to and so endorse existing expectations of roles. Thirdly, a criticism which derives from the issue of voluntarism is that role theory is unable to incorporate the notion of power as a central feature of the relationship between men and women.

The categories of 'male' and 'female' are treated as different but essentially equal. Role theory does not, therefore, accommodate ideas of oppression and exploitation other than in the sense that we are all (women and men) oppressed at having to conform to gender roles.

The weaknesses outlined have caused theorists to reject biological determinism and role theory in the search for theories of gender difference that focus on gender relations. In doing so the concern is not with ideas of 'natural difference' or with socially prescribed behaviour patterns but more with the power relations which exist between men and women and with the social institutions and structures through which such power relations are maintained (Whatmore, 1991). It is to these theories that the next section now turns.

Marxist theories

The most important extrinsic theories of gender inequality are, so Connell recognises, Marxist theories which see class as the central feature of social structure and, at their simplest level, interpret women's oppression as essentially a by-product of the operation of the capitalist system. At one extreme traditional Marxist theoretical perspectives have ignored gender relations reducing all male/female relationships to those of capitalist relations of production. Within such analyses, women's position is seen as irrelevant on the grounds that it is the family and not the individual that is the basic unit of social stratification (Walby, 1990). It is men's rather than women's economic power that is significant and women's class position is determined by their relationship to a male breadwinner.

From the late 1970s, many feminist writers (for example, Barrett, 1980; Eisenstein, 1979; Hartmann, 1979) began to criticise traditional Marxist approaches, arguing that such simple class-interest theories were insufficient to explain women's particular situation. What was needed, they argued, was a theoretical perspective that recognised women's position in the family and the division of labour *within* the household. In their view, since relations of production could not exist without being reproduced then Marxist analyses needed to incorporate an understanding of the relations of reproduction. In this way it was possible for women's subordination to be linked systematically with economic exploitation under capitalism.

Work in this area has been very important in demonstrating the economic significance of housework and has contributed to an extensive and fruitful debate on domestic labour within the capitalist mode of production. There is insufficient space here for anything more than a fleeting reference to this debate but it has been well documented elsewhere (see, for example, Barrett, 1980; Delphy, 1984; Redclift and Migione, 1985).

Walby (1990, p. 11) suggests that in attempting to incorporate a specific focus on women's subordination within the sphere of reproduction, some feminists have used the concept of class to "capture the nature of inequalities between women and men". She draws attention to Delphy's arguments that housework is a form of production and that husbands expropriate the *productive* activity of their wives within the home (see Delphy, 1984). Firestone, in a more extreme form, also seeks to conflate the categories of class and gender—this time through the classification of all women as one class and all men as another. Such a division clearly has overtones of the biological determinism for which Firestone was criticised earlier.

In their orthodox form Marxist theories fail to offer an adequate framework for the understanding of gender relations and women's oppression. Even the incorporation of a direct focus on relations of production within the household as advocated by structural Marxists, though a major advance on simple class—interest theories, cannot effectively explain women's subordination. Such approaches do not, for example, articulate the link between gender and capitalism—in other words they do not explain the sexual nature of oppression. As Connell (1987) notes, social reproduction is not a theory but an "object of strategy" which is not robust enough to carry the "explanatory weight" that is placed upon it.

Ultimately critics argue that the fundamental flaw of more orthodox Marxist theories is their reduction of gender relations to capitalism. Gender inequality is seen not as separate to but deriving from capitalist social relations. What such critics believe is called for is a theory of gender inequality which is logically independent of class theory. Such a theory would provide a framework for the understanding of gender inequality based on power relations between men and women *as* men and women and not as members of particular classes.

Dual systems theory

Recognising that gender inequality is not reducible to class relations and that capitalism and patriarchy are distinct systems of social relations has prompted some theorists to adopt what have become known as dual systems approaches (see Hartmann, 1979). These approaches, self evidently, attempt to analyse gender inequality in the context of two essentially separate yet interacting systems (capitalism and patriarchy). The extent and character of interaction varies according to the different emphases within dual systems analysis but theorists generally sustain the distinction of patriarchy and capitalism by, as Walby (1990) suggests, allocating them to different levels of society. Thus feminists who advocate the analytical separation of capitalism and patriarchy may argue, for example, that global economic relations are formed by capitalism while the ideological basis of women's domestic role is a function of patriarchy. Barrett (1980) includes a useful critique of dual systems theories in Marxist feminist analysis which identifies how different authors have attempted to unite (or not) the analytically separate structures of capitalism and patriarchy.

Dual systems theories, while helping to establish the importance of patriarchal gender relations as distinct from capitalist social relations, incorporate a number of serious difficulties. The belief that capitalism and patriarchy are influential on different levels cannot be sustained. This then presents difficulties in understanding exactly how the two 'systems' interact—where do the boundaries of each lie and which is dominant? The structures of patriarchy that have been incorporated in dual systems theories have, moreover, tended to be limited, with little emphasis being placed on areas such as sexuality and male violence. Again, the work that has been produced from discussions around dual systems theories should not be dismissed out of hand. Important insights into what Eisenstein (1979) termed "capitalist patriarchy" have emerged, especially in the context of housework and the domestic division of labour. These insights, so Connell suggests, are going in the right direction and if they are regarded as

"first approximations within a general type of theory, their potential can be developed in new ways" (Connell, 1987, p. 47).

The principal issue to emerge from Marxist feminism and in particular dual systems theory—at least the issue that most concerns us here in the evaluation of theoretical frameworks for the study of gender inequality—is the autonomy of patriarchy. It is seemingly obvious that in practice all our lives are fundamentally shaped by both class and gender relations and that, at some level, there is an interaction between the structures of capitalism and patriarchy. The preceding discussion of different theoretical perspectives has demonstrated the fact that there is widespread disagreement as to the relative importance of these structures. Radical feminists like Delphy, for example, argue that patriarchy constitutes *the* dominant structuring mechanism whilst Marxist feminists (e.g. Barrett, 1980; Connelly, 1986) maintain that it is capitalism. This debate will not be resolved here (or elsewhere). It does, however, serve to highlight the significance of discussions around the autonomy of patriarchy and its analytical separation from capitalism.

Foord and Gregson (1986) using a realist theoretical framework confront the issue of autonomy in proposing a 'hierarchy of abstraction' for the conceptualisation of patriarchy. They suggest, as part of this hierarchy, that the relationship between patriarchy and capitalism can be conceived of on three distinct but inter-related levels; general, particular (historically contingent) and individual (Whatmore, 1991). It is at the general level, so

Foord and Gregson argue, that these structures can be seen as auton-
omous. Consequently, at the level of historical analysis and of the individual, patriarchy and capitalism are contingently rather than necessarily
related.

It is perhaps helpful at this stage to consider, in a less abstract way, what
is actually meant by patriarchy and how the concept itself has helped us to
understand more about the relations of domination and inequality that
exist between men and women. The next section looks briefly at patriarchy
as a form of gender relation and then goes on to deal with two key issues
incorporated in ideas about patriarchy namely male violence and women's
sexuality. Again, space restricts the discussion of all these areas but in the
course of discussion the reader is referred to an extensive literature that
exists elsewhere.

Patriarchal Gender Relations
Defining patriarchy

Definitions of patriarchy as a theoretical tool tend to concentrate on its use
rather than its composition. Perhaps this reflects the difficulties inherent in
arriving at a conclusive definition of patriarchy—one which can accommodate change over time and one, moreover, which does not attempt simply
to assign people to a set of boxes or categories. Patriarchy at the most
general level of abstraction must be seen not as a rigid social system in
which all men consistently dominate all women in a way that is reminis-
cent of biological determinism, but as a set of social relations which are
constantly being reconstituted in response to changing social practice and
expectation.

Walby (1990) provides a useful starting point when she defines
patriarchy as a

> "system of social structures and social practices in which men dominate, oppress and
> exploit women" (Walby, 1990, p. 20).

She follows this with the assertion that the power relations through which
such domination operates are not universal in either strength or direction.
This is a point which Connell (1983) takes up as critical to the definition of
patriarchy. He notes the reporting by anthropologists of

> "sexual power structures which, if not unambiguously matriarchal, are also not simply
> patriarchal" (Connell, 1983, p. 40).

Even in societies such as Western capitalist societies where the predomi-
nant power is "unequivocally" held by adult men, Connell believes that
the differentiation and domination within genders must be recognised in
arriving at a definition of patriarchy. Thus the systematic oppression of
gay and effeminate men must be seen to offset the "hegemonic form of

masculinity" which some feminists have seen as the universal truth/essence of patriarchy.

In attempting to provide a definition of patriarchy that is more easily applied to the day-to-day operation of people's lives, Walby (1990) identifies six structures within which sets of 'patriarchal practices' are carried out. These structures are the:

(1) patriarchal mode of production
(2) patriarchal relations in paid work
(3) patriarchal relations in the state
(4) male violence
(5) patriarchal relations in sexuality
(6) patriarchal relations in cultural institutions.

The operation of a number of these structures (for example patriarchal relations in paid work and in the state) are taken up in future chapters of this book. Two of Walby's structures (male violence and patriarchal relations in sexuality) are considered in more depth in following sections of this chapter as patriarchal structures that underpin, to a large degree, the others mentioned.

Ann Ferguson, in her book *Blood at the Root: Motherhood, Sexuality and Male Domination* (1989), proposes a rather different interpretation of the composition of patriarchy. Taking an historical perspective, Ferguson argues that there has been a shift in what she calls "father patriarchy" through "husband patriarchy" to "public patriarchy". This shift represents a change, over time, in the primary power relations within different modes of social formation. Thus, Ferguson argues that there have been three main periods of male domination in the history of the US from the colonial period.

> "Each of these periods involves a different sort of patriarchal relationship between men, women and children and each of them has its different basic mechanism for maintaining male dominance. In the colonial period, father patriarchy was reproduced by fathers' legal and economic control of children's marriages and inheritance through family property vested in sons, not daughters. In the romantic Victorian period, husband patriarchy was reproduced by the institutions of the 'family wage', which was vested in husbands who were the family breadwinners" (Ferguson, 1989, pp. 101–2).

The contemporary form of male domination is public patriarchy which is not based to the same degree on male control of women in family kinship networks but is dependent on 'the public mechanisms of the patriarchal welfare state'. State institutions, the operation of welfare systems and the media are, so Ferguson argues, important constituents of public patriarchy and consequently the mechanisms through which male power over women is exercised. This is not to deny that men continue to dominate and oppress women in the family, through domestic violence, and in paid work, but that there has been a shift away from the direct power of men in the family as the primary mechanism of patriarchy.

Whatever the relative importance of the different 'structures' or 'mechanisms' through which patriarchy operates, this discussion has highlighted a number of issues—the centrality of which necessitates their further investigation. The next section picks up on two of these issues—male violence and the control of women's sexuality. Both are closely related to biological reproduction and heterosexuality which many feminist writers have identified as the "material basis of patriarchal gender relations" (Whatmore, 1991, p. 37).

Male violence

In discussing the role of male violence as a 'patriarchal structure' we are obviously interested in the nature and extent of male violence—which men and women are involved and with what frequency? We need also to consider the different explanations of male violence against women and how these accord with differing conceptualisations of patriarchy.

Before it can be measured, male violence must of course be defined—a task which as the literature confirms, is by no means straightforward. Violence in the form of physical assault and rape is obviously most clear cut and easily definable (although, as will be seen below, the recognition of even rape as male violence is not always without question). But abusive and sexist language towards women, unwanted attention (particularly where this involves touching) as well as flashing, kerb crawling etc. should also be seen as forms of male violence since such behaviour, while not necessarily resulting in physical harm to women, is generally used to assert male power over women and is predicated on the ability to instill fear (see Halson, 1991; Kelly, 1987). In this context, many feminists believe that pornography is also a form of male violence towards women. As Coveney *et al.* (1984, p. 17) write:

> "Sexual harassment of women on the street can take the form of whistles, catcalls, comments, touching up, rape, kerb crawling, following, indecent exposure and physical violence. All these forms of male behaviour serve to remind women that men are powerful. They undermine women's confidence and self-esteem, they remind us of our vulnerability and of the necessity to continue to adopt survival strategies."

The fact that a high proportion of reported violence (and presumably an even higher proportion of unreported violence) takes place in the home makes it even more difficult to identify. As Hall (1984) notes, the idea of a 'dark[1] stranger' is largely a myth. From a survey into violence against women conducted by the London Rape Crisis Centre it was discovered

---

[1]The author distances herself from the racist implications of this term. She does note, however, the racist reporting of rape ... "Race is more often noted when a black man is involved than when the assailant is white, and white men, when they rape, are commonly described as 'swarthy'" (Hall, 1985, p. 69).

that of the 694 women who had been raped or assaulted, 64% knew their attacker.

Clearly this has huge implications for the recognition and reporting of all forms of violence against women. The reluctance of the legal system in Britain to recognise some forms of violence (the obvious example being rape within marriage) only serves to further obscure our knowledge in this area (see Rhodes and McNeill, 1985 for a discussion of sex law).

Research has indicated very strongly the underestimation, particularly within official statistics, of the extent of violence against women. The fact that rapes are frequently not recorded has attracted a good deal of attention (see Hall, 1984; Hanmer and Saunders, 1984; Rhodes and McNeill, 1985; Segal, 1990), but much less well documented is the almost routine level of violence that some women are subjected to. Hanmer and Saunders (1985) undertook a detailed survey of a local area to "bring together the various forms of violence to women" with the aim of understanding the patterns that had emerged in the experience and recording of violence. They interviewed 129 women, 84 of whom had witnessed or personally experienced an incidence of violence—76 of these women had actually been the subject of threats, violence or sexual harassment.

In their study, Hanmer and Saunders deliberately allowed women to set their own definitions of violence—to determine themselves whether a particular incident constituted 'violence'. Disaggregation of the incidents cited revealed about half to be verbal encounters, a quarter were visual and the remaining quarter involved physical assault. Although the survey recorded that over half the incidents had taken place in a public place, Hanmer and Saunders are sceptical of this result believing the frequency of violence in the home to have been underestimated by the women taking part in the study.

Like Hanmer and Saunders' study, work by Hall (1984) identified a high incidence of violence against women. Reporting on a survey of 1236 women carried out by the London Rape Centre, Hall found that more than one in six had been raped and nearly one in three sexually assaulted. In addition the survey also asked women about 'invasions of their sexual privacy' (interpreted here as male violence). Eighty-three per cent of respondents had received "unwelcome sexual remarks" (usually more than once or frequently) and seventy-six per cent had been grabbed or touched up against their will (Hall, 1984).

The fact that we really know very little about the extent and form of violence against women generally (notwithstanding the research referred to) says much about the nature of male violence as a patriarchal structure. As has been noted already, the legal definition of violence is very narrow— particularly in relation to sexual assault or rape. This narrow interpre- tation is largely mirrored in institutional and social reactions to violence with women being encouraged to downplay or ignore incidents like indecent exposure, touching up or verbal abuse. Treatment of rape and domestic violence victims by the police is an obvious example of the lack of recognition and low priority given to male violence against women (see Edwards, 1991). The London rape survey found that of the 145 women who had been raped, only 12 (8%) had reported the attack to the police. When violence is experienced, women are encouraged to believe that they 'asked for it' by, for example, dressing or acting provocatively or just by being female. They are also made to feel guilty that an assault ever happened.

The recognition of male violence is particularly low in the case of certain groups of women. Black women are less likely to receive sympathetic treatment from the police (Hall, 1984) and, as Adams (1985) notes, the rape of a prostitute is "completely ignored". She writes:

"Always the judgements in the court are made using all the prejudices of sexist, racist, classist, ageist society, and these prejudices have already decided what kind of women are raped and what kind of women are lying or guilty of 'provocation'" (Adams, 1985, p. 32–33).

The lack of recognition is reinforced as women in these groups are less likely to report an attack.

Attempting to understand *why* men use violence against women is fundamental to the examination of patriarchy. Researchers have noted the importance of violence—and in particular rape—as the ultimate proof of men's power and women's insignificance. They talk about the idea of men's over-riding sexual needs, of violence at times of stress and of women as men's property. Walby (1990) attempts a systematic review of alternative explanations of male violence—linking these explanations to different interpretations on the basis of patriarchal gender relations.

One common explanation of violence against women that Walby considers is that the men involved are abnormal—possibly psychologically deranged and very different from 'ordinary men'. Such a view, however, is not compatible with evidence either on the *extent* of violence or its treatment by the legal system, the police and society in general. As has already been seen, there is evidence to suggest that the extent of male violence against women is significantly underestimated. According to Walby, the majority of convicted rapists are not referred for psychiatric care/investigation. In discussing rape, Adams argues that while men

"make it clear that they are horrified and upset by other men's violence....they laugh at jokes about rape, cover up and excuse other men's violence and punish women for daring to suggest that they have been raped. **These are all the same men** not a minority of sex starved maniacs."

She continues:

"if men really thought rape was so bad then the other men that get involved with dealing with rape would not behave as they do.... the police, doctors, judges etc. They would not *english das focus instead of crue.*

punish us with cruel jokes, humiliating medical examinations and refusals to believe our story. They wouldn't pass judgements on a woman's behaviour, life-style, clothes and sexuality if they did not in some way want to prove her guilt and his innocence" (Adams, 1985 pp. 33–34, author's emphasis).

Another set of explanations for male violence revolve, Walby suggests, around social class. Some theorists have argued that men are violent at times of economic stress and that working class men — those most vulnerable to unemployment, loss of housing etc. are more likely than middle class men to act violently towards women. Again, however, the empirical evidence that has been produced to support this view is inconclusive.

Explanations which endeavour to link male violence and class position fail to explain the gendered nature of violence — why, when a 'crisis' occurs, is it *women* whom men attack rather than other men. Moreover, if violence is to be associated with levels of economic and social disadvantage in this way, why are women not more violent than men since it is women who are *most* prone to redundancy/low pay/poor housing etc.

"The fact that women are much less violent than men suggests that the thesis that social disadvantage breeds violent behaviour needs re-thinking" (Walby, 1990, p. 134).

A third group of explanations for male violence against women is provided by radical feminists. Authors such as Brownmiller (1976) have argued that violence is socially constructed and that, in all areas of their lives, men are encouraged in the physical domination of women — the control of women's sexuality which culminates in rape. Such explanations have been criticised for their biological determinist overtones (all men are rapists) and for their failure to incorporate other forms of social division especially class and race. Yet they are important in their emphasis of the social forces behind men's use of violence to control women. What they fail critically to do is to suggest why some men and not others individually commit acts of violence against women.

Walby rightly argues that radical interpretations of male violence are most useful when accompanied by an analysis of the state's role in supporting male control over women. Indeed, it is impossible, so the range of theoretical perspectives ably demonstrates, to fully understand male violence as a form of patriarchal power without also recognising the role of the state in supporting male control. As noted above, the state, in the context of the operation of the legal system, reinforces male violence by failing to recognise or adequately punish attacks on women. Thus rapists "operate within an institutionalised setting that works to their advantage and in which a victim has little chance to redress her grievance" (Brownmiller, 1976, p. 256). In addition, in devising and maintaining a welfare system which ensures women's dependency on men and their inability to escape violent situations, the state further perpetuates male power.

Male violence is quite clearly fundamental to the establishment and maintenance of patriarchal gender relations and as such central to women's inequality. A number of points have arisen from this brief discussion that are perhaps worth emphasising. The extent of male violence against women is consistently underestimated at all levels. Many acts of 'violence' are not interpreted as such by either the British legal system or by society generally. It is important that explanations of male violence recognise this underestimation and see acts of violence not as isolated incidents but as part of the systematic control of women by men. In addition, explanations must prioritise the gendered nature of violence but must also acknowledge the importance of race and class divisions. Undoubtedly the most useful explanations of male violence against women are those that prioritise the social construction of violence and, moreover, emphasise the state's role in sustaining and perpetuating that violence. Finally, it is essential that we do not underestimate the enduring nature of male violence against women. While some argue that official statistics demonstrate a decline in forms of violence against women others claim the opposite—stressing the continued failure to acknowledge violence which is itself part of the problem.

Many issues discussed in later chapters of this book return to the question of male violence (either directly or indirectly) and to its continuing role in shaping patriarchal gender relations.

Sexuality

There are, quite clearly, strong links between male violence and the control of women's sexuality as patriarchal structures. Violence, and in particular rape, may be used by men to enforce certain forms of sexual relations and sexual practices and to ensure the dominance of male sexuality. Sexuality is, so some feminists argue, the medium through which male power over women is established and reinforced. As such it is central to the discussion of patriarchy and to the understanding of gender relations. While Segal (1987), amongst others, argues against the interpretation of sexuality as the *primary* social sphere of male power, she acknowledges the central place of sex in our lives and its role in defining who we are as individuals. The following section looks briefly at the ways in which men seek to control women's sexuality—particularly the practices which maintain heterosexual gender relations. It then goes on to suggest different theoretical interpretations of the basis of this control.

At a very simple level it is easy to see that women have in the past and continue to be judged according to various assumptions about their sexuality. They have been valued for their virginity, purity and submissiveness. Their ability to perform as a good wife and mother is assessed in terms of their conformity to sexual stereotypes of innocence and passivity. Much has been written in the moral codes which governed the sexual behaviour of women in the eighteenth and nineteenth centuries and on the divisions that were created between 'pure' and 'fallen' women (see, for example, Davidoff and Hall, 1987; Wilson, 1990) Authors have also noted the continuing power of Victorian attitudes in the context of women's struggle for liberation at the beginning of the twentieth century and of the enduring nature of the association of sexual purity with femininity (see Coveney *et al.*, 1984).

While major changes have occurred in the second part of the twentieth century, and particularly since the 1960s, in attitudes towards sexual freedom, women's sexuality is still surrounded by a range of sanctions and constraints—legal, social and ideological (Segal, 1987). Women's involvement in pre-marital sex or their experience of more than one sexual relationship may not be frowned on in the same way as it was thirty years ago, but tolerance only extends in certain directions and in a way that ensures women's sexuality remains within the control of men. As Segal (1990, p. 274) writes:

> "The tangled sense of sexual freedom, inferiority and confusion women felt then (in the 1960s)—suddenly freer than ever before to engage in sexual encounters with less fear of pregnancy, moral condemnation and guilt..... yet still, and even more blatantly, surrounded by media messages of themselves as little more than the belittled playthings of men."

A principal element of the continuation of male power over women's sexuality is the dominance of heterosexuality. The construction of adult sexual relations, within which male and female sexuality are located, revolve around male pleasure in a pattern where the "man's arousal and control of movement is central" (Connell, 1983, p. 24). Eroticism and satisfaction are focused on the penis and on penetration in a

> "practice of sexual encounter that begins with erection and ends with ejaculation. and in which the woman's pleasure is marginal to what the man does, or is assumed to be guaranteed by powerful ejaculation" (Connell, 1983, p. 24).

Again, the woman's role in such encounters is generally a submissive one—or at least her activity is controlled by the man in a way that is primarily designed to give him pleasure. This point is vividly illustrated by Coveney *et al.* (1984) in their discussions of the male magazine, Forum.

The images and expectations of masculinity that emerge from heterosexual relations are, some would argue, equally restrictive to men. Women's passivity and submissiveness is mirrored by an image which sees men as forceful dominant and aggressive, and which equates 'success' with some arbitrary notion of sexual prowess. Although men's behaviour is clearly restricted by the images of masculinity that dominate heterosexual relations (see Hearn, 1987 and Jackson, 1991 for further discussion on this point), it can not be denied that men generally benefit from those images and from their implications for sexual practices. The acceptance by women of heterosexuality as the dominant form of sexual relations between adults is more complex. Some radical feminists believe that women's 'preference' for heterosexual relations is itself a function of male control. As Rich (1980) writes

"for women heterosexuality may not be 'preference' at all but something that has been composed, managed, organised, propagandised and maintained by force" (quoted in Segal, 1987).

Sexual liberation for women, it is maintained, can only be achieved through challenging the conception of the sexual act as the moment of penile penetration of the vagina and acknowledging and encouraging other forms/causes of arousal in women.

During the 1970s radical feminists called for a re-appraisal of the nature and sources of women's sexual pleasures. This, they argued, involved women learning more about their own sexuality and about their relationships with other women. Such knowledge would begin to effect changes in the power relations between men and women and lead to a wider acceptance and tolerance of different types of sexual relations. Radical feminists' interpretation of sexuality is to see intimate relations between women as to be expected—in effect reversing the acceptance of heterosexuality as the norm and of lesbianism and male homosexuality as 'deviant'.

Central to the process of gaining more control over their own sexuality is women's knowledge and control of fertility. Traditionally men have controlled the conditions and circumstances surrounding reproduction and childcare. To ensure social acceptance women were (and to some extent still are) required to give birth only within narrowly defined situations—establishing their legal, social and economic dependence on men. Facilities for contraception and abortion have, by the same token, been available to women largely within circumstances prescribed by men. Since the 1970s, due partly to the campaigning effects of the feminist movement, women's access to contraception and abortion in Britain have improved. Furthermore, advances in technology, together with increasing acceptance of techniques such as insemination, have reduced the significance of the nuclear family and of women's dependence on men.

Discussions of women's sexuality inevitably incorporate questions about change. Advances in the area of contraception and childbirth together with a greater general tolerance towards women's sexual activity both within and outside marriage have been seen as positive changes in terms of women's control of their own sexuality. And yet, as many authors point out, progress has been very slow and patchy. Sylvia Walby (1990) writes of the "continuing pressures on women to engage in heterosexual activity and to marry or cohabit with a man". According to Walby the "sexual double standard" is alive and well—while male promiscuity is taken for granted and even praised, women who are known to have (or have had) more than one sexual partner still face criticism and abuse. Similarly, as other authors have demonstrated (see Bell, 1991; Valentine,

1992) relationships that step outside the bounds of 'normal' heterosexual activity—lesbian and male homosexual relationships—are far from universally accepted or tolerated.

One major obstacle to changes in the control of women's sexuality is the continued expansion of pornography. The commercial exploitation of women's bodies by men represents in itself a highly visible expression of male power while the nature of pornography—its focus on heterosexual (often violent) relations in which women's primary purpose is the satisfaction of men's sexual desire—reinforces conventional sexual relations. While both radical and liberal feminists have long campaigned against pornography, such is the power of the industry and its effectiveness in persuading men and women of the innocence and impotence of its imagery that recent years have seen an increase rather than a decrease in the volume of pornography (Dworkin, 1981). There is insufficient space here to do anything more than note the continuing power of pornography in shaping men and women's sexuality, other authors have taken up issues around the extent and form of pornography which are of course relevant here (see, for example, Coveney *et al.*, 1984; Griffin, 1981).

As with the discussion of male violence, it is important to consider the different perspectives that have been put forward to try to explain the basis of sexual relations and of male and female sexuality. We have seen very clearly the ways in which male power is used to control women's sexuality—what haven't yet been explored are the underlying processes which determine, at a more fundamental level, where male power originates. Again, treatment of these issues will inevitably be brief.

The many different theories that have been put forward to explain the basis of sexuality can be divided essentially between those that emphasise the primacy of sex as a bodily drive and those that stress the primacy of the social in the creation of the sexual (Ferguson, 1989). Central to the development of theoretical thought on either side of this 'divide' is the work of Freud. Traditional readings of Freud quite clearly advocate the notion of sexuality as an instinctive drive, while later theorists move away from this interpretation in attempts to emphasise social factors in the formation of sexuality, they remain influenced by debates around psychoanalysis and the role and significance of infantile experiences.

Freud's biological drive interpretation of sexuality argues the importance of an unconscious system of mental activity formed by the social repression of infant sexual experience. The sensual feelings and desire felt by young children is channelled in conventional ways, as they grow up, into a love for the mother. This love, however, is subject to immense conflict as the child grows up and has to shift to transform previous attachments to the parents repressing their sexual content. This situation is seen by Freud to be at the heart of the Oedipus complex. At this stage, men and women are neither simply masculine or feminine but acquire their adult identity with the transformation of incestuous relationships with their parents. It is at this point that boys and girls take on differing sexual identities cemented by the boy's fear of castration and the girl's 'penis envy'.

Feminists have challenged Freud's arguments on many grounds denouncing early work on sex roles which sees, as Segal (1987) notes, the whole psychoanalytical tradition as a bastion of male supremacy. The idea of the existence of an innate sex drive has been criticised as biologically determinist since it rests almost entirely on differences in male and female anatomy and appears to afford no possibility of change. Too great an emphasis is placed on childhood experience at the expense of a recognition of the importance of adult learning and the altering of an individual's conscious and unconscious desires. As well as the more conventional interpretations of Freud's ideas, however, there have been other, less physically determinist, attempts to use parts of Freudian theory in the explanation of sexuality. Such interpretations can offer greater insights, it may be argued, into the understanding of sexual relations and of male control of women's sexuality.

Juliet Mitchell, for example, argued strongly during the 1970s for a Lacanian interpretation of Freud in which a structuralist rather than a biologist account of sexual difference is advanced and in which the cultural aspects of his theory are given greater emphasis. Lacanian feminists opposed the simplicities of the conditioning approach arguing that it is the underlying social structure of patriarchy that is responsible for the construction of social identity (Segal, 1987). They support what they see as the main tenet of Freud's work — the importance that is attached to the subconscious and to infant experience in the shaping of sexuality and to psychoanalysis as a tool in the interpretation of male and female sexuality. Lacanian feminists place considerable emphasis on the role of language in both the conscious and the unconscious and in doing so see Freud's references to anatomy as symbolic in a way that overcomes biologism (Walby, 1990).

Other feminist interpretations of sexuality move further from Freud in the importance that is placed on social construction. While they recognise the possible value of psychoanalysis and the need to acknowledge child-hood thoughts/experiences, they reject the 'psychic essentialism' of Lacanian feminism claiming that it exists outside changing social institutions such as the family and thus outside women's lived experience (Segal, 1987). Sexuality is seen as something that is learnt rather than biologically determined and consequently negotiated on an individual basis according to particular sets of social experiences. The work of Foucault on the analysis of sexuality is seen by Walby (1990) as deriving in part from this view. What makes Foucault's approach more acceptable is that, by using the concept of discourse he provides a way into "large-scale social

patterning, large-scale historical change and systematic power relations" (Walby, 1990, p. 115).

There is insufficient time here for a more detailed analysis of the different theoretical explanations of sexuality. Those directions referred to, while individually valuable in various ways in stimulating debate on the basis of sexuality, all pay insufficient attention to the importance of gender relations and particularly patriarchy in the formation and expression of sexual identities and sexual relations. Here we return to the issues discussed above—to the centrality of heterosexuality, pornography and male violence, for example in the formation of sexuality. The importance of such structures demonstrates that sexuality can not be fully explained in terms of the individual (whatever the nature of early sexual experiences) but must be seen as fundamentally rooted in broad patterns of gender inequality. In what has been written it is also clear that sexuality can not be treated as a private matter but as a public issue which both contributes to and is shaped by power relations throughout all areas of our lives.

This section has explored the notion of patriarchy and of male violence and sexuality as important structures through which male power is exerted and inequality between men and women maintained. The section was not, as mentioned earlier, intended to provide a comprehensive review of the various patriarchal structures, but simply to select a number of issues of key theoretical importance in order to work towards a better understanding of patriarchy as the basis of gender relations. An issue that has not received direct attention here and yet is very important to the construction and operation of patriarchal gender relations is paid work. Theoretical perspectives on women's role in the labour force and the operation of patriarchy in the work place are incorporated in the first part of Chapter 5. It is sufficient here simply to note that the choices of employment available to women *and* their experiences within paid work are both partly a function of the operation of patriarchy and cannot be fully understood without some recognition of underlying patriarchal structures.

Thus far there has been a tendency, in the discussion of the derivation and maintenance of male power, to see women as passive recipients of patriarchy. Clearly, in terms of the operation of certain patriarchal 'structures' (the obvious being male violence), women are, in all senses, victims of male oppression. But to see women continually in this light is to ignore the reality and potential of the struggle against patriarchy and to deny the possibility of change. Women's fight against patriarchy is highly important to the operation of male power and any discussion of gender inequality must recognise its influence. It also provides a valuable link between the theoretical and conceptual understanding of patriarchy and its practical outcomes. The feminist movement, as a major facet of women's struggle against patriarchy, asserts that what are generally seen, in industrial/post industrial western society, as personal issues (the family, domestic violence, childcare, sexuality and reproduction ......) are also—especially for women—important political questions. Such an assertion challenges, in a very positive and often practical way, the values of contemporary male dominance.

The following section focuses explicitly on the nature of women's struggle against patriarchy. While it is recognised that an important element of this struggle takes place on an individual level as women fight against the particular inequalities they themselves experience at work or in the home, the discussion here concentrates on women's collective response to male oppression. In doing so it can portray more effectively the extent to which women's struggle constitutes a unified political movement and a systematic challenge to the basis and expression of male power. Chapter 4 will take up some of the issues raised here, especially the role of the feminist movement in initiating women into formal politics in Britain, in further discussion of women's access to power.

The Women's Liberation Movement and the Development of Feminism

There is certainly no shortage of texts documenting the history, composition and political orientation of the women's movement in Britain (see, for example, Bryson, 1992; Campbell, 1987; Rowbotham, 1989; Rowbotham *et al.*, 1979; Spender, 1984). Many texts on contemporary women's liberation note the long history of feminist ideas and their evolution through various stages of political action. Juliet Mitchell (1971) has argued that feminism as a conscious protest movement arose in England in the seventeenth century and should be seen as running parallel to struggles for equality in general. At this time feminism was concerned with what Phillips (1987) describes as "formal equality"—the right to equal treatment in the eyes of the law and, as time progressed, to other rights such as the vote, to own property, to education and so on. The idea of equal rights formed the essence of women's protest through the nineteenth and early twentieth centuries. Campaigns staged around suffrage, housing conditions, welfare and childcare were all premised on the view that women should, as a matter of principle, have equal rights to men, and that behind this belief lay notions of justice and morality. While an important 'starting point' for early feminist campaigns, the principle of equal rights has not necessarily, even when achieved, resulted in a marked improvement for women. The formal acceptance of equal rights is not an automatic guarantee of equality of experience.

In accounts of the evolution of feminism a distinction is often drawn between the nineteenth and early twentieth century campaigns and the Women's Liberation Movement (WLM) of the 1960s onwards. While the essential interconnectivity of women's struggles throughout history is recognised, feminism of the 1960s is, in Britain and the United States, seen as distinct from anything that had come before it. In documenting her own participation in the women's movement of the 1960s, Anne Phillips describes how she saw feminists of earlier generations as a

"strange and alien breed (who were) a pretty dull lot: not so much radical visionaries but sensible reformers.... confined by limited aims..... a few reforms here and there; just a moderate improvement in the status of women" (Phillips, 1987, p. 4).

She goes on to recall how feminists of the 1960s, by contrast, believed that they would "challenge everything" in much more ambitious demands for reform. Coote and Pattullo (1990) also suggest that the 1960s constitutes the beginnings of a "distinct phase" of the continuing women's movement. They argue, however, that Mary Wollstonecraft and feminists of her genre had had the same ideas and had fought the same battles as the women of the 1960s. The 1960s WLM seemed different because:

"news had not travelled down the years (and) because women lacked the power to determine what was 'history' and what was not" (Coote and Pattullo, 1990, p. 86).

Whatever the reason or the reality, there is a very real feeling that feminists of the 1960s were striving for something radical and new. At the time feminist politics did not exist as part of the political culture in Britain. In the 1960s feminists were striving to re-discover their political history but they were also searching for new ways to fight inequality and overcome their powerlessness.

As already noted, the WLM of the 1960s took as its guiding principle the idea that the 'personal is political'—enshrining a belief that women's personal experience and feelings should form the starting point for understanding women's situation and for potential action in response to that situation. The 1960s had in the provision of contraception, the availability of education and paid work for women and of labour-saving domestic technology, provided the opportunities for greater freedom for women. This opportunity was at the same time, however, constrained by attitudes surrounding women's domestic role. The inconsistencies between the opportunities opening up for women and the expectations of their behaviour, together with a general political discontent amongst the young, encouraged dissatisfied women to come together to discuss their problems and share experiences. Small 'consciousness raising' groups soon developed as the backbone of the WLM.

At the centre of this movement was women's belief that sexual politics constituted a significant and legitimate area of struggle and that equality for women would only be achieved through an attack on male violence and men's control of women's sexuality. The WLM's most articulated demand was the right of women to control their own bodies. In fighting for this control, feminist political activity during the 1960s included demonstrations in favour of the 1967 Abortion Act as well as the celebrated disruption of the Miss World contest. Women's groups attacked media images of women and, in particular, the commercialisation of women's bodies through pornography.

By the time of the first national women's liberation conference in 1970, four basic political demands had emerged from the movement; equal pay, equal education and job opportunities, free contraception and abortion on demand and universal flexible childcare. Three other demands were later added to the list; these were legal facilities and financial independence for women, an end to discrimination against lesbians and the right to a self-defined sexuality and an end to rape and all violence against women (Barrett, 1980). In a sense what matters here is less the actual details of women's demands but the broader purpose of the movement. It was, as Coote and Pattullo (1990, p. 90) note, more than a pressure group with a preoccupation for reform, but a movement to "increase the power of women in both the public and the private spheres".[2] The WLM gave women a chance to come together for discussions and consciousness raising and to learn how to organise politically (on both local and national levels) around their demands (this point is taken up further in Chapter 4). Equally important was the fact that the WLM helped many women to understand, in a broad theoretical sense, more about the nature of their oppression. It taught women to recognise the relationship between their problems and their powerlessness and it taught them something of the link between inequality and patriarchy.

> "As a political apprenticeship, involvement in the WLM was a uniquely rich experience. It led women to develop a theoretical perspective on male power and the forces that sustained it; by analysing 'patriarchy' as a system of male power which pre-dated capitalism and helped to form its character, they gained new insights into the causes of female subordination" (Coote and Pattullo, 1990, p. 91).

But while feminists were developing the skills for political activity they were not using them, so Barrett (1980) argues, in a major assault on the central state. She believes that the politicisation of the personal that has been the 'hallmark' of contemporary feminism has led to a critical stance on civil rights politics and a reluctance to engage in campaigns based on formal constitutional issues. The organisation of the WLM into small, 'grass roots' groups and its rejection of what are seen as male oriented working practices has also ensured that the focus of feminist action has been at the local rather than the central state level. While recognising the importance of the WLM in national political issues such as the campaign for free, legal and safe abortion, it is clear that the main thrust of feminist action has been in local campaigns organised around, for example, housing for battered women, the provision of childcare and so on.

---

[2]It could be argued that in campaigning around the 'personal as political' women were seeking to break down the false dichotomy between the public and private spheres. As Campbell (1987) notes, feminism's challenge to both left and right was as a politics which integrated the public and the private.

This local emphasis in women's political activity is obviously of central importance to the analysis of women's role in the policy process and as such is discussed in more depth in Chapter 4.

There is no space here for further discussion of the direction and achievements of the WLM. Its importance in the context of this chapter is in the role it has performed in raising women's awareness of the nature of gender inequality and in providing a vehicle for the translation of the theoretical understanding of patriarchy into political action. Although the contemporary women's movement has been united under a common celebration of womanhood, it has also been fraught by internal divisions and disagreement. The dilemmas faced by the women's movement need brief consideration here as they are important to the recent history of the development of feminism in Britain and to the current health of the women's movement.

The WLM in Britain has always encompassed a variety of theoretical positions in terms of the explanation of women's inequality. These have inevitably resulted in the advocacy of differing political strategies from amongst the membership. Roughly speaking, there has been a division between radical and socialist feminists which stems from differing beliefs as to the underlying causes of women's oppression—whether women's oppression is primary and underpins all other forms of domination or whether it is interconnected with other equally basic forms of oppression in capitalist society (Segal, 1987). The radical/socialist division clearly reflects aspects of the theoretical divide discussed earlier with radical feminists often being criticised for descending into biological determinism and socialist feminists for reducing women's inequality to the issue of capitalist economic relations.

During the early 1970s, the division between radical and socialist feminists was manifest in debates around political organisation. Radical feminists argued for the political autonomy of the women's movement and for the exclusion of men from meetings and campaigns. Some radical feminists supported the idea of 'personal separatism' in lives without men, believing that the adoption of socialist feminism would inevitably involve losing sight of their aims in what would become a liberal take-over of the WLM. Phillips (1987, p. 122) argues that the growth of Women's Aid Refuges and Rape Crisis Centres during the early 1970s "brought the real violence in men's relations with women out in the open" and in doing so added weight for radical feminists calls for political separatism.

Socialist feminists, while supporting the goals of radical feminists, have argued that there is no conflict between feminism and socialism. Indeed, they suggest that since socialism is concerned with the redistribution of wealth, power and resources, then it must encompass the demands of feminism in the support of disadvantaged groups such as women. During the 1970s, women were becoming more active in the Labour party and in socialist politics generally, perceiving a need to engage with power directly. They used debates within the labour movement to argue women's position in relation to, for example, equal pay and sexual discrimination and also to advance 'women's issues' within the Trade Union movement. The relationship between feminism and the politics of the left inevitably created divisions—not only between radical and socialist feminists but between socialist feminists of different classes.

The women's movement in Britain has always suffered from the criticism that it is middle class. It was inevitable, so Coote and Pattullo (1990) argue, that a movement, initially started by middle class women which was aimed at discussing personal experiences, should reflect middle class needs and problems. The demands and expectations that emerged from the feminist movement were not, they argued, exclusively middle class—they reflected the interests of all women. But, whatever its intentions, the WLM clearly had problems making connections 'across classes' and assimilating working class women into the movement. The reality was that while middle class and working class women shared common interests *as women* their experience of oppression differed considerably. Working class women were aware of the conflicts incorporated in fighting *against* men for equality and *with* them in pursuit of class based interests. Alternatively, middle class women

> "could struggle to change their men in the interests of liberation **without** at the same time struggling to defend them in the interests of their own class. They could understand the need to fight with and against working class men **without** having to confront them in their own kitchens" (Coote and Pattullo, 1990, p. 96).

The relationship between feminist and socialist politics remained a major issue in the development of the women's movement and one which has been seen by many commentators (see, for example, Segal, 1987; Phillips, 1987) as central to its decline. Class divisions have not been the only source of fragmentation within the WLM, however. Black women, lesbians and old women have been amongst those who have argued that the WLM in Britain has not only failed to meet their needs, but has succeeded in compounding their disadvantage. As Segal (1987, p. 58) writes, during the 1970s such women

> "began to speak, write and organise around their specific oppression. They spoke of domination not just by men but by groups of women who were more powerful than they, including feminists. Although universally subordinated as women within their own class and ethnic groups, their lives were also affected by women who held power and privilege in the wider world".

The differing, sometimes conflicting needs of groups of women have presented feminism and the WLM in particular with difficulties. Feminism has always been about identifying common concerns amongst women and sharing experiences. The identification of major differences amongst women has presented problems not only in political organisation but also, as is shown below, in the evolution of feminist theory.

From the late 1970s the women's movement has been in crisis. Anne Phillips questions whether it can still be seen as a 'movement' at all, such is the extent of the divisions within feminism. The fragmentation of women's political activity has led to the dissipation of much of the cohesiveness and energy of the WLM. While many women have experienced very real gains in relation to, for example, economic independence and sexual liberation, and young women in particular have considerably more 'freedom' today than they did in the past, the strength and unity of the feminist movement has declined. Segal believes that the way forward for the women's movement must be in embracing socialism and furthering women's interests from within organisations such as the Labour Party and Trade Unions. This debate is taken up in Chapter 4. In conclusion here it is important to acknowledge the role and influence of the women's movement in women's struggle for equality and to recognise the part it has played in fighting against the forces of patriarchy. At the same time we must realise the limitations of the movement and acknowledge the continuing social and economic subordination of women.

Feminism and Difference

The preceding observations on the women's movement in Britain have commented on its fragmentation, demonstrating how the movement has traditionally failed to recognise differences between women. Black women in particular have criticised white feminists for ignoring their needs and for supporting a women's movement with which they cannot identify. The issue of difference has thus emerged as a key political question with considerable relevance for the nature and direction of feminist activity. Recently feminist writers (see, for example, Barrett, 1987; Bondi, 1990; McDowell, 1991; Stefano, 1990) have recognised that differences between women are also central to the construction and use of theoretical feminist perspectives with important implications for the conceptualisation and understanding of gender relations.

Linda McDowell (1991, p. 126) has noted how an acceptance of "experiential diversity" in women's oppression is not new in research on gender within geography. What is much less commonly appreciated, she argues, is that the divisions based on class, race and ethnicity "are not additive". The experiences of black or working class women cannot simply be superimposed on top of existing feminist perspectives since the experience of being black or working class in itself transforms the experience of being a women. Nevertheless, work by socialist feminists within geography has, in negotiating the relationship between class and gender (see, for example, Bowlby *et al.*, 1989) started to "break down monolithic categories of masculinity and femininity, and to explore different constructions associated with different places and class positions" (Bondi, 1990, p. 164).

Recognising the diversity in women's experiences leads, ultimately, to a questioning of the very categories 'male' and 'female'. Work, mainly by anthropologists, on the cultural construction of gender has noted how ideas and images of the behaviour and attributes of 'women' are culturally and historically specific and how the recognition of this specificity necessitates that we begin to challenge key dualisms and dichotomies that have been used in the discussion of gender relations. Bondi (1990) cites the work of feminist post-structuralists who argue that the binary opposition of 'men' and 'women' is a patriarchal construct and that there is no essential femininity or masculinity.

Post-structuralism has been drawn on quite heavily in recent years by feminists in attempts to inform the debate on difference and diversity and to aid the dismantling of dualisms. The importance of language in the construction of meaning and in the organisation of cultural processes has been a particular focus of attention (McDowell, 1991; Scott, 1988). Bondi (1990, p. 164), in a critique of post-structuralist work, sees the different accounts as

"negotiating a knife-edge between positional and experiential concepts of difference, as exploring the relationship between gender as a symbolic construct and as a set of social relations, and as attempting to reconcile femininity as a condition and as a process".

A protracted debate on the role of post-structuralism in feminist analysis is not appropriate here. What is important is that we acknowledge the debates that have taken place as a way of recognising the importance of diversity within women's position and within feminism itself. Our analysis of women's subordination and our understanding of gender relations must be informed by the notion of difference. We must recognise the specificity of our own observations in terms of race, class, ethnicity and time and be aware of the cultural construction of the everyday concepts that we take for granted. As McDowell (1991, p. 131) writes:

"There is not uniformity or sameness and the sets of meanings and structures that result in women's subordination have to be specified in each instance."

Having put the case for the acceptance of difference, however, we must be careful not to descend into a sort of "atheoretical pluralism" (McDowell, 1991). While difference is important, the recognition of difference does not preclude unity. Acknowledging that women have different needs, different interests and different experiences, and indeed that the very experience of being 'a woman' varies across and within cultures, can strengthen rather than dissipate the power of feminism both as a theoretical tool and as a political force.

Conclusion

The discussions incorporated within this chapter appear, at first sight, far removed from the issue of land use planning, dealing as they do with general theoretical explanations of women's inequality. As stressed in the introductory chapter, however, one, if not *the*, critical argument of this book is that the relationship between women, planning and policy can not be understood in a vacuum. In order to recognise the extent and nature of women's inequality within the built environment and to start to identify planning's contribution to maintaining and alleviating that inequality we must appreciate something of the broader relations through which inequality is created and sustained. This, as has been explained, necessitates the examination of patriarchal gender relations as the underlying basis through which male power over women and hence women's inequality is reproduced.

The following chapters deal much more directly with 'planning' and 'policy' — moving from a broad examination of the physical structure of the built environment to a more detailed analysis of particular policy sectors. It is inevitable that, in focusing on actual planning practice, we depart from the theoretical debates that have been developed in the course of this chapter. This is not to undermine the relevance of these debates. Parts of the remaining chapters have very clear and direct links with what has already been discussed — the power of women in the planning process, for example, or the issue of planning for women's safety — in other areas the links are less obvious. It must be argued, however, that whatever the *apparent* relationship between theories of women's subordination, planning and the policy process, an acceptance and understanding of that relationship is central to any attempts to appreciate both women's experience of the past and contemporary built environment, and the significance of planning in shaping that experience.

3

Women and Land Use Planning

Introduction

In Chapter 3 we move away from the underlying theoretical concerns surrounding women's inequality to a more direct discussion of land use planning; the intention being to apply the arguments debated above to the evolution and operation of planning within the built environment. The broad aim of the chapter, as described in the introduction, is to examine the way in which gender relations both affect and are affected by land use planning. Chapters 5, 6 and 7 focus on particular areas of policy (employment, transport and housing) in a sectoral approach. Here we concentrate on broad, physical planning and design related issues as they concern both the city and the neighbourhood. In particular, the different functions of the city are examined in a consideration of the gendered use of space. Various authors have, over the past ten years, discussed the division of the city into separate spheres/zones, relating this physical evolution to the organisation of people's lives. These debates form an important starting point for the analysis of the relationship between gender and planning and are examined in some depth here.

Having looked at land use planning on a macro-scale, the second part of the chapter will go on to discuss more localised expressions of the relationship between gender and the built environment. Here concern will be not so much with the particular functions of the city as a whole, but with the use and purpose of individual buildings and local spaces. Attention will be drawn to aspects of the design of the built environment, to the constraints particular characteristics place on their use and the expectations concerning elements of gender role that they reinforce.

A major issue to emerge in terms of the gendered use of space, both at a macro- and a micro-level, is that of physical control and personal safety. People's relationship with particular parts of the city—their feelings towards them and, often, their very ability to use or occupy them, is closely related to perceptions of fear and feelings of safety. For women, in particular, constraints surrounding safety can dominate their experience of and access to parts of the city. While recognising the underlying power relations which govern spatial accessibility and lead to the growth of territoriality, this chapter considers the role of planning in the creation and amelioration of hostile environments for women. It discusses how particular planning goals or strategies (or simply the withdrawal of the planning process) have inadvertently led to the production of unsafe and threatening environments and how planning itself has not only capitulated in the creation of a gender-blind city but one which actually poses particular threats to the safety of women's lives.

In accordance with the specified aims of the book, the chapter attempts to illustrate the arguments made through the use of examples of planning policies. To some extent this task is more straightforward in relation to the second part of the chapter and the discussion of the design and use of local environments. The early part of the discussion, in its consideration of wider city functions, the evolution of different zones and their reinforcement of specific gender roles and relations, is less easily related to direct planning strategies. Important links can be made, however, between the actual planning process, the goals and principles it espouses and the mechanisms by which its aims are achieved, and the gendered use of space—even if such links are not immediately articulated in published plans. Finally, again as one of the purposes of this book, suggestions will be made as to the ways in which planning policies can alleviate some of the problems that have been outlined. Use will again be made of actual examples, although some suggestions will inevitably represent more 'ideal propositions' that have yet to be implemented.

Gender and the Evolution of the Urban Environment

In the light of the issues raised in Chapters 1 and 2 the starting point for this chapter must be the basic assertion that urban form, its development and planning, cannot be divorced from the organisation and operation of gender relations and from the power relations that are embodied therein. The evolution of the contemporary city, socially, economically and physically, is fundamentally linked to the changing form of the domestic household. There exists, in effect, a two-way relationship between land use planning and gender. The way in which we plan our cities and design our buildings and open spaces imposes, as will be shown below, severe constraints on the organisation of the lives of both men and women and, consequently, on the operation of the domestic household. At the same time, the city has, it may be argued, been planned *as a response* to the changing demands of the household and of social relations within it. The emphasis of this current chapter is with the first part of this two-way relationship. But, as will become clear, it is impossible to discuss the interaction of gender and land use planning in terms of cause and affect. While planning policies, decisions about the location of services and the nature of land uses, form powerful influences on our lives, such policies are themselves influenced by social and economic relations within society. Moreover, such relations have served to shape not only day-to-day decisions by planners but the evolution of the planning process in general.

With the growth in feminist geography documented in Chapter 1, came the emergence of a number of publications, both in Britain and North America, on the relationship between gender and urban spatial structure. Noting the previous neglect of the specific affects on women's lives, authors began to document the evolution of the contemporary city from a perspective which incorporated not only the productive but also the reproductive sphere (see, for example, Women and Geography Study Group, 1984; Wekerle, 1984; Wekerle *et al.*, 1980; Mackenzie, 1980; Stimpson *et al.*, 1980). Such work gave explicit recognition to women's activities within the domestic household, drawing attention both to the ways in which women's lives were influenced by the evolving urban environment and to the extent to which that evolution was itself constrained by the gender relations of the household. Some of this work focused on the pre-capitalist city but the majority concentrated on the industrial city from the early nineteenth century up to the present day. A common feature of these studies was the identification of important links between the gender division of labour in the domestic household and the wider relationship between gender and urban land use.

The pre- and early industrial city

The Women and Geography Study Group (1984) note that the pre-industrial city was characterised by a jumble of land uses without clearly demarcated residential, commercial or industrial areas. The now familiar separation of home and workplace was not a feature of the emerging city and consequently, at least for the artisan classes, the roles of husband and wife were far less rigidly differentiated.

> "For the artisans, home either *was* the workshop or was physically close to it. Wives often helped in the business and even where they did not, they lived surrounded by the same activities that were part of the daily experience of their husbands" (WGSG, 1984, p. 47).

As trading activities increased, however, important changes in the organisation of family life emerged amongst the wealthier merchant classes. Business and domestic work became increasingly separate and men's and women's roles more detached. With this change in the organisation of the household, incorporating in itself deepening expectations concerning the relationship between women and the home, were important implications for land use within the urban area. For the wealthier classes, the requirement to live at or adjacent to the scene of production was diminishing—indeed, the incorporation of physical distance between home and workplace was becoming a powerful symbol of wealth and success.

As the process of industrialisation gathered pace so a new form of city emerged. With the development of the factory system as the major form of manufacturing came the numerical explosion of urban populations. The old mixed use areas were replaced by more strictly segregated commercial, manufacturing and residential districts. The middle and upper classes moved out to new housing on the periphery of the urban areas while the poor occupied dwellings just outside the core of the city. For all classes the separation of home and work was firmly established and the segregation of particular land uses became a feature of the first attempts to plan urban space. The growth of the city in this way resulted in new and distinct patterns of population movement necessitating the creation of transportation networks.

These major developments in urban form and structure clearly had very important and far reaching implications for gender roles. As noted, the separation of home and work was encouraging greater demarcation in the activities of men and women and reinforcing emerging beliefs surrounding the appropriateness of women's domestic position. The family, more than ever, was held up as the model form of social organisation and women's role within it very firmly articulated (see Davidoff and Hall, 1987). Not only women's role but their behaviour in general was scrutinised. The state of affairs is well summed up by the WGSG as follows:

"Their (women's) proper role was in serving men either as wives or servants. The home, wife and children were seen as a refuge for men from the brutalizing influence of work. Home and female society constituted the private sphere in which emotions could be expressed; work and male society constituted the public sphere of rationality, science and intellect. These two spheres were becoming, both literally and metaphorically, separate areas of life" (WGSG, 1984, p. 49).

Those writing about the development of urban areas and the implications on gender roles and, more specifically, on women's lives have made considerable use of the concepts of 'public' and 'private'. Different spheres of activity have been associated with either the 'public' world of employment and of economic and political activity, or with the 'private' world of the home and domestic life. While the general use of such concepts has been criticised by some, particularly in terms of their firm theoretical separation and their association with actual physical spaces, they are useful in helping to articulate the extent to which women's lives, with the growth of the contemporary city, became compartmentalised. The denotion of 'public' and 'private' implied that some form of spatial pattern accompanied the separation of women and men into different activities and also helped to emphasise the difficulties women faced in attempting to move out of the domestic sphere.

Important in the context of this debate is the extent to which many conventional studies of urban development and planning together with associated political activity, have focused almost exclusively on the *public* sphere—ignoring for the most part the private sphere and consequently the dominant needs and activities of women (see Bondi and Peake, 1988; McDowell, 1983). This point is taken up again in Chapter 4.

Elizabeth Wilson (1991) writes at length of women's contradictory experience of the city. She notes the strong pressures that operated on women's presence in the city—the links with morality that have already been mentioned, the associations with poverty and disease and the fears of physical abuse and violence—but argues that the city also represented for women a place of liberation and change. It had the potential to offer women excitement and enjoyment. Women's presence in the city was seen as a threat to traditional values and to family life and consequently as a challenge to the patriarchal system (Wilson, 1991).

There can be no denying the power and pervasiveness of the organisation of social relations and spatial structures that resulted in women's concentration within the private sphere of the home. It is not the case, however, that this went unchallenged. By the late nineteenth and early twentieth century there were signs that some women were becoming dissatisfied with their alienation from the world of commercial and industrial activity. Opportunities for paid work for women were increasing in the factory and office with employers ever keen to exploit cheap sources of labour. Such opportunities offered women not only the chance to enhance the household income but also to escape the restrictive sphere of the home. Working class and then, increasingly, middle class women began to take advantage of these opportunities and to acquire jobs in manufacturing and service industries (see MacKenzie, 1980).

While for some women the decision to become involved in paid employment was simply a response to the financial demands of the household, for others it was more closely linked to a desire for freedom and equality with men. The growth of women's employment during this time can not be totally divorced from the early activity of the feminist movement in both Britain and the United States—more will be said on this topic in Chapter 5. Serious opposition arose from those who saw women's involvement outside the home as a threat to established social order and most importantly to the security and continued existence of the family. Middle class and working class men alike spoke out against what they saw as the 'unnatural' involvement of women in paid employment.

Sympathy with this view was found amongst urban reformers of the early twentieth century. Women's participation in waged work was interpreted as symptomatic of the physical problems of urban squalor and poor housing conditions. The 'solution' to what was seen as an undesirable change in the accepted social order was not a reorganisation of gender roles and of the existing household division of labour, but a planning response incorporating new urban residential development. The following thirty to forty years saw an attempt to use the built environment to shape patterns of family life. The new suburbs of British and American cities sought to provide an environment for the sustainability of the *ideal* family household and in so doing reinforced a particular set of gender relations and gender roles. As Dolores Hayden writes in the context of the planning of the American city:

> "...the private suburban house was the stage set for the effective sexual division of labour. It was the commodity par excellence, a spur for male paid labour and a container for female unpaid labour. It made gender appear a more important self-definition than class, and consumption more involving than production" (Hayden, 1980, p. 169).

The following section briefly considers the impact of suburban growth on the daily lives of women in the first part of the twentieth century. In so doing, it demonstrates not only the interaction between planning policies and gender roles but also the way in which gender relations are reflected in and reinforced by aspects of the organisation of urban space.

The growth of the suburbs

The period of early suburban growth within British and American cities represents for a number of authors a distinct phase in the relationship between women's activities and urban planning. Miller (1983) writes of the radical transformation that occurred in women's roles during the second half of the nineteenth and early part of the twentieth centuries linking this transformation to the process of suburbanisation that was taking place in American cities at the time. In Britain, the development of the suburbs was partly a response to the rise in home ownership and consequently incorporated a particular ideology which can not be divorced from particular assumptions concerning the roles of women (see McDowell, 1983). Clearly, suburbanisation cannot be studied simply as a form of residential development but as a process whose significance is as much to do with the organisation of social and economic relations as with the form and composition of the built environment.

This being the case we should not overlook the fact that the evolution of the suburbs had important *physical* impacts on women's lives. The separation of residential areas from not only employment but from other urban activities such as retailing and leisure increased the need for travel and made demands on women's mobility. Early suburban development posed fewer problems, being closer to the city centre. As the suburbs grew in size, however, distances between different functions increased, constituting a real barrier to women's involvement outside the home. Land use within the suburbs was more extensive than in the city centre—the low-density building exacerbating the problems of accessibility. Miller (1983), writing on early American suburbanisation, argues that these problems meant that suburban wives "tended to be severely constrained in their daily activities, especially when compared with their counterparts in urban apartment settings" (Miller, 1983, p. 83). He also suggests that constraints on suburban women were increased due to the problems of attracting, and affording, domestic help.

Physical distance encouraged feelings of isolation amongst women living in the suburbs. The dream of the self-sufficient household removed many of the opportunities for social interaction amongst women in the performing of daily tasks, while the ideology of personal ownership reinforced the notion of privacy that became associated with the home. As Miller again writes:

> "The dispersed residences of the suburbs were not very conducive to formal visiting, one of the mainstays of city social life. The greater focus on the nuclear family meant that home-bound activities were likely to be solitary activities. Opportunities in residential suburbs were limited and many of them, if not most of them, focused attention on women's domestic roles" (Miller, 1983, p. 84).

The domesticity of early twentieth century suburbia helped to create and was itself reinforced in Britain and America by the appearance a whole range of new consumer durables. The growth of manufacturing industry made available items of domestic technology such as refrigerators, washing machines and vacuum cleaners, which revolutionised daily domestic tasks. Coupled with these innovations was the provision of municipal services such as water, gas, electricity and mains sewerage. Linda McDowell again links these changes (not, perhaps in the early part of the twentieth century but certainly following the war) to the growth in home ownership in Britain, arguing that the appreciation of house prices for the first time provided many households with disposable income with which to purchase the new 'labour saving' devices. Similarly, in America, the emergence of "a home-buying, home-owning middle class represented the major market for manufactured goods .... Buying a house was only the first stage in consumer development" (Miller, 1983, p. 82).

While particular items of domestic technology took some of the hard manual work out of some housework tasks, they did not lead *per se* to a reduction in the time spent by women on domestic work. On the contrary, by encouraging women to assume direct responsibility for work that would previously have been undertaken by servants, they tended to reassert women's domestic role. The 'cult' of domesticity put immense pressure on women to perform their household duties efficiently and skilfully. The health and happiness of the family was, more than ever, the responsibility of the woman—inextricably linked to the smooth running of the home.

Advertisements and women's journals constantly reinforced the assumption that women should be judged and valued above all else by their abilities in the domestic sphere.

The introduction to the 'Be–Ro' booklet of Home Recipes (undated) states that

"The women who can cook well and bake well has every reason to be proud of her cooking. In ninety-nine cases out of a hundred she has a happy home, because good cooking means good food, and good food means good health".

It goes on to add that

"there is no more pleasing sight than that of a happy family around a well stocked tea table, all enjoying their food; and the mother who is responsible for the cooking, and who has prepared it with her own hands, has every right to survey the results of her culinary skill with pride and satisfaction".

While these expectations were clearly not unique to suburban women, this form of residential development gave physical expression to the social relations from which they were derived. The constraining influence of land uses, together with cultural and ideological aspirations surrounding the form of housing development, trapped women within an environment which provided space only for the development of domestic roles. This relationship between spatial form and gender relations that characterised suburban residential development has been articulated in a number of studies of specific cases. Philip Wagner (1984), for example, discusses the American Greenbelt Towns, planned in the 1930s—a project, initially calling for the building of several hundred new towns aimed at offering "a viable, low-cost, socially desirable solution to the problem of urban residential congestion" (Wagner, 1984, p. 36). According to Wagner these Greenbelt Towns re-asserted the social values of the suburban communities, imagining women only within the home and aspiring to encourage a strong family life.

Ironically, the cost to the individual of maintaining home ownership threatened the very social values enshrined in suburban development. In many cases families could not rely simply on the income of the male partner and it was necessary for women to obtain paid employment to meet what McDowell refers to as the "high cost of the suburban ideal" (McDowell, 1983, p. 67). By the 1950s the single-earner nuclear family was becoming a rarity. The dominant form of residential development, however, militated against women's participation in waged work. The location of employment opportunities and the poor provision of public transport between residential areas and the city centre meant that women's choice of job opportunities was severely restricted. The expectation that women would remain the primary domestic worker, continuing to assume responsibility for the reproduction of the domestic household, placed additional time constraints on women's availability and further limited their job choices. In the main, women's entry into the world of paid employment was as poorly paid low-status workers whose jobs frequently duplicated the caring and servicing aspects of their domestic role.

> "The post-war expansion of the service sector was built around this kind of wage labour and the predominately domestic type of tasks involved fuelled the assumption that because their jobs mirrored their continuing responsibilities in the home, women were not 'real workers'. The home and community were still 'women's place', ensuring that their ventures into the public sphere were both constrained and poorly rewarded" (MacKenzie, 1989, p. 111).

These issues are taken up in later chapters on employment and housing provision. It is sufficient here to note the inherent contradiction for women in the development of a suburban lifestyle and to recognise the major difficulties it imposed on their organisation of time and space.

Despite these contradictions, suburban development continued to dominate post-war housing provision in Britain. Early twentieth century attempts to move away from the conservative principles incorporated in the design of residential areas were few. Ebenezer Howard had, in the first of the planned Garden Cities, advocated experiments with communal living and co-operative living in the form of centralised kitchens and apartments arranged around quadrangles (see McDowell, 1983). Such experiments were, however, short-lived and after the first two Garden Cities, concern for community participation degenerated, as McDowell notes, "into a purely physical arrangement—the neighbourhood principle".

The Garden Cities were predicated on the belief that:

> "The answer to the chaos of urban life was to reduce the size and density of cities and somehow restore the relationship of city dwellers to the countryside" (Wilson, 1991, p. 100).

As in the case of the suburbs, it was felt that planning solutions could be applied to the serious urban problems of squalor and poverty—in the case of the Garden Cities the solutions involved the even more extreme zoning of physical land uses and the separation of residential and industrial/ commercial areas. Early town planners like Unwin, Parker, Howard himself and, later, Abercrombie, were driven by a profound sense of anti-urbanism and a desire to prevent, at all cost, the continuation of urban sprawl. The Garden City, incorporating a break with existing built-up areas, was seen as an ideal planning solution. Indeed, as Wilson (1991, p. 104) notes, the Garden City became "hugely influential" both in Britain and abroad as a "dominant model of how all good cities should be".

Despite the reputation of the Garden Cities, they largely failed to live up to the Utopian dreams that had inspired their early planning. While they provided improved standards of housing for some individuals, they constituted no simple or automatic solution to the problems of urban areas as was hoped. The Garden Cities assumed a yearning for rural life styles amongst city dwellers that was often not present. In attempting to combine the 'best' of the towns and countryside in separating new development from existing urban areas, they served to replicate in many ways the characteristics of suburban lifestyles. For women this meant a continuation of conventional assumptions about the appropriateness of their domestic role and of the existing gender division of labour.

There was some hope that the later generations of 'New Towns' might provide the setting for some sort of departure from the form and function of the conventional suburbs and in doing so challenge the established relationship between urban structure and women's roles. This hope was, however, not to materialise as is described below.

New town development

The profound changes that took place in the lives of women during the Second World War failed to find expression in post-war housing and planning policies. The participation of women in all forms of industrial activity and the release from many of their conventional domestic duties during the war, prompted some recognition by those involved in social welfare policy of the constraints that characterised their traditional roles (Women and Geography Study Group, 1984). Such recognition did not, however, go as far as supporting any major reorganisation in the division of labour between men and women nor to any radical re-thinking of assumptions regarding women's domestic role. On the contrary, far greater concern was attached to the need to ensure the post-war return of men to the jobs that had been temporarily filled by women.

Thus, on the face of it, new town planning policies continued to reinforce an established set of gender relations and the associated male and female division of labour. Communities were planned, as were the earlier suburbs, on the assumption that individual households supported a full-time domestic worker (the wife) and a full-time (male) bread winner. As McDowell writes:

> "Neighbourhoods were designed as self-contained groups of several hundred houses with associated local facilities of shops, parks, a primary school, and primary health care, interpreted by their male architects as reducing travel time and costs for women and children, but actually reducing choice and mobility" (McDowell, 1983, p. 64).

Studies of particular new towns (see, for example, work on Milton Keynes by Matrix (1984) and Foord and Lewis's research on Peterlee (1984)) have provided much evidence to support these assertions, noting the way in which service provision assumes traditional gender roles and how planning policies encourage a "self-fulfilling prophecy" by ensuring that women's activities are locally based (Matrix, 1984). Women's mobility, or lack or it, is seen by the Matrix group as the central issue in the design of Milton Keynes. Since planning priorities for the new town have endorsed the conventional separation of different urban activities, high levels of mobility are required. Women's inferior access to private transport (see Chapter 6) and the poor provision of public transport means that they are restricted to the home environment, frequently unable to access employment and leisure activities available in other parts of the town. When women are required to travel, the design of transportation networks—a design that emphasises routes to and from the city centre rather than radial routes—makes journeys complex and time consuming.

Despite the assumptions concerning traditional gender roles, the reality of life in the new towns is that many women are involved in paid work outside the home. Foord and Lewis, in their discussion of East Kilbride and Peterlee new towns (Foord and Lewis, 1984) note the contradictions that this implies for planning. Such new towns were designed partly as a response to the economic restructuring of old industrial regions. One of the priorities being the provision of a pool of cheap, available labour to work in the new light manufacturing and service industries. Women, as elsewhere, constituted just such a source of labour. Moreover, the particular economic characteristics of the areas discussed by Foord and Lewis— principally their former reliance on heavy industry—meant that women's incomes were a necessity for household survival. And yet, little was done, in the physical design of these towns, or in the provision of public services to encourage or facilitate women's entry into paid work.

"While the creation of employment for women was a priority in Peterlee's development and a consequence of East Kilbride's growth, the provision of facilities enabling women to combine child-care with wage work has been accorded no such priority. So far as the planned physical and social development of the towns is concerned women as mothers responsible for young children and women as wage earners have been dealt with separately" (Foord and Lewis, 1984, p. 51).

Women, in response, have been forced very often to enter part-time employment. The problem of coping with dual roles has been exacerbated by the physical structure of urban development and as a result women's work has become marginalised. While this situation has not gone unnoticed (Foord and Lewis cite a Development Corporation report published in 1973 in which the need to increase the availability of public transport and to provide childcare to facilitate women's entry into employment were noted) the public sector has failed to take appropriate action. Transport to and from factories has been provided by some employers but only in isolated incidents. Women have been able to exercise little freedom in their employment choices. In many cases this situation has been further exploited by employers to their own gain—a topic which is taken up in Chapter 5.

The following section of this chapter continues this theme looking at the implications of economic restructuring on women's use of time and space. In doing so it will bring the analysis of the relationship between gender roles and relations and land use planning up to the present day. Throughout the discussion so far, emphasis has been placed on the two-way nature of this relationship. Thus it has been asserted that while women's lives have clearly been constrained by the conventional development of the built environment, it is also the case that the changes occurring in women's roles have placed new demands on the use and planning of space in and around our towns and cities. These new demands and the responses to them are particularly important, as documented below, in the contemporary context.

Gender relations and the re-structuring of urban areas

Economic restructuring has encouraged important changes in the relationship between production and reproduction. While women's entry into waged work has been gathering pace throughout the twentieth century and particularly since the Second World War, the restructuring of British industry led to the creation of mass employment for women, linked primarily to the rise in the importance of the service sector (see discussion in Chapter 5). It also heralded far reaching changes in the distribution of employment opportunities amongst men and women and challenged the notion of the sole *male* breadwinner within the household. As more and more women have taken advantage of the shifts occurring in the labour market, so the changes they are making to their daily lives to accommodate new opportunities are becoming more pervasive. Women have always had to balance the requirements of their different roles. Increasingly, however, they are demanding that employers, service providers and the state take some responsibility for these adjustments. The question that must be asked here is to what extent has land use planning been affected by the changes occurring in women's use of space as they attempt to re-organise their lives around new demands and pressures.

Industry has to some extent responded to the greater involvement of women in waged work by moving out of the city centre to sites on the periphery of urban areas—although this is by no means the sole motivation for this move. Relocation in search of cheap labour has not necessarily made employment opportunities more accessible to women since industries have tended to be sited on estates away from residential zones. So rather than being part of a zone of mixed land uses that would be beneficial to women, industries are sited in isolation imposing even more constraints on women by separating employment from other city centre functions (for example banking, retailing and some forms of leisure).

More important than the changing location of industry is what Suzanne MacKenzie refers to as the shifting of the boundaries between public and private spaces. She argues that as women have become more involved in 'productive' work so the division between production and reproduction has blurred. With this has come a merging of public and private activities and hence the spaces within which they take place (MacKenzie, 1988, 1989). She uses the example of childbirth and childcare to demonstrate how, by assuming control over their own lives, women's use of time and space alter. Fertility control and childcare networks have allowed women to become involved in a range of activities outside the private sphere and in doing so have changed the nature of workplace and other 'public' environments.

> "The lives of women with dual roles are complex, involving intricate arrangements in space and time, and severe constraints on space and time. In an attempt to cope with these constraints, women have created networks and places that cut across and actively alter the boundaries between 'home' and 'public places', which lie at the basis of the constraints" (MacKenzie, 1988, p. 53).

The implications of these trends for the use and planning of the urban environment are considerable. Most significant, perhaps is that women are choosing to live in neighbourhoods where the sort of support mechanisms mentioned can be sustained and reproduced. Such neighbourhoods are characteristic not of the suburbs but of the city centres (see Wekerle, 1980). Work by Saegert in the USA concluded that the higher density, mixed-use residential environments of the city centres give women more options and when questioned about residential preference, men opted for the suburbs while women were likely to chose city centre locations. Such conclusions are supported by Wekerle (1984) who argues that inner city neighbourhoods are most likely to incorporate the sort of support networks and public services essential to most women and particularly to single mothers. These authors go on to note that the attachment of women to such neighbourhoods acts as a prime force for their revitalisation—not only do lone women and women-headed households provide a *demand* for city centre housing, but their skills and energy in local political activity are likely to help in obtaining finance for rejuvenation.

Liz Bondi takes up these ideas in analysing the relationship between gender and gentrification (Bondi, 1991). She notes the importance of changes in women's participation in the labour market and associated patterns of child-birth and child rearing to the process of gentrification, suggesting that the new patterns of activity amongst middle class women have important implications for the extent and location of urban gentrification. Bondi cautions, however, that studies should not be confined to middle class women who constitute the gentrifiers but should include those poorer women displaced by the process—they should look, in short, at both 'agents' and 'victims'. Central to these arguments is an appreciation of the fact that gentrification involves "a process of gender construction as well as class construction" (Bondi, 1991, p. 194) and one which demands that attention be paid not only to class relations but also to changing power relations between women and men.

Once again it is clear that the relationship between women and the built environment—the interaction between women's roles and the development of urban and rural areas—cannot be divorced from the power relations within which this is set. Just as the growth of the suburbs and the subsequent influence on women's lives reflected and reinforced a set of patriarchal gender relations which saw, very simply, women at the centre of the home and family, so gentrification incorporates a new, but not, some would argue, significantly different set of power relations between women and men.

The changes occurring in women's use of space and time, however they are conceptualised and explained, need to be evaluated in terms of their impact on the built environment. While new ways of analysing urban environments by feminists have led to a greater appreciation of the different demands women are making on the organisation of services and land use, we must not lose sight of the extent to which these are reflected in any real change in the planning of the built environment.

"Cities are still planned by men for men. While the lives of women have changed radically, the urban environment in which they live has not" (Wekerle, 1984, p. 146).

The majority of women still live in residential areas planned as single rather than mixed use zones. Women's lives continue to be shaped by the separation of different activities and the need to travel, generally on a daily basis, between home, work, childcare facilities, shops etc., etc. They are still disadvantaged in their use of the built environment through being primarily associated with the domestic sphere and consequently alienated from 'public' activities and spaces. These points are taken up later in the book, here we are primarily concerned with demonstrating the contribution of land use planning to the organisation of women's lives and to the restrictions it imposes upon them.

So far consideration of the separation of different functions in the British city past and present has focused mainly on residential areas and the isolation of the 'private' world of the home from the 'public' world of employment, decision making and political activity. A further example of such separation, and one which aptly incorporates very contemporary planning decisions, is the location of retail facilities. Much discussion has taken place concerning the relative merits of centralised versus decentralised shopping provision and, in particular of the value of out of town regional centres. Major planning battles have been staged over proposals for such centres in some areas involving lengthy appeals and challenging entrenched planning principles such as Green Belts.

The implications for women of the decentralisation of retail facilities in the form of both the existing retail parks and the largely hypothetical regional shopping centres (with the notable exceptions of Brent Cross in London, Metro Centre in Gateshead and Merryhill in the West Midlands that have been built), while not the chief concern amongst practising planners, have inspired discussion in academic publications and the planning press (see for example, Bowlby, 1990a,b). The main issue for women surrounding the use of such centres is accessibility. Their location away from both residential estates and centres of employment necessitates special journeys and while this is not necessarily a problem for those with access to private transport, it may be for the less mobile—the car-less and the old. A second fear is that out of town shopping facilities will undermine the viability of existing provision in town centres. Again, an absence of retailing functions in the city centre will mean extra journeys for women complicating their patterns of daily travel.

Bowlby (1990a) believes that it is too early in the development of out of town shopping facilities to come to any firm conclusions as to their real impact on the lives of women. The implications of their growth are contradictory. While access may be a problem for some, there is no doubt that the new centres that have been built have generally provided an improved environment for shoppers incorporating a range of shops, facilities for baby changing and play areas for children in what is generally a cleaner, safer and more comfortable environment than traditionally exists. New facilities may threaten existing town centre provision but can also act as a stimulus to the revitalisation of such environments. Finally, in a way that demonstrates the merging of 'public' and 'private' activities, the new shopping centres may be an important source of employment for women and their evaluation must take into account potential workers as well as users.

From a planning point of view, it is often, with considerable justification, argued (see for example, Bowlby, 1990a) that, whatever the implications for women, it is the *commercial* success of such developments that will decide their future. The case study of Birmingham city centre re-development, discussed below and in Chapter 8, demonstrates this point. The influence of planners is mainly restricted to locational issues.[3]

Such influence is, however, important in at least attempting to facilitate women's access to out of town centres, in, for example, arguing for sites that maximise the potential for public transport connections.

The final part of this section has introduced the importance of local design and the planning of individual developments in the context of women's experience. Until now we have been largely concerned with broad land use functions in the separation of productive and reproductive

---

[3]Recent Government advice on housing policy (Circular 7/91) suggesting a role for planners in determining tenure have no equivalent in a retailing context and cannot be seen as representing a radical extension of planning responsibilities.

activity and its consequent implications for our use of what have become seen as 'public' and 'private' spaces. In the next part of the chapter the intention is to focus on local issues. To look at the use and design of space in specific neighbourhoods, relating the needs of women and a consideration of gender issues not only to localities but also to individual spaces and buildings.

Women, Urban Design and the Built Environment

The purpose of this next section, then, is to examine the relationship between gender and urban design—in particular the extent to which the planning of spaces and buildings places constraints on women's use of the built environment. These issues constitute a growing area of interest amongst academics and practitioners but one which remains poorly developed. Remarkably little attention has been given, moreover, within the emergence of the topic to the wider explanations of the constraints urban design place on women. Other than in the context of *dangerous* environments, work has rarely attempted to explore the underlying basis of the problems faced by women, nor to link aspects of their interaction with particular spaces and buildings to the operation of patriarchal gender relations as has occurred in the study of broader land uses.

Many of the priorities for the design of our towns and cities reflect what Matrix (1984) refer to as the "macho myths of metropolitan architecture" and it is not hard to compile a catalogue of disadvantages that such design poses for women. Fundamentally, city centres have been constructed to facilitate the primary interests of industry and business. Emphasis in many cities has been placed on the development of transport links to ensure that urban areas function as efficiently as possible as a centre of productive activity. The siting and design of individual buildings and the use of intervening spaces has served to reinforce economic priorities leading frequently to a very alienating physical environment. The dominance of these interests, and in particular of circulatory routes, result in unattractive and hostile city centres. John Punter in his study of urban design in Bristol (Punter, 1990) provides useful examples of the way in which priorities for the re-development of city centres have helped to exclude the users—particularly pedestrians—in effect removing the street from the public realm. It is clearly not just women who are affected by these planning and design priorities. It is, however, the case that the pattern of women's daily activities, together with the fact that their lives are more likely to be divorced from the principal productive uses of the city centre, increases the impact of such alienation.

Problems of mobility within the city are felt more seriously by women as the dominant users of public transport and as pedestrians (and consequently, not the beneficiaries of the 'efficient' road systems). The sheer size of the city centre can be a major problem for some women (Bowlby, 1990)—particularly where different uses are segmented by major roads. Pedestrianisation schemes hold obvious benefits in this respect, but even where schemes are designed they are frequently restricted to small areas and don't provide links between different uses such as offices and shops. The childcare responsibilities of women frequently serve to reinforce their problems of mobility. Roads become even more impossible to manage. These difficulties are shared by many elderly people and by those with disabilities.

At a more detailed level, added difficulties for women in the use of the built environment are apparent. Steps—in particular in and out of subways—curb stones and buildings with poor access and narrow entrances can all prove problematic to women with children. Shopping can become more arduous due to a lack of street furniture and play space. The design of 'public' buildings can be profoundly off-putting to women. Many are imposing and uninviting with poor sign posting and reception areas (one prime example being DHS buildings). The general decay of some city centre environments, making them dangerous and unhealthy places can magnify the difficulties experienced by women and help to reinforce their sense of alienation.

Of course not all these problems can be directly attributed solely to planning—a point that is stressed at the end of this chapter in a discussion of planning 'alternatives' and in the conclusion to the book. Planners, however, as professionals primarily concerned with the development of the built environment, must be aware of these issues and must recognise, in the interconnection of the different contributory processes, their powers to influence and direct the ultimate form of the design of urban and rural space. In the production of a safe and healthy environment the planner may only be one of a number of different actors—and often not the most powerful—but it is within the remit of planners to reinforce the sort of priorities for development that minimise the difficulties articulated above and promote equality of use.

The examination of the impact of design on women's experiences must obviously be extended beyond the city centre to incorporate suburban and rural residential areas. Concern here lies with both the layout of housing estates and the design of individual houses. Attention in this chapter, however, concentrates largely on the former aspect—the principles of house design being incorporated in a wider discussion of housing in Chapter 7.

Given the assumptions noted earlier concerning the extent to which residential provision has reflected the belief that 'women's place is in the home', it is surprising how little influence women have had on the actual *design* of residential environments. The result has been that many residential environments serve to complicate the reality of women's role and have a negative affect on the quality of women's life within the home. A very simple yet pertinent example is the replacement of Victorian back to back housing (so called slums) with the tower blocks of the 1950s and 1960s. Much has been written about the social problems that resulted from the re-housing of people into these new high rise developments. Worst affected were women whose domestic role became more arduous and isolating in the new tower blocks with their squalid lifts and walkways and their lack of play space for children.

Suburban development and post-war housing estates are generally an improvement on the tower blocks in terms of the quality of the physical environment (nevertheless some large estates, particularly of public housing, are very rundown and unattractive). Both have been designed to reflect the importance of privacy. Individual dwellings, often detached, stand in their own plot with their own driveway and private garden. The amount of public 'shared' space (for example children's play areas) on estates is minimal and its location and quality rarely encourage its regular use by women. Some more contemporary residential development has attempted to adopt more imaginative ideas in the layout of houses and the use of space between dwellings. As Jos Boys notes, during the late 1970s the thinking on the design of public housing estates was that

> "houses should be grouped around a series of protected outside spaces enclosing 'nature' which are linked informally and which together make a separate territory visually divided from the surrounding environment" (Matrix, 1984, p. 44).

She argues, however, that such specifications incorporate problems for women's use of residential areas. The type of design encouraged was a reaction against the "visual monotony and coldness" of much housing built in the past. It aimed to provide protected spaces where women could escape the isolation of the individual house and children play together safely. In reality, however, such spaces may, as public places, hold hidden dangers for women. The failure of designers to recognise the gender inequalities incorporated in the use of space has resulted, as Boys observes, in the building of estates that are "no-mans, or rather no-woman's lands".

The problems encountered by women in the design of both residential and non-residential areas appear again to stem largely from what have become the dominant expectations regarding gender roles. These expectations are reinforced by a set of power relations which serve to control women's use of space and restrict them to 'appropriate places'. Women are thus alienated from the public sphere by design priorities which neglect many of their principal concerns. Unequal use of public spaces and the protection of male dominance are self-reinforcing and lead, ultimately, to the production of environments that are dangerous to women. Thus, at its extreme, women's inequality is reflected in their exclusion.

The following section of this chapter looks at women's safety in the built environment, drawing attention to the role of planning and urban design in the production of dangerous or safe environments. Again, constraints on the ability of planners to influence the outcome of complex social relations which derive ultimately from inequalities in access to power, must be recognised. But so must their role as contributors to the physical expression of such social relations. Planners, as will be argued in the following section, do have the ability to ameliorate or reinforce the extent to which gender inequalities successfully exclude women's access to particular environments although they clearly have very limited influence over the actual derivation and perpetuation of those inequalities. As the WDS note, women can feel threatened by:

> "casual intimidation or the threat of actual violence from men which has nothing to do with the design of the environment. However, it is also clear from talking to women, that particular environments are more unpleasant and unsafe than others, for a complexity of reasons, including design" (WDS, 1988, p. 6).

The details of particular planning responses to problems of unsafe environments are included in the chapters on housing and transport.

Planning and women's safety

Right from childhood, boys and girls are taught to conform to the different expectations that society places on their use of space.

> "Girl children are socialised off the street through an implanted fear of men, by restrictions on street games and activities and by an emphasis on activities that concern grace rather than speed. Girls soon learn to take up as little space as possible.... (while) boys soon learn that they can prove their 'boyness' by taking up lots of room, particularly outside on the street" (Boys, 1984, p. 41).

These rules are carried into adulthood when male expectations about what is appropriate female behaviour restrict women's use of space. These expectations are adopted widely by society—for example, women are advised not to go out alone after dark—those who do are frequently seen as 'asking for trouble'. Even codes regarding dress influence women's access to certain environments. The established 'norm', as was discussed in Chapter 2, is that women are out of place in certain public spaces and at certain times. It is acceptable for women to be out shopping during the daytime but not in the city centre at night (especially alone). While it is permissable for (white) men to hang around in groups on the street, women doing so are thought highly suspect and throw themselves open to abuse—cat calls, whistles and physical violence. Chapter 2 has already looked at the roots of such physical violence—here concern is with the relationship between that violence (and with the exclusion of women from public space) and the ways in which the environment is planned.

The Women's Design Service conclude from talking to women living on three council housing estates in London that there is "an almost infinite number of factors affecting women's feelings about their safety" WDS, 1988, p. 9). In this instance, the extent of fear was such that a majority of women were afraid to go out after dark and a sizeable number were scared to venture out at any time. These conclusions are reinforced by other studies of women's use of the built environment—Trench, for example, reports the findings of research undertaken on the Milton Court housing estate in Lewisham, London, in which 53% of women said that they did not leave the house after dark and 18% avoided going out 'whenever possible'. The British Crime Survey undertaken in 1983 reported that 48% of women surveyed felt unsafe walking alone at night—this compares with 13% of men (Atkins, 1989).

Recognising the extent of women's fear is relatively simple—attempting to pin down causes of fear and isolate those causes that relate directly to planning and design of environments is more problematic. Factors tend to be inter-related making causes difficult to identify and solutions hard, if not impossible, to implement. The following factors are some of those most frequently cited by women as contributing to their fear both in residential areas and in the wider built environment. The list is by no means exhaustive nor are all the examples universally frightening to women. It does serve at least to draw attention to those areas of greatest potential concern and provides a starting point for the discussion of practical responses.

One common cause of women's fear is the lack of adequate lighting in public places. Dark environments are more threatening to women than light environments, increasing the fear and likelihood of being attacked. In a survey of over 1,200 women living in London, Hall (1985) discovered that 75% of women felt unsafe in dark (public) environments. Fear was experienced by women not only outside their own residential areas but also in the vicinity of their homes. A number of local authorities currently taking part in a Home Office sponsored 'Safer Cities Scheme' (see below) also identify a lack of street lighting as contributing to women's fear. The problem is seen as particularly serious in 'enclosed' environments such as multi-storey car parks, subways, alleyways etc. By contrast well-lit environments reduce fear and help create a greater sense of security amongst women. The likelihood of attack declines in places where visibility is good and where people are unable to lurk in dark corners. Visibility increases women's confidence encouraging them to use public places and, simply by raising their profile, reduce frequency of attacks.

On a related issue, women's fear may be increased by other environments that offer 'hiding places' to would-be attackers. Blind alleys, 'interesting' corners, blocked views and thick vegetation, for example, represent potential dangers, while on housing estates women may fear pram sheds, communal garages and rubbish areas for the same reasons

(WDS, 1988). Again, dangers associated with such places may be reduced through the use of sensitive lighting.

Clearly, dangerous environments are not simply those in which women feel at risk from physical attack from men. Women may also class as 'dangerous' those places which threaten the health of themselves or their children. Busy roads, pollution from traffic and industry together with generally rundown towns and cities can all constitute 'dangerous environments'. Very few places (if any) can be seen as totally safe at all times — some are renowned; subways, dark car parks outside pubs and nightclubs — but even ordinary residential areas and town centres can be unsafe for women.

Not all women experience or perceive dangers in the built environment in the same way. Lesbian women, for example, often feel more threatened than straight women in 'public' spaces. Their 'geography' of fear will consequently appear very different (for discussion see Pain, 1991; Valentine, 1992a).

Gill Valentine (1992b) looks at the coping strategies that have been adopted by women to minimise the feelings and realities of danger within the built environment. She categorises such strategies into three groups:

(1) Time space avoidance strategies — reducing the perceived threat by simply not going out, or at least not alone.
(2) Environmental response strategies — walking more quickly, alert and aware of possible attackers and of 'dangerous' and 'safe' places.
(3) Physical defense strategies — adjustment of physical appearance to pass as a man or the carrying of weapons for self defense.

Clearly, these coping strategies represent a response to the built environment as it currently exists and do not include the option of changing the nature of urban space — simply people's behaviour within it.

Planners (and academics) may disagree over the extent to which design based solutions can eliminate or reduce danger — and, consequently, the need for women to adopt 'coping strategies'. Oc and Trench (1992), for example, put considerable faith in the ability of 'mixed uses' and the design of environments which encourage busy streets to deter violence and increase women's safety. Others (see, for example, Valentine, 1992b), are less convinced of the capacity of planning and design to achieve such a measure of control. This debate is taken up again in the next section. What is important here is to recognise the spatial dimension to women's fear that is incorporated within the evolution and planning of our towns and cities. Planning has not created women's vulnerability, nor is it totally responsible for the continuation of women's fear. It does, however, have a responsibility, through the powers it possesses, to finding ways of increasing safety for women through thoughtful and sympathetic design.

Finally it is worth noting that one response to the perceived dangers in some areas has been the privatisation of space — for example restricting access to housing estates or the use of entry phones on individual buildings and, in effect, by-passing the planning system. As the Women's Design Service points out, however, such measures don't necessarily create safer environments for women. Restricting entry to spaces or buildings *may* deny access to attackers but will more likely simply remove people from earshot. Privatising spaces reduces the numbers of people using those spaces for legitimate purposes, transforming them from public thoroughfares to hostile unpeopled environments.

Planning Responses: Where Do We Go From Here?

This chapter has sought to identify the relationship between land use planning and women's experience and has focused largely on the problems created for women by the basic priorities endorsed by conventional urban planning. While local examples have been cited, discussion has been largely confined to broad planning principles rather than individual decisions and has commented on the ways in which general trends have reinforced the creation of an essentially gender biased form of the built environment. The next section of the chapter now considers some of the ways planning has begun to respond to the problems created for women in their use of the built environment. It documents instances where planners have acted against established trends and finally makes a number of suggestions as to how planners could do more to contribute to the creation of a non-sexist built environment.

One of the major difficulties here concerns the question of recognition. Chapters 1 and 2 have already considered the essential invisibility of women's needs in a society where male lives, needs and expectations are seen as the norm and where this is reflected in the distribution of power and allocation of resources. The problems faced by women and, perhaps more importantly, the fact that planning in the built environment perpetuates and reinforces women's traditional role in society, go largely unnoticed. The sort of issues discussed in the preceding part of this chapter are, in one sense, non-issues, since they almost fail to reach the planning agenda. Debate concerning the appropriateness of particular policies or principles in terms of the differing needs of men and women is rare. In short it is hard for planners to devise solutions to land use problems that they and most of society don't even know exist. This being the case, the examples documented below are exceptions that go against the direction of conventional planning responses. They are not generally widespread although some are notably growing in popularity/acceptability.

Work cited in the discussion of gentrification and the revitalisation of urban areas (see McKenzie, 1989; Bondi, 1991; Wekerle, 1984) has noted women's preference for inner city residential locations. Such locations, it is suggested, often provide women with greater access to employment, childcare, health and retail services etc. facilitating the co-ordination of their dual roles. It is here, moreover, that women are most likely to be able to develop informal support networks to replace dwindling public service provision. Women's needs, it would appear, are best met through mixed use development; environments that incorporate housing, employment and services. Such environments are most likely to be found, at present, in inner city locations—this need not be the case however—especially given the spatial characteristics of industrial restructuring and the provision of employment opportunities for women on the periphery of urban areas.

MacKenzie (1989, p. 118) refers to the "new form of city divided into a patchwork of communities containing both public and private resources" that emerges as shifts occur in the division of labour and women play a greater part in productive activity outside the home. Planners clearly have a role to play in the development of this kind of city—assisting the move away from what Wekerle calls "exclusionary zoning".

At a local level, the point was made earlier that women frequently find town centres alienating places—especially at night. The Birmingham pressure group, Cities for People, believe that encouraging a diversity of uses in town centres helps to create a more vibrant atmosphere and reduces feelings of alienation and fear. The post-war planning and development of Birmingham is criticised by Birmingham Cities for People (BCP) women's group in a report entitled Women at the Centre (BCP, 1990). In this report the authors describe how the city centre has been planned to respond to the needs of the business visitor. Communications—in particular the famous inner ring road—have been seen as a priority and the historic Bull Ring with its cheap, lively markets "obliterated by a concrete jungle and 1960s shopping centre".

The report goes on to consider ways in which planners should respond to the mistakes of the past, advocating in particular that new development give priority to creating a mixture of uses including housing, community centres, employment, shops and green spaces. Residents in the city centre, it is suggested, would automatically attract a diversity of services and amenities.

> "The city would be alive and thriving at all hours instead of day-time tension and frantic escape, followed by deserted night-time streets cruised by taxis and crowds of youths" (Birmingham Cities for People, 1989, p. 9).

The BCP report notes the importance of public participation in the redevelopment of urban areas. It draws attention to the need to include women in seeking solutions to the problems that exist and in designing a non-sexist built environment. Without women's active involvement in land use planning at *all* levels, the kind of priorities that have characterised the evolution of the modern city will prevail. Chapter 4 looks more closely at the whole topic of women's participation in decision making. Here it is important in considering planners' response, to recognise the need for women to assert their own views as to what may be appropriate solutions. As noted above, many existing inadequacies stem from the invisibility of women's problems and needs. While that invisibility continues the sort of measures devised by planners will, as demonstrated in the Birmingham case, be unlikely to improve the lives of women to any significant degree.

The WDS in their survey of housing estate design in London also note the importance of involving women in the identification and implementation of design solutions. Their conclusions from speaking to women about the problems they face in the environments around their home, is that the relationship between women's needs, and in particular their safety, and design is much more complex than might at first seem. They write:

> "Clearly there are basic improvements to lighting and security to buildings which should be carried out as a priority where tenants feel it is appropriate, but there have been many examples of costly design changes which have had little effect on tenants' feeling of satisfaction with their estate" (Women's Design Service, 1988, pp. 11–12).

The first task for planners and architects is to find out what women want and *then* to implement appropriate solutions. Many such solutions may be simple and small-scale—the very act of involving women in the design of these environments, as the WDS demonstrate, makes them feel happier about using them and helps to reinforce a sense of security.

The problem of dangerous environments is in some senses more tangible and planners are provided at least with more practical opportunities of devising responses to the problems women face. Requesting the installation of street lighting or pedestrian crossings is more likely to be within the scope of day-to-day planning activities than dealing with the separation of residential areas from centres of employment. In 1988, as part of the Government's 'Action for Cities' initiative, the Home Office introduced a series of Safer City projects. These projects have been designed to identify the main types of crime occurring within selected cities and to suggest strategies for dealing with the crimes that exist. Women's safety, while not initially the primary focus of these projects emerged as a key issue—the main motive for the initiative itself was to attract people back into the city centre, thereby assisting urban economic regeneration. Women are most likely to avoid the city centre through fear of violence and so women are the people who need to be attracted back in. Briefly, the projects have identified various planning measures that can be adopted to reduce violence and crime and to promote 'Safer Cities'.

Trench believes that the strategies identified by the Safer Cities initiatives can be divided into two distinct types. The first of these is what she refers to as a "fortress approach" with "segregation and separate protected provision for women". This might include, for example, women-only sections of car parks, safe women's transport schemes (see Chapter 6 for a discussion), walled estates with guards and, more commonly in Britain, entry phones. Such an approach leaves "the environment as dangerous as it ever was but exempts women from its consequences" (Trench, 1990, p. 4). This type of solution is generally not directly one of *design* but rather of service provision. The creation of privatised space, however, as implied by some 'solutions' within this category, is a design issue and as noted earlier, one which may reduce rather than increase women's safety.

The second type of approach advocates measures that "improve the environment for all and therefore provide benefits for other vulnerable groups, or indeed benefits other than just in terms of safety" (Trench, 1990, p. 4). Here suggestions clearly fall within the remit of planners — the abolition of subways, the provision of better street lighting and of more salubrious places to wait for buses, for example. Measures of this sort have been recognised by planners in some authorities and are beginning to be more commonplace. Some examples are included in Chapter 8.

Clearly, as Trench recognises in her discussion of the Safer Cities initiative, planning measures of the sort described, however effective in themselves, cannot be introduced in isolation. Indeed, one of the dangers of looking at planning and design 'solutions' is that they reduce the problem of violence against women to a technical one. Such measures must, therefore, be seen as part of a package that includes support and counselling services for women who have experienced attack and attempts to address the problems of domestic violence and rehabilitation. Further attention will be given to these issues in the conclusion to this book. It is sufficient here to acknowledge that planning *is* important in the creation of a built environment that is both safe for women and meets their daily needs. Planning, and urban design cannot alone produce such an environment and whatever technical measures can be taken will undoubtedly be mediated by wider forces that contribute to women's fear and control their use of the built environment.

The idea that planning, while not entirely responsible, can exert a fundamental influence over inequalities in the built environment is one which is central to the arguments put forward in this chapter. Later chapters contain more specific detail as to the nature of planning's role in reinforcing and/or alleviating gender inequalities. Here the purpose has been to provide a general overview of the relationship between land use planning and women's experience of the city, noting areas where planning has contributed to the gendered use of space and to emerging gender roles and relations.

This final section has raised the issue of change. An important consideration must be the potential offered by planning for changing the relationship between gender and the planned environment as described here. The point has been made that progress in addressing women's needs depends to a large extent on the inclusion of women in the planning process. The next chapter looks at the involvement of women in planning both as professionals and as members of the public. Their role in influencing planning decisions is seen as critically bound up with their wider political role and brings us back inevitably to questions surrounding access to power.

4

Women, Power and Decision Making

Introduction

In identifying various planning responses to the problems and dangers experienced by women in their use of the built environment, Chapter 3 has asserted the importance of women's involvement in the planning process. The 'invisibility' of many of the constraints that land use planning imposes on women (together with their constant re-adjustment of their lives and aspirations) means that effective planning solutions will only be achieved where women are fully incorporated into decision making. Women's particular needs must be identified and addressed as part of mainstream planning policy. Solutions, whether they relate to broad land use or design issues, or to sectoral policies, must be included within normal planning objectives and not be left to appear as a benevolent afterthought.

This chapter directly considers the question of women's participation in plan making and policy implementation. It documents women's role in the planning process both as professionals and as members of the public. Just how much say do women have in determining planning decisions either at a strategic or a local level? The chapter also examines the status of what are generally termed 'women's issues' in planning. To what extent are women's needs incorporated into the planning system and what kind of frameworks have been established to address the particular problems women face? Central to these issues is the question of women's marginality. The chapter discusses the most effective way of ensuring that gender issues are given serious attention throughout the decision-making process, arguing that, where necessary, the planning process should be adapted to ensure that this is achieved. Particular attention is given to the need to avoid 'tokenism' and the 'adding in' of women's issues.

Women's participation in planning can not be divorced from their wider access to power. Their lack of involvement in the past and the low priority given to gender issues in planning is symptomatic of the powerlessness of women. This chapter considers the underlying reasons for this powerlessness—returning to some of the questions raised in Chapters 1 and 2. It identifies expressions of women's lack of power and discusses the possibilities for change in relation to planning decisions. In questioning women's access to power we are naturally brought into contact with debates surrounding their political involvement and, in particular, how changes in their political participation interacts with changes in their life styles and economic position.

In turn, the examination of women's political activity cannot be undertaken without reference to feminism and to the Women's Liberation Movement (WLM). Chapter 2 has looked at the importance of feminism in relation to women's power and as a reaction to the inequality between women and men in society. Here attention is given to the relationship between feminism and women's direct political activity. Particular attention is devoted to the way in which feminism, through the WLM has enabled women to recognise and to demonstrate the political nature of what are generally seen as 'personal' issues.

Women, Power and the Parliamentary System

Perhaps an appropriate starting point for the discussion of women's access to political power is the 1918 Representation of the People Act which allowed women over the age of thirty to vote for the first time. This assumed starting point should not, however, be allowed to obscure the fact that women had been involved in political activity long before this date—not least in the campaigns surrounding women's suffrage that took place in the nineteenth and early twentieth centuries (see Bryson, 1992). Radical working class movements (e.g. the Owenites and Chartists) incorporated some (limited) calls for women's suffrage, while some years later, middle class women began to campaign for an increase in women's rights. In 1869 women were granted the municiple vote, allowing them to participate in local politics, but it was not until 1918 that women were permitted a formal role in the national political activity of the country. Following this Act, however, progress towards women's greater representation was slow and it must be remembered that it wasn't until 1928 that the vote was extended to *all* women.

Women's political activity during the early and mid twentieth century was dominated by campaigns around suffrage but was not confined to this issue. Increasingly, women began to organise around issues of employment, contraception and childcare. The early twentieth century saw a proliferation of welfare reforms aimed at improving the health of children and young people and consequently the quality of labour power. Legislation focused on childhealth and conditions of child rearing and procreation

(Rowan, 1982). Such reforms, however, saw existing problems mainly as a result of mothers' ignorance, rather than poor material conditions. Their solution—to instruct women in the 'skills of motherhood'—served not to empower women but simply to enforce the dominance of their domestic role. Linked to these views on the importance of women's domestic role was a support for the 'family wage'—the belief that every family should be in receipt of a single wage (to be earned by the male worker), a wage sufficient to support the whole family. The underlying ideology was, again, the maintenance of women within the home as wives and mothers, and *not* as wage earners.

In response to the attitudes from which welfare reform had started to emerge, women's political organisation gained strength. Amongst the most influential organisations established by women for this purpose was the Women's Co-operative Guild (WCG), founded in 1883. The WCG was determined to go beyond immediate domestic concerns and sought to campaign for wider social reform that would provide *practical* solutions to the needs of women. In doing so they aimed not to ignore the private sphere of the home but to challenge what they saw as the false dichotomy between women's public and private lives. Amongst the early campaigns of the WCG was the provision of maternity benefit directly to all mothers and a comprehensive national scheme of maternity care. The WCG became a well established and supported organisation (with over 50,000 members by the 1930s). It is seen as unique for its time, demanding reforms not only from the state but also from men as individuals. The WCG stood alone in tackling personal relationships between husbands and wives as crucial to women's rights and well-being.

The spirit of the WCG campaigns—the issues around which its members mobilized—was supported by other working class women's organisations in the early twentieth century, so moving away from the "laissez faire individualism of early, mainly middle class, feminists" (Bryson, 1992). One organisation which took up the demands of what became known as welfare feminism was the Women's Labour League (WLL). Founded in 1906, the WLL (to be replaced by the Labour Party women's sections in 1918) was closely allied to the labour movement in its aims and organisation. The League's early activity centred on increasing women's involvement in organised politics and in the Labour Party in general. Its arguments, however, did not challenge the dominant assumptions of women's domestic role; on the contrary they emphasised the value of women's contribution as wives and mothers within political life. As Rowan writes:

> "Reversing the priorities of the WCG, which were to transcend domestic responsibility to 'the world beyond the family and even beyond the store', the League stressed that political activity was necessary for women to carry out their domestic duties fully" (Rowan, 1982, p. 74).

Opposition to this focus was expressed by a group of women within the League who argued strongly for a married women's right to work. But the experiences of women's mass involvement in war work (the long hours, unhealthy conditions and opposition from male unions) hardened opinion against mothers' employment within the labour movement generally.

In other respects the First World War helped women within the labour movement to gain influence — marking the beginning of a new tendency for women to work with, or even within government. Several women were appointed on government committees such as the Women's Housing Advisory Committee, The Central Committee on Women's Employment and the Consumer Council's Sub-Committee on Municipal Kitchens. Attitudes towards working women within the labour movement were beginning to change and the gains won by women during the war years were staunchly defended by organised campaigns once the war was over.

The organisations mentioned here were by no means unique, nor did they represent the extent of women's political activity during the early twentieth century. 'The Primrose League', for example, was important in campaigning for a voice for women within the Conservative Party, while the Union Women's Associations also fought vigorously for women's political representation. Such organisations did not, however, have the mass working class appeal of the Women's Cooperative Guild and Women's Labour League (Campbell, 1987).

The value of political groups and campaigns in improving women's health and welfare (especially amongst the working classes) in the early-mid twentieth century cannot be denied. More progressive women's organisations had some limited success in changing attitudes towards women's economic and political roles. It may be argued that the gains that were made in terms of the state adopting greater responsibility for health care and child welfare (for example in the provision of health visitors and midwives) served simply to establish new norms of mothering which trapped women more firmly within the domestic sphere. But, as Rowan argues, these changes initiated a "shift in the patriarchal centre of gravity from the individual family to the political and ideological levels" (Rowan, 1982, p. 82). She goes on to assert that:

> "The working-class home was opened up, not only to closer state regulation, but also as a legitimate sphere of political struggle. If child-rearing and housewifery were civic duties, they could demand civic rights in return" (p. 82).

The link between the importance of motherhood and votes for women, while not explicit in the demands of many of the women's organisations and political groups, thus became apparent.

During the inter-war years and directly following the Second World War, women continued to organise around welfare issues, demanding resources to assist 'women's work' within the domestic arena, while at the same time, opening up the private sphere of the home. Successful at times in relation to specific demands, women's political activity remained largely confined to issues concerning consumption, the family and the home. From the 1950s control over fertility emerged as a major focus for women's political activity, giving rise to a new wave of women's networks and fundamental to the development of the women's liberation movement (Mackenzie, 1988). Campaigns around the control of childbirth, contraception and, later, abortion, were absorbed into mainstream political activity and women's liberation itself re-emerged as a political as well as a social objective.

Despite the parliamentary time given to issues such as abortion, the focus of women's political activity has remained, by and large, the local state. Women have been important actors within community action groups, local protest movements etc. As studies of urban politics have demonstrated, however, (see, for example, Dunleavy, 1984; Saunders, 1982; Duncan and Goodwin, 1988) major political parties have been slow to associate with extra parliamentary activity and consequently consumption issues, those issues that are, disproportionately, the concern of women, are depoliticised (Button, 1984).

As Bondi and Peake (1988) note problems surrounding 'reproduction' are relatively isolated from mainstream political life. Various commentators have attempted to explain such isolation in terms of the tension between local state and central state activity (see Cockburn, 1977; Saunders, 1982), seeing protest over consumption (local state) issues as basically transitory, issue-specific and geographically constrained. Bondi and Peake (1988, p. 34) argue, however, that such arguments have tended to ignore the relationship between gender and reproduction. Thus, the "political isolation of issues of reproduction also involves the isolation of interests stemming from gender interests".

The low political profile of consumption issues relates, fundamentally, to the limited political power of women. Women, while constituting 52% of the electorate in Britain remain poorly represented in positions of political power. The numbers of women occupying political positions is inversely proportional to the power of these positions. At the time of the 1987 general election, women accounted for about 40–50% of local Labour and Conservative Party membership, about 15% of local councillors and less than 7% of MPs (Bondi and Peake, 1988). While the 1987 general election saw a record (at that time) number of female candidates contesting parliamentary seats, 327 compared with 267 in 1983 and only 90 in 1964, the figures must, as Coote and Patullo (1990) point out, be put in perspective. In 1987 there were 1,997 male candidates — 594 of these went on to become MPs as opposed to 41 women. The 1992 general election showed a further improvement in women's representation in parliament. The total number of women candidates was 548 and 58 of these were successfully elected — 17 more than in 1987. While important in continuing an upward trend, these gains are small and still leave women very severely under represented. In the House of Lords women's representation is even more marginal; in 1987 only 67 (5%) of the 1186 peers were women.

Within the Government itself, the situation is comparable with far fewer women than men holding key posts in the Cabinet. During the 1980s the position of Margaret Thatcher as Prime Minister was frequently held up (by non-feminists) as illustrative of the fact that women can and do command positions of political power. On looking closely at Thatcher's background and rise to power, however, it is evident that her position is not typical of all or indeed many women. Her education and early introduction into political life were very unusual for a women of her generation and as Coote and Pattullo (1990) argue:

> "Mrs. Thatcher's phenomenal success does not show that any woman .... can become powerful in British politics. It demonstrates only what one particular woman can do in one particular — and by no means typical — set of circumstances" (p. 7).

Perhaps more importantly, once in a position of power, Thatcher essentially did nothing to increase the power of women generally. She appointed no women to her cabinet(s) and promoted very few women to top Civil Service posts. Many of Thatcher's policies worked *against* the interests of women, attacking public service provision and eroding the base of community power. Since Thatcher's resignation, pressure has been placed on the Prime Minister, John Major, to include women within his Cabinet. Following the 1992 election he could no longer afford to ignore this pressure and appointed three women to key posts within the Government. Unfortunately, as will be seen in the remaining chapters of the book, there is little evidence to suggest that such a move reflects a real commitment by those in Government to improving the position and power of women more widely.

While the majority of women's political activity, then, has been in the more accessible arena of 'informal' politics; locally based campaigns around issues of collective consumption, there are notable instances of their participation in national (mainstream) issues. Two obvious examples pertinent to women's recent political experience in Britain are the anti-nuclear protests at Greenham Common and the 1984/5 miners' strike. In both cases women emerged to take a leading role in campaigns and, at times, to re-orientate the protest in accordance with their own interpretation of the issues and their particular needs and interests within the struggle. Important here is not so much the influence women had on these political campaigns — although this says much about women's particular approach to conflict and negotiation — but the actual power and experience afforded to women through their involvement.

The Greenham Common Peace Camp and the Miners' Support Groups were established by collections of women who felt alienated and frustrated by the workings of a male dominated political system. In a sense they can be seen as a reaction by women against the traditional male domination of political activity in Britain and a strong desire by women to organise differently. The campaigns drew many women into formal politics for the first time, collective action giving them the confidence and strength to assert their belief and needs within a male world. As Lynne Segal (1987) writing on the women's peace movement asserts:

> "The strength of the Greenham Common Peace camp undoubtedly derives from the fact that it is organised only by and for women. It is perfectly obvious that many women are silenced within the more formal structures of most mixed groups, and cannot experience the control, confidence and solidarity they more often share with one another" (Segal, 1987, p. 167).

A number of authors, including Segal, have written at length on the links between political campaigns such as Greenham Common and the feminist movement (see, for example, Snitow, 1985; Cook and Kirk, 1983; Harford and Hopkins, 1984) attempting to assess the importance of such action for women's equality generally. There is disagreement over the extent to which women are fundamentally (and permanently) empowered by campaigns such as Greenham Common. While some authors have argued that there can be no denying the positive impact of women organising together to control their own lives, others believe that such single issue campaigns—and the women's peace movement in particular—have simply succeeded in diverting attention and energy from the *real* struggle against male power.

There is disagreement, also, as to the extent to which the political power acquired by women from campaigns, such as Greenham Common, or the miners' support group is really sustainable. Individual women's accounts of the impact that being involved in an intensive political campaign had on their lives confirms the immediate liberating effect of such action (see for example, Leonard, 1991; Stead, 1987). Coote and Pattullo (1990) document the attempts that were made by women involved in the miners' strike to perpetuate the organisations that had evolved by building links to other women's groups including the Greenham women and groups campaigning against apartheid in South Africa. In terms of women more broadly, however, "when women's collective struggles die down .... the confidence and sense of purpose they generate begins to fade" (Segal, 1987, p. 233). The degree to which male power is seriously eroded as a result of women's political action in these cases is minimal. While the involvement of women in the miners' strike, for example, encouraged the National Union of Mineworkers to support attempts by women to gain greater equality within the Trade Union movement more generally, outside *this* particular union (and hence further from the focus of women's involvement) neither the Labour Party nor the TUC were prepared to change their own internal practices to strengthen women's position. The following quote from Segal aptly sums up the situation:

> "In terms of overall political power there has been little change in the position of women in Britain at the top of any state institutions. The continuing growth of women's political consciousness and activism in local politics and diverse campaigns and movements is not reflected in any parliamentary, legislative judicial or senior civil service elites, where their representation remains under 5%. This contrasts with the position in Sweden, Norway, Denmark and Finland where women's representation in Parliament is over 25%" (Segal, 1987, p. 229).

Women and the Planning Process

Having looked, on a fairly general level, at women's access to political power and channels of decision making, we now turn in the following section to a more detailed analysis of women's power within the planning process. This analysis will include an assessment of women's role in the structures of decision making and a consideration of the centrality of women's issues within the planning agenda. Both will involve an examination of the mechanisms of policy making—in particular the channels through which women's needs and demands are heard. Discussion will be based on a variety of different sources including published research, planning documents and the results of interviews with women directly involved in the planning process—both as planning officers and as members of pressure groups.

A central concern in the analysis of women's influence in the planning system is the examination of their role as professionals/employees within that system. A study by Greed (1992) revealed that in 1971 women constituted just 5.4% of the corporate membership of the Royal Town Planning Institute (the professional organisation of the planning profession). By 1991 this figure had risen to 16.5%. Clearly not all these women were necessarily practising planners at the time and many other women currently employed in planning departments may not have qualified for or taken up membership of the RTPI. The figures do, however, demonstrate the dominance of male members within the profession. This domination is particularly pronounced within it's 'upper echelons' with a heavy concentration of men within more senior posts. Greed's research indicates that only 5% of senior planning posts are held by women (Greed, 1993).

These figures are not particularly surprising—men being numerically dominant in the majority of professional occupations and, within these professions, at higher grades. In addition to her special focus on planning, Greed has traced this trend through the main professions concerned with land development. Her results are summarised in Table 4.1.

The figures for those employed in planning echo a bias in favour of men in planning education. A study undertaken in the late 1980s (see Hillier *et*

TABLE 4.1 *Membership of the Built Environment Professions (1991)*

Body	Total membership	% Female
Royal Town Planning Institute	16764	18.0
Royal Institue of Chartered Surveyors	86323	6.8
Institute of Civil Engineers	77595	2.8
Institute of Structural Engineers	21503	2.8
Institute of Housing	10352	41.0
Royal Institute of British Architects	31266	7.5

Source: Greed (1992, p. 12).

al., 1988) found that the ratio of women to men on full-time undergraduate planning courses in the UK was 1:3. Contrary to general trends surrounding women's participation in higher education, this proportion was apparently not on the increase. Women's participation on part-time postgraduate courses in planning was, however, rising slightly (the ratio of women to men on part-time courses rose from 1:3.7 in 1985 to 1:3 in 1986).

Of course, as has already been pointed out above, the presence of women within the decision-making process is no guarantee that women's initiatives will be adopted or even fought for. As Halford (1989, p. 169) points out:

> "On its own, the participation of women in the formal process of local government policy making is not enough to ensure that positive policies for women are developed and implemented."

What is more certain, however, is that a lack of women in the planning profession may result in the neglect of women's needs and in the automatic acceptance of planning strategies which perpetuate stereo-typical assumptions concerning the gendered use of space. Women in planning and related jobs may not universally push for non-sexist planning policies, but their presence in the profession provides an important reminder of the changing role of women and their related needs and experiences.

The positions of individual women within the planning profession is only one, albeit very important, factor in influencing the adoption of positive policies for women by local authorities. Another key factor is the commitment to equal opportunities across the authority generally and the extent to which such commitment is reflected in the formal strategies and structure of the council. Of relevance here is the adoption of an equal opportunities policy — together with the mechanisms to implement such a policy — and the existence of a special women's unit and/or committee (or sub-committee). 'Equalities' strategies are again no guarantee that women's issues within *planning* are given a high profile, especially if the channels of communication between departments are weak, but are at least an indication that the issues are formally recognised within the wider organisations.

The following section considers the role of formal initiatives in promoting the needs of women within the built environment and in increasing their power within the planning process. It draws on both published research and original empirical data.

Women's Committees/Units in Local Government

While it is very difficult to quantify or compare the prioritisation of women's issues by local authorities it can be argued that a women's committee generally demonstrates a higher level of commitment to furthering women's needs and equality than does an equal opportunities (EO) strategy. Equal opportunities policies, and indeed EO units, are involved primarily with raising women's issues *within* the authority—principally securing greater equity in job appointments, promotions etc. and working to advance more favourable deals for women in relation to, for example, childcare and flexible hours of working. They deal in the main not only with issues of gender but with inequalities based on race and (often) disability too. Consequently, the attention that can be given to women's needs in society by an EO policy/unit is relatively limited. By contrast, women's committees and units do at least concentrate primarily on gender inequality (although within this wider remit they may at times focus on black women or disabled women). Their 'target', moreover, is women in general and not just women within the authority and they tend to have more scope for intervention. The division between EO and women's units/committees does not always follow this pattern (especially given the recent tendency of local authorities to incorporate women's and race initiatives within one equality unit). It is important, therefore, in attempting to classify local authority initiatives, that attention is paid to the actual remit of the different formal structures and that assumptions are not made based on titles alone.

The emergence of women's units and women's committees within local government is a relatively recent phenomenon—only since the beginning of the 1980s have formal initiatives of this type been properly established. Research by Susan Halford (see Halford, 1987, 1989) examined the early development of women's initiatives within local government, identifying the number, form and geographical distribution of such initiatives. This work discovered three basic types of initiative; firstly, full women's committees, secondly, women's sub-committees and thirdly, a group of what were described as "miscellaneous initiatives"—equal opportunities initiatives, women's working parties etc.

TABLE 4.2 *Women's Initiatives in Local Government, 1986*

Full women's committee	Women's sub-committee	Other initiatives
Derbyshire CC	Nottingham	Norwich
Camden LB	Brent LB	Leicester
Ealing LB	Greenwich LB	Rochdale MBC
Hackney LB	Newham LB	Tameside MBC
Haringey LB	Newcastle MBC	Manchester MBC
Islington LB	Southampton	Basildon
Lambeth LB	Wolverhampton	Reading
Lewisham LB	Leeds	Bradford MBC
Southwark LB		Kirklees MBC
Waltham Forest LB		Sheffield MBC
Brighton		
Bristol		
Birmingham MBC		
York		

Source: Halford (1989).

Table 4.2 summarises the number and spatial location of the three different forms of women's initiative in England as recorded at the time of Halford's research; the mid-eighties. Halford discovered, through this research, that only 8% of all local authorities in England, Scotland and Wales had introduced some form of women's initiative (the table only lists those authorities in England for comparative purposes). The table demonstrates a clear bias in the location of initiatives, with the vast majority, 85% of the total, occurring in local authorities which can be described as 'urban'. Also very apparent is the concentration of women's initiatives in London with 30% of all initiatives falling within the Greater London area (Halford, 1989).

Kathryn Riley (1990) has also studied the introduction of women's committees and units in local government, identifying not only the early pattern of growth but also the basic aims and objectives of these initiatives. Riley describes the emergence of the first women's committees — all in London — and notes how the emphasis at the time was primarily on getting women's issues on the political agenda. Focusing on the local authority as an employer, councils such as Camden and Lewisham started to push for equality of opportunity in "the removal of institutional obstacles which blocked women's career progression" (Riley, 1990, p. 51). By 1981 the GLC's Women's Committee was pushing for more "politically ambitious" objectives, seeking to increase the power and resources available to women in an attempt to address, more broadly, the social and economic problems experienced by women.

Riley argues that it is possible to distinguish between the ultimate aim of equality of *outcome* that was supported by the women's committees and that of equality of *opportunity* as endorsed by councillors or by council officers. These, she suggests, are not necessarily compatible:

TABLE 4.3 *Women's Committees in Local Authorities (with Dates of Formation)*

Full committee		Sub-committee	
Greenwich	1987	Southampton	1986
Islington	1982	Manchester	1986
*Hackney	—		
*Southwark	—	Leicester	—
Lewisham	—	Birmingham	—
Newham	1985	*Bristol	1990
W. Forest	1986		
N. Tyneside	1988		
Wolverhampton	1985		
Basildon	1989		
Sheffield	1986		
*Brighton	—		

*No 1991 questionnaire returned but authorities contacted separately to ascertain if the former Women's Committee still existed.
Source: Questionnaire survey (1991).

> "The assumption behind the equality of opportunity strategy was that equality would be achieved by the introduction of rigorous officer controls and procedures on recruitment, selection etc. and by the removal of obvious bias in housing allocation policies etc. Equality of outcome, however, would require *specific actions* to redress the balance of past discriminations" (Riley, 1992, p. 53).

A review of women's committees, undertaken in 1983 (see reference in Riley, 1992), identifies the common aims of the eleven committees then established. These aims indicate quite clearly that it was equality of *outcome* that was supported by the women's committees at that time. There aims were essentially to

(1) promote the welfare of women and women's rights
(2) work for the elimination of discrimination against women in legislation and practices
(3) encourage the adoption of positive action to promote real equality of opportunity for women
(4) encourage and support the development of women's groups and organisations
(5) open up the Council decision-making structure to women in the community.

It is beyond the scope of this book to undertake a detailed examination of the actual achievements of individual women's committees (but see Halford, 1991; Riley, 1990). What is of more immediate concern here is the nature of the evolution of women's committees (and other initiatives for addressing 'equality' issues) as a formal part of the structure of local government—to what extent and in what form have they survived?

To answer this question and to try to discover more about the nature of local government commitment to women's committees and women's units, the survey of local authorities in England (as described in Chapter 1) was undertaken. This allowed Halford's information to be updated (albeit on a partial basis), in the identification of those authorities in which there was a women's unit,[5] women's committee or other form of initiative.

The incomplete coverage of the questionnaire survey means that it is difficult to make direct comparisons between the 1991 survey and Halford's research as regards total numbers of women's full- and sub-committees. It has been possible, however, to follow up all those authorities where full women's committees existed in 1986 and directly compare the 1986 findings with those of 1991. At times the authority committee structure did not fit happily within the division imposed here—some 'sub-committees' were not named as such but appeared to have the same role and position in the hierarchy as other 'named' sub-committees. While the following classification is as accurate as the information available will currently allow, some variation from this position may have taken place since the time of writing, in particular in the numbers of sub-committees and 'other' initiatives.

The research revealed that, in 1991, full women's committees existed in twelve authorities with sub-committees in a further five (see Table 4.3). Comparing this to Halford's 1986 survey it appears that there has been an overall reduction in the numbers of women's committees from twenty three to seventeen. Eight councils have lost their full women's committee (see Tables 4.2 and 4.3) — by and large these have become sub-committees of equalities committees. Three women's sub-committees from 1986 have now become full committees (Wolverhampton, Greenwich and Newham) while a further four have been abolished completely. Manchester is the only authority that now has a women's sub-committee where previously no initiative existed (although, as noted earlier, this information is not as easy to check where authorities failed to return questionnaires).

The distribution of women's committees was, as Halford (1989) had earlier pointed out, strongly biased in favour of London Boroughs and Metropolitan Borough Councils with only five authorities *outside* these areas having either a full or sub- women's committee.

As Riley's (1990) research has shown, commonly women's committees are supported by women's units. Of the 270 authorities who responded to the questionnaire, nine (3.3%) have a formal women's unit as part of the council organisation. The authorities and the years in which the women's units were established are listed in Table 4.4.

Again an important observation to be drawn from this list is that it includes only two authorities (Basildon and Bristol) that are neither London Boroughs or Metropolitan Districts. Significant is the absence of

---

[5]It is unclear from Halford's research whether 'women's units' are included under other initiatives. Here they are discussed separately.

TABLE 4.4 *Local Authority Women's Units*

Authority	Year of formation
1983	
Islington	1982
Newham	1985
Waltham Forest	1986
Birmingham	1984
North Tyneside	1988
Sheffield	—
Wolverhampton	1985
Basildon	1989
Bristol	1986

Source: Questionnaire survey (1991).

County Council representation. So women's units are concentrated entirely within urban authorities, with Basildon being the only authority included which is not a major city in its own right or part of London.

Like women's committees, the establishment of women's units is concentrated temporally as well as spatially with the majority being formed in the mid to late 1980s. As far as *this* survey is concerned then, the local authority women's units that do exist all came into being during a period of just eight years between 1982 and 1989.

The degree of overlap between authorities with women's units and those with women's committees is high; all authorities with a women's unit also have a women's committee and only three (or six) authorities, Lewisham, Manchester and Southampton, have just a women's committee and no women's unit.

As Halford recognised in her research, there are other forms of 'women's initiative' within the structures of local government, in addition to women's units and women's committees. Eighteen authorities[6] in the 1991 questionnaire survey reported the existence of groups which, while not actually women's units or committees, are structures within the council with a responsibility for women's issues/equality. Some of these groups are specifically *planning* initiatives while others are authority-wide (see Table 4.5).

The status of the eighteen initiatives included here varies significantly. A number are informal groups set up to consider women's issues either within planning or more broadly, and act wholly or partly as support networks for women working in the authority. They share, with many of the groups identified, an advisory function, and like such groups have little direct influence on policy making within the authority. Other groups, for example, Barking and Dagenham's Women's Liaison Group, have a more

---

[6]Included in this 18 were only authorities that did *not* have either a women's unit or a women's committee.

TABLE 4.5 *Other Forms of Local Authority Women's Initiative*

Authority	Initiative
Barking & Dagenham	Women's Liaison Group
Bedfordshire	Women's Consultative Group
Calderdale	Women and Planning Group
Derbyshire	Women and Planning Action Plan
Dudley	Women's Network
Hounslow	Women and Planning Group
Northampton	Women Planner's Group
Norwich	Women and Violence Group
Nottinghamshire	Women's Issues Consultative Group
Oldham	Forum for Women
Rutland	Women's Advisory Group
Thamesdown	Women's Advisory Panel
Thurrock	Women in the 90s
Wandsworth	Informal Women's Group
Welwyn Hatfield	Women's Officer
Dorset County Council	Women Principal Officers Group
Gloucestershire C.C.	Women Manager's Network
Suffolk County Council	Women in Management Group

Source: Questionnaire survey (1991).

TABLE 4.6 *Authorities with an Equal Opportunities Committee or Unit*

Luton	Avon	Merton	Bradford
Reading	Cumbria	Lambeth	SouthTyneside
Pendle	Humberside	Sutton	Dudley
Rosendale	Derbyshire	Harrow	
Peterborough	Lancashire		
Stoke on Trent	Northumberland		
Norwich			

Source: Questionnaire survey (1991).

formal role to play in the decision-making process with a direct link into identified committees within the authorities. In general, as Halford argues, such groups are likely to be less effective than women's units or full committees due to their low status, poor resourcing and the fact that they are "unlikely to be centrally integrated into the council committee structure" (Halford, 1989, p. 167).

In addition to those groups already mentioned a further three specific women's groups were identified—these were aimed at women in management within the authorities. All three were in County Councils; Dorset, Gloucestershire and Suffolk.

Interestingly, while the number of authorities with women's committees and sub-committees is declining, the number developing other types of initiative is increasing. Halford's work identified only ten women's initiatives in English authorities, over and above the formal committees and units. Again, although *direct* comparisons are not really appropriate, the results do indicate a swing from the support of conventional structures to more *ad hoc* groupings with varying emphases in terms of personnel and topic.

In addition to those local authorities with women's units, committees or another form of women's initiative, were a number of councils who claimed to be addressing women's needs through some kind of equal opportunities unit or group. As already noted, equal opportunity initiatives can take a range of forms and can represent very different levels of commitment on behalf of authorities to women's issues. Some councils have established structures within the organisation to handle 'equality issues'—equal opportunity units and committees. Others have restricted their involvement to equal opportunity working parties or nominated EO officers, while a third group appear committed only to policy statements on EO. It is very difficult, on a general level, to evaluate the relative strengths of the different approaches. It is possible, however, to distinguish between those EO initiatives that are essentially internal to the council and focus purely on current and potential local authority employees, and those that exist to promote EO in the district/county more widely.

This division between types of EO initiative is critical. The raising of the EO profile amongst public and private agencies and employers during the 1980s has prompted many to produce some kind of declaration or statement on the issue (Stone, 1988). The existence of a written policy is not necessarily a guarantee that an authority is developing strategies aimed at addressing women's needs generally. Such strategies are more likely to emanate from units and committees established for the purpose of advancing EO beyond the authority. These formal structures are closer in organisation and purpose to the women's units and committees already discussed, although by definition (that they deal with all forms of disadvantaged 'minority' group) their commitment to women's issues specifically is likely to be less.

Of those authorities responding to the questionnaire survey, twenty reported that within their organisation there was an EO committee or unit. The twenty included seven district councils, six county councils, four London boroughs and three metropolitan councils (see Table 4.6)

In at least two cases, Reading and Lambeth, the EO or equality unit had *replaced* pre-existing women's units. The position of Bristol is that restructuring within the council has resulted in the loss of the women's and race committees as full committees and their incorporation into a new 'equalities' committee. Within this committee, as discussed later, 'Women' and 'Race' are retained as sub-committees. It is too early to say whether reductions in local authority funding together with changing political priorities mean that this is a pattern likely to be repeated elsewhere. The fact that no new women's units have been created since 1990 is perhaps an indication of a change of direction towards equality units and a consequent down grading of both women's and race issues. As Riley (1990, p. 61) again notes:

> "Even scarcer resources will force Women's Units and Committees to decide on the best organisational arrangement for the continuation of effective work on gender equality and for the most effective links with other aspects of equality work. The decision whether to establish a Central Equal Opportunities Unit or Directorate, bringing together all aspects of equal opportunities, or to have separate free standing Units, is a complex one, dependant on a range of factors including the type of authority, the culture of the organisation and its stage of development in tackling equal opportunities issues".

This theme is taken up again later in the chapter.

In addition to the twenty authorities mentioned a further nineteen have either an EO working party/monitoring group, fourteen, or a designated EO officer, five. The distribution of EO working parties is weighted towards the district councils; eight of the fourteen are from districts, four are from metropolitan boroughs and two from counties. Of the EO officers, two are located in county councils, two in London boroughs and one in a District.

Combining all types of initiative discussed here a total of seventy-one authorities currently have some form of established women's or equal opportunities initiative (other than a simple policy statement of equal opportunities). This represents 27% of those authorities responding to the questionnaire. As mentioned earlier, as a proportion of all 405 authorities this is likely to be somewhat of an over-estimation since those with a positive approach were more likely to respond to the survey. A clear urban bias has been identified in the distribution of the different initiatives. Overall, of those authorities responding to the questionnaire, 57% of both London boroughs and metropolitan councils currently have a women's or equal opportunities initiative. The same applies, by contrast, to 41% of county councils and only 13% of districts. It is important to note, moreover, that the initiatives belonging to the county and district councils were generally those concerning equal opportunities rather than women's issues — consequently, as argued above, those with least power to address the general needs of women within the broader community.

The extent to which the existence of formal structures such as women's units and equality committees can provide impetus and support for planning departments is influenced partly by the links that exist between them. The survey of local authorities revealed quite a wide variation in the ways in which individual planning departments related to the recognised women's initiatives. In some cases links have been established within the organisational framework of the authority and there are clear channels through which information is passed. Some authorities operate a system of designated officers within planning departments whose role it is to liaise between women's initiatives and planning, to receive information and often to represent the planning department in formal meetings of women's committees and groups. Other authorities appear to reinforce links through the exchange of reports and minutes of meetings and others simply through casual communication and advice when needed.

It is very difficult to evaluate the relative effectiveness of the different ways in which planning departments relate to women's initiatives. What is apparent, however, as stressed in the responses to the questionnaire survey and by the officer from Bristol City Council's women's unit (see below), is that in order to raise awareness of women's issues amongst planners and for the policies and advice emerging from women's initiatives to be taken on board by planning departments, links need to be both formal and firmly established. As a respondent from a London borough remarked, "links between the planning department and women's unit need to be structured—ideally for one or a group of planning officers to be responsible for work on women's issues. Unless this is formally established the relationship is dependent on the personal commitment of individuals" (for further discussion of this point, see Chapter 8).

While the majority of planning departments appeared to relate to the authority's women's initiatives either via a nominated officer or simply through casual advice, a few had more extensive and well developed links. Islington Council, for example, have established an explicit link between the two in their Local Plan and Development Control consultation procedures. In addition, they operate a system of working groups on specific issues of relevance to planning and the women's unit and while there is not a specific group or individual in planning with formal responsibility for overseeing women's issues, in practice this work tends to be co-ordinated by one person.

One of the clear messages to emerge from the study of linkages between planning departments and women's initiatives where they exist is that the strength of the relationship is to a large extent dependent on the commitment of individuals. A number of authorities claimed that the work/advice of the women's unit or committee had a very direct route into the planning department because a planner happened to be acting as a key member of that initiative. This obviously begs the question as to whether the links would be retained if the particular individual changed jobs.

The details of specific local authority planning policies geared to the needs and interests of women are discussed on a subject-by-subject basis in the following chapters. It is important, however, in concluding this discussion of women's initiatives, to make a few observations about the general relationship between the existence of organisational structures and the development of positive policies for women within planning departments.

Perhaps not surprisingly, the questionnaire identified strong links between the existence of a women's unit or committee and explicit planning policies on women's issues (only 7 authorities of the 35 with a women's initiative had no explicit planning policies for women (with a further 4 unknown)). The relationship was less well developed in the case of authorities with EO units or committees and less developed still amongst those where only an EO monitoring group or working party had been established (8 out of 20 of the former and 9 of 19 of the latter had no planning policies directed specifically at women's needs). Conversely, 32 authorities were identified who claimed to have introduced policies concerning women's issues but did not have any form of women's or EO initiative in either the planning department or the council at large.

Women's Initiatives and the Local State

So far the discussion has concentrated largely on the presence or absence of formal structures for addressing women's needs within local authorities. Other than to identify the original aims and objectives of women's committees, little has been said about the ways in which such structures work and how they fit within the environment of local government and local state politics. In terms of positive gains for women, however, this is an area of key importance. Central to the efficacy of women's initiatives is the nature of their interaction with other local government machinery and their status and acceptability within the political arena of the local state. Again, this area provides potential for an entire book and its limitation here to a small part of a chapter is difficult. The whole debate incorporates wider questions not only on the relationship between formal politics and community action but also the way in which academics have chosen to portray or interpret women's political activity.

As was pointed out earlier in this chapter, the fact that women's political activity has revolved mainly around consumption issues has served to devalue their contribution. Women have been associated with what are regarded as 'private' and thus non-political issues. Where they have been involved in political battles their activity has consistently been labelled informal. Struggles by feminists have sought to re-define the boundaries as to what is political (and in some cases they have made considerable ground); to increase recognition that issues around 'the personal'—issues of childcare, reproduction and sexuality for example—are deeply political issues. As such, they argue, these issues should be debated as part of legitimate mainstream local and national political activity.

Brownhill and Halford (1990) criticise the use of the formal/informal dichotomy to describe political activity, and in particular the categorisation of women's involvement within the informal sphere. They suggest that such a categorisation is impossible to implement given the complexity of the political issues within which women are active. Furthermore it denies the struggle which women have fought to re-define the personal into the political and conveniently sidesteps (by reducing it to a 'private' matter) the challenge of the women's movement.

The introduction of women's initiatives into local government represented, in some senses, a greater acceptance of women's issues as a part of the local political agenda. The main period of their introduction—the early to mid 1980s—was a time when the 'new urban left' had reached its height and was able to express a commitment to more radical 'grass roots' politics within the structures of local government (Duncan and Goodwin, 1988). The contribution of women's initiatives; their ability to achieve the sorts of gains for women for which they were established, must be seen within the context of the changing fortunes of the left within political activity. Moreover, women's initiatives can only be judged within a wider recognition of the changes that they were attempting to make to the whole way in which local politics operates and in particular to the relationship between local government and the community.

From the outset, women's initiatives have sat uncomfortably within a local government which while (perhaps only partially) supportive of their aims and objectives, was not prepared to sanction or even recognise their challenge to the existing structures of political power. The major contradiction that has been faced by women's initiatives has been that their operation and existence has been determined by an essentially patriarchal state whose own mode of operation runs largely counter to their essential beliefs. As Brownhill and Halford (1990) note:

> "Both state and mainstream politics are male dominated, operate using political forms which are the antithesis of the women's movement and, maybe most importantly, devise and implement policies which maintain the unequal position of women in society" (p. 401).

Some commentators have suggested that, in the light of the inherent contradiction between the aims of women's initiatives and the allegiances of local government, the former are bound to be tokenistic. Similarly, a belief that in introducing women's initiatives the aim is to detract women from the 'real struggle' (against male dominance) has caused sections of the women's movement to reject local government women's initiatives. It is, however, important to recognise that while their gains will be arguably small and inevitably constrained within the traditional structures of local government, it is an explicit aim of women's initiatives to *challenge* these structures. Women's committees and units have sought, through the use of feminist practices, to transform not only the priorities but the operation of local government in Britain.

Women who reject the 'tokenism' label argue that it is only through the introduction of feminist ways of working—as characterise women's initiatives—from within local government that change will be achieved. These ways of working incorporate many ideas from the women's movement such as non-hierarchical structures, collective decision making and women only groups. Perhaps, more importantly, as Brownhill and Halford (1990, p. 401) assert:

"Underneath these (styles and methods of working) lie a commitment to transform the relationship between local government and the broader community from the operation of power and control by the authority over the community to use the authority's resources (in the widest sense) to empower local people"

As part of this attempt to empower local people women's committees have frequently co-opted women from the local community and attempted to devolve financial resources.

Looking back from the early 1990s allows us to reflect on the development and achievements of women's initiatives as a part of the operation of local politics and decision making. Later chapters will comment in more depth on their contribution within specific policy areas as part of the planning process but here we are concerned with their broader role within local government organisation. The concentration of women's initiatives in space and time indicates their close relationship with the political fortunes of the 'new urban left'. The decline of this movement under the ideological, political and financial attacks of the central state has had predictable implications for individual elements such as women's initiatives. But even during the early 1980s, when local government remained *relatively* strong, political support for women's initiatives was patchy and the new styles of working often the cause of distrust and suspicion. Given these constraints, could women's initiatives ever hope to maintain a lasting influence?

Susan Halford (1991) has looked at why women's initiatives have generally failed to extend their power within local government. She uses a case study of the London Borough of Camden's Women's Committee—one of the first to be established and a "flagship of municipal feminism" (Brownhill and Halford, 1990)—to suggest reasons for this failure. Three main reasons are identified. Firstly, Halford argues, the setting up of the Women's Committee in Camden never had total commitment from Labour Party councillors making its operation difficult from the start. Secondly, the various sections of the council did not agree on a clear strategy for the Women's Committee resulting at times in 'open conflict' over priorities. This conflict was played on by those hostile to the Women's Committee to effectively "immobilize independent feminist activity" (Brownhill and Halford, 1990). Finally, in line with the comments already made, constraints on finance resulting from rate-capping were used by councillors who had never supported the Women's Committee to oppose its existence.

While these arguments have been developed to account specifically for the problems of the London Borough of Camden's Women's Committee, they can be applied more broadly to help explain the fortunes of women's initiatives in local government. The following case study of Bristol City Council's Women's Committee reveals very similar divisions and conflicts as experienced in Camden. The study provides a brief account of the history of the Bristol Committee illustrating not only the nature and source of conflict but also, the priority that was placed on close links with the community and with 'grass roots' political organisations.

Bristol City Council's Women's Committee

The Bristol City Council Women's Committee was established in 1986 after the Labour Party gained control of the city in the local elections. The Labour Party manifesto included a commitment to establishing women's and race committees—both to be supported by a 'unit' composed of professional staff. The commitment to establishing such committees was very much representative of the kind of more radical grass-roots local politics mentioned earlier and associated particularly with the early to mid 1980s. Even so some Labour Party councillors, especially on the right of the party, were opposed from the beginning to the women's committee and, just as Halford observed in Camden, internal wranglings within the different factions of the party contributed to the committee's stormy life and eventual re-structuring.

When it was established, the BCC Women's Committee was allocated a relatively substantial budget of £300,000. From the beginning the Women's Committee received considerable criticism, especially from the press, regarding the allocation of the budget and the decisions surrounding support for different groups. In particular, the Committee was attacked for its funding of lesbian groups and for its perceived indiscriminate prioritisation of working class projects. In reality this criticism (whether or not it is 'legitimate') is not even supported by the breakdown in funding allocation—in 1987/8 less than 2% of committee funding went to lesbian groups while the majority of supported projects were health related and available to all women in the city. The criticisms were, however, used by unsympathetic Tory councillors in attempts to discredit the Women's Committee and, assisted by an ever willing press, to generate public hostility.

1990 was a key year in the life of the BCC Women's Committee. In this year a study was undertaken by an external body designed to consider options for the re-structuring of the council. The study included negotiation with existing members of the council as to what would be appropriate for Bristol. The review supported a *stronger* structure for equal opportunities, suggesting that within the existing framework a number of broad concerns such as EO throughout the council and issues relating to sexual orientation, were not currently being addressed. According to one councillor, however, this review process was highjacked by the groups hostile to EO as a way of down grading the Women's Committee. This, in fact, reflects a response favoured elsewhere and was justified by Bristol councillors on the basis of its acceptance elsewhere. Riley (1990) notes that the integration of the Women's Committee with an equal opportunities committee has served to stifle "contentious issues raised by the women's lobby". The structure that emerged in Bristol City Council consisted of a central 'Equalities Committee' with women, race and disability retained as separate sub-groups. Critically, the Committee budget was to be handled by a separate group again.

Links can be drawn between the changes taking place in the Women's Committee and those within the broader Labour movement. The setting up of the Women's Committee represented, as noted, a time of more radical ideas and of considerable energy amongst the Labour Party and amongst individuals. However, tensions evident within the Labour Party in the late 1980s and early 1990s were also apparent in the Women's Committee where, increasingly, problems emerged between different groups. Councillors sitting on the Women's Committee at the time have identified a major rift between some of the co-optees on the Committee and other more moderate women, claiming that "left wing factions" of the Labour Party were attempting to use the co-optees to attack the Women's Committee. This again has parallels with what was happening generally within Labour Party politics. Frustrated with the extreme attitudes of some of the co-optees, a number of committed women resigned from the Women's Sub-Committee at the beginning of 1992. Action supported by some of the left wing members had become, they claimed, increasingly difficult to defend, endangering the credibility of the Equalities Committee.

There are, it is clear from the history of the Women's/Equality Committee as described above, two highly related issues. Firstly was the general re-structuring of the Committee and secondly the internal operation of the Women's Committee/Sub-Committee. The process of re-structuring was not, as noted above, entirely hostile to the existence of the Women's Committee and was generally supportive of EO within the Council. The process did, however, provide an opportunity for opponents of the Women's Committee to challenge the existence and overall power base of the Committee. Most Tory members were unfailingly negative towards the Women's Committee. Liberals on the council perceived a need for EO to be taken seriously but believed that this would happen within an Equalities Committee and that no separate focus on women was necessary. Splits within the Labour Party meant that even some Labour councillors objected to the continuation of the Women's Committee in its original form. The fact that the Women's Sub-Committee survived under the re-structured Equalities Committee is, however, an indication that high levels of commitment and support did remain—the end result representing a compromise but one that did at least protect the idea of a separate 'women's' structure.

What took place in this process of re-structuring cannot be divorced from the internal disputes within the Women's Committee. The problems caused by the co-opted members have their parallels elsewhere—Riley (1990) notes the difficulties experienced in the London Borough of Camden by the co-opted left wing women. The severe disagreements over spending priorities and financial management divided the Committee and while some criticism of the allocative practices have simply been the preoccupation of a reactionary press, there has been some genuine concern amongst progressive and committed members of the committee.

Although the new Equalities Committee represents a down grading of Women's Issues *per se* within the council, it retains, in itself, a valuable commitment to EO work and remains an important vehicle through which women's needs can be addressed. Some councillors believe that in its current, more stable form, the Equality Committee can do more for the needs of women than was possible before re-structuring (one clear example is described in Chapter 6—the reintroduction of a safe women's transport scheme by the Equality Committee that had previously been criticised out of hand as a *Women's Committee* initiative). This, however, will be dependent on the individuals involved and the continuing commitment from those in key positions. So far the Equalities Committee has done little but manage the activities of the sub-groups (women, race and disability). The opportunity does exist for a more positive stance on EO across the council itself and the Equalities Committee has indicated a willingness to make links with other Committees, including planning. The current chair of the BCC Planning Committee is optimistic about the future of links between the Equalities Committee and Planning. A more 'progressive' Planning Committee ('not just old men') has meant that there is a greater overlap than ever before between the two committees. This 'phase' in the battle for equal opportunities is again indicative of a more general attitude to local politics by the left—symbolically and very significantly represented, according to the Chair, by the election of a black middle class *male* councillor to the chair of the Equalities Committee. The relationship between planning and equal opportunities in Bristol is discussed again in Chapter 8.

Conclusion

This chapter has argued that women's initiatives in planning can only be understood in the context of a wider appreciation of women's role in decision-making and their access to power within the formal policy-making and political processes. Chapter 2 has discussed the concept of power and considered theoretical debates surrounding women's unequal access to power, influence and control. This chapter has attempted to apply aspects of these discussions to the more practical operation of power—particularly in relation to the planning system. Attention has been devoted to the under representation of women in key, influential, posts—both as politicians in national and local politics and as professionals within local government—and to the patriarchal nature of decision-making structures and practices.

In considering the formal mechanisms through which women can press for greater recognition of their needs, discussion has focused on women's committees and other initiatives in local government. The analysis of such initiatives has introduced a number of inter-related issues – for example, the commitment of women's initiatives to less rigid, hierarchical styles of working, the change of emphasis within local government away from women's to equal opportunities committees and the problems of ensuring that the aims and principles of women's initiatives are picked up within the local authority generally. What is clear from the discussion of women's initiatives is that their role, status and ultimately their survival must be seen in the context not only of the operation of gender relations but also of the evolution of local politics. The extent to which positive gains for women may be achieved through the formation and implementation of 'women's initiatives' in local government is dependent not only on women's access to power *per se* but on the expression of that power in the relationship between the central and the local state.

This chapter has been limited to the analysis of women's initiatives in local government/planning. While reference has been made to women's prominent role in 'informal' or community politics, no systematic discussion of this role has taken place. Clearly, however, questions surrounding the success or failure of formal initiatives in planning—and the extent to which these represent an expression of women's power within decision making—must recognise the importance of initiatives *outside* this formal sphere. In Chapter 8, in the conclusion of this book, we briefly consider the contribution of groups and initiatives beyond the local planning process. Before then the next three chapters look in more depth at the nature of the specific policies that have been introduced to address women's needs. Each chapter adopts a particular topic area and sets the planning initiatives within broader theoretical and practical consideration of women's experiences within that area.

5

Women and Employment

Introduction

In the academic debate surrounding women's roles and gender relations, employment has emerged as possibly the most important single issue. A wealth of material has been published in the last 15 years looking at all aspects of women's contribution to and experiences within the labour market. The whole question of waged work has been recognised as crucial to the wider organisation of gender roles and to our understanding of women's oppression and the evolution of gender relations. As noted in Chapter 2, paid work forms an important 'patriarchal structure' through which male power over women is expressed and reinforced.

Similarly, in the case of planning, employment and economic development constitute key issues. The planning process performs a major role in the location of economic development in general and in the distribution of particular forms of employment. As a statutory function planning has a significant input not only into decisions regarding the siting of employment related development but also, at a more strategic level, into the creation of job opportunities and the generation of conditions for economic growth. Planning in any number of guises, is bound up in influencing and reacting to trends in job provision.

It follows, therefore, that planning can contribute both directly and indirectly to employment provision for women. In influencing decisions surrounding the location and form of employment growth and by encouraging measures to stimulate local and national economic development, planning can help determine the number and range of job opportunities available to women. In the provision and siting of other resources and facilities (retail, housing, community and medical facilities, for example) planning can often play a decisive role in shaping the employment patterns of women.

The purpose of this chapter is to examine the contribution of planning to the involvement of women in waged work within the framework of feminist analysis. It aims to apply theoretical debates on the constraints and opportunities experienced by women in the labour market to the evaluation of planning policies. It argues that in order to understand what planning has done and can do to address women's employment needs, we must know more about the nature of problems faced by women in paid work. In turn, an appreciation of these problems must itself stem from an examination of theoretical debate surrounding the operation of the labour market and of women's position within it.

Again, the scope of the subject means that there is a need to be selective in terms of the material covered. In particular, the analysis of different theoretical perspectives on women's entry into the labour market must, by necessity, be limited. This having been said, it is nevertheless important that this discussion be included here, for while it appears to incorporate a range of issues that are beyond the scope or influence of the planning process, these are issues that are themselves critical to a broad understanding of women's employment. As has been argued several times already, a feminist analysis of planning which is prescriptive as well as descriptive must include key debates in feminist theory on the underlying reasons for women's inequality. The discussion here of the theoretical underpinning of explanations for women's participation in the labour market looks to provide a summary of such debates.

The discussion of theoretical work on women's entry to and experiences within waged work is followed by a review of relevant government policy. These sections look mainly at contemporary policy—the Equal Pay and Sex Discrimination Acts, for example— in an attempt to identify the principal national responses to women's employment needs. The point is made that while state policy and legislation over a range of issues (such as welfare benefits and childcare) has a bearing on women's availability for and performance within waged work, concern here is primarily with policy which focuses directly on employment. The final part of the chapter moves on to a more indepth analysis of actual planning policy with the intention of examining the planning response to the particular needs of women in relation to employment. As explained in Chapter 1, use is made of original examples of policy drawn from local authority planning department documentation in an effort to demonstrate and explain the direction and priorities of current initiatives.

Before turning to the theoretical debate it is worth examining some of the principal trends in women's participation in the labour force in Britain this century.

Trends in Women's Employment Participation

In 1951 26.9% of women in Britain were economically active. By 1971 this figure had risen to 36.5% (Walby, 1986) and by 1991 it stood at 71%. Over 10 million women had a paid job in 1991, representing almost 40% of the

economically active population. During the twentieth century there have
been several short-term fluctuations in women's rates of economic activity.
There can be no disputing, however, the general trend which shows a
steady increase in the numbers of women who have a paid job. It is
primarily, although not exclusively, variations in the numbers of *married*
women in employment that have accounted for the fluctuations over
time — in 1911 just under 10% of married women had a job; by 1981 this
figure had reached 50% and in 1991 it stood at 67%. (Labour Force
Survey, Department of Employment, 1991.)

Another salient characteristic of the growth in women's employment
participation is the dominance of part-time work In 1991 41.8% of women
in employment worked part-time as opposed to just 4.3% of men. It is, so
the data suggest, an increase in the numbers involved in part-time work
that is primarily responsible for the increase in women's participation in
the labour market *per se*. It may be wrong, therefore, to assume a major
increase in the range of employment opportunities available to women
since the observed growth may indicate, more accurately, a greater
'sharing out' of jobs for women rather than a movement by women into
whole new areas of work (McDowell, 1991). The growth in part-time
employment is particularly important in the context of the economic re-
structuring of industry in Britain and the move to a more 'flexible'
workforce and is a topic to which we shall return in later theoretical
discussion.

A close examination of the data shows that the increase in women's
participation in the labour market this century has not been even but has
been characterised by periods of very significant growth. One well documented period of expansion in women's participation in employment was
between 1939 and 1945, the time of the Second World War (see Brown,
1992; Summerfield, 1989; Walby, 1986). During this time, women's
civilian employment rose from under five million in 1939 to six million at
its peak in 1943, a growth of 42.4% (Brown, 1992). In 1931 women
constituted just under 30% of the employed population but by 1943 this
had risen to 38.8% (Summerfield, 1989). Changes also occurred, at this
time, in the age and marital profile of women in the labour market. The
proportion of employed women who were married rose from 16% in 1931
to 43% in 1943. In line with this shift, the average age of employed women
also rose with an increase in the percentage of the female workforce aged
25–44 from 43 to 57 (Brown, 1992).

The most recent period of rapid growth in women's participation in the
labour market has come at a time of contraction in the workforce overall.
Some commentators argue that, changes in the economy notwithstanding,
this growth is set to continue. The so-called 'demographic time-bomb' —
the decline in the numbers of young people set to come into the workforce
will have very serious implications for the availability of, in particular,

skilled labour by the turn of the century. The labour force aged under 25 is projected to fall by 1.2 million (approximately 20%) between 1987 and 1995 (Employment Gazette, 1988). Within such a context the contribution of women, especially married women, to the workforce is expected to become increasingly important.

Estimates suggest that, even taking into account the reduction in young women (as part of the demographic dip), the number of women in the labour market is expected to increase by about 0.76 million. More striking is the anticipated rise in the number of economically active women aged between 25 and 54. This cohort is expected to grow by 1 million, meaning that by 1995 women will constitute 44% of the 'prime age' workforce.

Just as the increase in women's participation in employment in the UK has shown fluctuations over time, so has it tended to vary over space with some regions (and, indeed individual towns and cities) demonstrating much more rapid growth than others. The geographical unevenness in women's involvement in the labour force is an important facet of economic re-structuring and extremely relevant to the work of planners and policy makers. Doreen Massey, in her book, *Spatial Divisions of Labour* (1984), provided one of the first and perhaps best known accounts of the gender implications of the re-structuring of local labour markets.

Massey argues that national and even regional trends often obscure important local variations in the composition of labour markets. Particular historical, cultural, social and political characteristics combine to influence the local patterns of job creation. Such local variation is not only highly pertinent to the distribution of female employment but may also encompass specific local forms of gender relations.

Future increases in women's activity rates are projected to continue in all regions of the country. In three regions; the South West, Wales and East Anglia, it is anticipated that this rise will bring the activity rate for the female population of working age within 10 percentage points of the male rate (Employment Gazette, January 1990). The spatial variation that has occurred and continues to occur in women's employment participation is not simply regional but has other dimensions. For example, variations have been recorded (see Errington *et al.*, 1989; Little *et al.*, 1991) in female activity between urban and rural parts of the country with generally fewer women involved in paid work in rural areas than in towns and cities.

The various trends that have emerged in women's participation in paid work—the involvement of married women, the increases in part-time working and the concentration within particular sectors—are obviously not only of considerable interest to planners and policy makers, but are also extremely complex. As noted in the introduction to this chapter, in order to understand and explain trends in women's employment it is important that certain theoretical discussions surrounding the circumstances of women's involvement in the labour market must be examined.

The following section aims to do two things; firstly, to examine the debate surrounding women's entry into the workforce—under what circumstances do women take up a paid job and, in particular, what is their role in the process of capital accumulation. Secondly, to consider the experiences of women *within* paid work—what sort of jobs they do and how easily do they gain promotion. The two areas are in some senses theoretically inseparable. The fact that they are separated in the text here is for practical reasons and in recognition of the emphases of existing work. The main argument raised here is that past theories have been largely inadequate in explaining either the conditions of women's participation in paid work or their experiences within it. What is required is a theory of patriarchy which sees gender relations and male power over women as a key factor in explaining all aspects of women's employment.

Theoretical Perspectives on Women's Employment Participation

Chapter 2 has put forward a range of positions that have been used by different theorists to explain the basis of women's subordination. Links can be made between these wider perspectives and the theories that have been applied to women's involvement in employment; the principles of sex-role theory, for example, are reflected in what have been termed 'sociological approaches' to women's participation in the labour market. Central to the development of theories on women's employment is the role of capital accumulation and the relationship between the needs of capital and the influence of gender. As we shall see, the theories considered take differing perspectives on this debate.

In her book, *Unequal Work*, Veronica Beechey (1987) identified three particular types of theoretical approach that have characterised the analysis of female waged labour. Firstly, there is what she describes as "classical sociological analysis" in which a structural functionalist approach is adopted. Secondly, Beechey identifies theories of the dual labour market which together constitute a "radical critique of neo-classical economics". Thirdly, drawing heavily on the 'dual systems' theory of women's subordination, there are Marxist analyses of the labour process in which emphasis is placed to varying degrees on "specifically feminist questions". These three approaches form a useful framework for the discussion of existing theoretical explanations of women's role in the production process and are briefly reviewed below.

Sociological theories

Those theories that Beechey collectively terms "sociological" centre on the analysis of women's two roles and attempt to explain women's entry into the labour market as a function of their domestic role. Changes in women's involvement in paid work are interpreted in relation to role conflicts experienced within the family and to varying demands of the domestic household. Such approaches are criticised for divorcing the family from "an analysis of the forces and relations of production" (Beechey, 1987, p. 18) and for paying insufficient attention to the *economic* importance of women's waged and non-waged labour. They fail to question the existence of women's 'dual role' or to ask why it is women whose entry into the labour market is dictated by role conflicts and by the need to sustain the domestic household. In documenting women's participation in employment, sociological approaches have introduced some important and interesting information—especially concerning the day-to-day problems women experience in balancing their dual roles and in the separation of home and work—they are less helpful, however, in actually explaining the reasons for women's involvement in paid work or in interpreting the constraints on that involvement other than as a function of women's domestic circumstances. In general, then, 'sociological' approaches to the study of women's entry into the labour market have, as Barron and Norris (1976) maintain, "concentrated on the supply side of the situation and paid less attention to the demand side" (quoted in Beechey, 1987, p. 32).

Dual labour market theories

The second category of theoretical approach to be considered revolves around what is termed the dual labour market (DLM) approach. Theories of the dual labour market, while varying in terms of their sophistication, collectively offer an interpretation of women's participation in the labour market which goes beyond an analysis of their role as wives and mothers. Instead of reducing women's employment experiences to their domestic roles, dual labour market theories argue that such experiences derive fundamentally from the internal operation of the labour market. Thus it is the economics of the labour market that control women's position within it.

   Developed initially in the 1960s in the examination of the employment characteristics of black workers in parts of the USA, DLM theory sought to explain the concentration of certain groups of workers into particular low-wage, low-skill sectors of the economy. The work identified an essentially segmented labour market with the existence of a primary and a secondary sector; primary sector jobs being characterised by high levels of pay, good working conditions and favourable employment prospects, and those in the secondary sector by low pay, low skill levels and poor working conditions. Dual labour market theory was offered initially as an alternative to the neoclassical model of the 1960s which saw the labour market as a self-equilibrating system where supply and demand factors would balance themselves in a process of free competition. It was argued (see Doeringer and Piore, 1971) that DLM theory recognised, to a far greater extent than existing theories, the inbuilt structural obstacles to individuals gaining access to different parts of the labour market. It thus was seen to explain the exclusion of certain sectors of society from particular jobs and the inability of individuals to enter the labour market on equal terms and with equal chance of securing appropriate employment to match their attributes or qualifications.

It was not until the 1970s that dual labour market theories started to be used to explain the experiences of *women* in gaining access to the labour market. Important in this respect was the work of Barron and Norris (1976). They argued that women are basically concentrated within certain parts of the labour market and as a group constitute a secondary sector whose access to employment is confined to poorly paid, low-skill jobs. Clearly, this argument introduces a whole series of issues in relation to the actual conditions of women's paid work that are not tackled by the 'sociological approaches' and dual labour market theories have been seen as significant in drawing attention to the fact that women's employment situation is not equal to men's. Various reasons have been advanced in order to explain why women can be regarded as 'secondary' workers. Barron and Norris (1976) argue, for example, that

(1) women are easily dispensable
(2) they are clearly differentiated from other workers as a group
(3) they have little interest in acquiring job training
(4) they have little interest in economic rewards
(5) they lack solidarity with each other.

Despite attempting to analyse women's employment position in relation to the dynamics of the labour market (or perhaps because of this) dual labour market theories provide little by way of explanation as to *why* it is women who possess the attributes listed above that result in their positions as secondary workers. Even if these characteristics can be accepted (is it true, for example, that all women are unconcerned with training and income?!) *why* do women comply with them? Moreover, such theories are largely descriptive and thus do not articulate the actual processes by which women are constituted as a preferred source for the secondary labour market. While important that they attach some weight to the needs and workings of the labour market, DLM theories can be criticised for becoming too immersed in the 'demand side'. They fail to appreciate the interaction between the labour market and the domestic economy in explaining women's entry into employment and consequently why some women are more available or attractive to the labour market than others.

The third group of theories identified by Beechey as important in explaining the pattern of women's involvement in the labour market are based on Marxist interpretations of the economy. While this group includes a number of 'approaches' which individually pick up on different aspects of the nature and explanation of women's involvement in paid work, central to them all is the belief that women's employment is critically structured by the relationship between capital and labour in the pro-duction process. The main arguments raised by Marxist interpretations are developed in the work of Bravermann, in particular in the reserve army of labour theory. These arguments are briefly examined below.

Marxist theory

In his book, *Labour and Monopoly Capital* published in 1974, Bravermann asserts that women's relationship to the labour market has been pro-foundly altered by two particular trends in the development of capitalism. Firstly, capital has sought (and effectively achieved) the de-skilling of jobs such that they can be performed by machines and *cheap* labour power. Secondly, technological progress that has been a feature of the evolution of capitalism has enabled household tasks to be carried out with greater ease and within a much shorter space of time.

> "As a consequence of these two parallel processes, women freed from domestic work are available to take up the new deskilled work in offices and factories. Thus their labour force participation rate rises. At the same time the labour force participation rates for men drop as they are expelled from skilled labour and become unemployed or retire early. Bravermann foresees a convergence in the proportions of men and women in the paid workforce" (Walby, 1990, p. 34).

In conjunction with these changes, Bravermann argues, the family loses its function as a unit of production, remaining simply an "institution for the consumption of commodities" (Beechey, 1987, p. 76). By the same token, the role of the housewife changes from the production of use values within the domestic economy to the contribution of wage labour (more directly appropriated by capital).

Bravermann's ideas are important to the understanding of women's entry into the labour market in that they draw on the relationship between domestic and waged work *and* attempt to locate women's employment within a much broader understanding of contemporary capitalism. There are, however, major inconsistencies in his arguments that cannot be ignored. These inconsistencies derive from, firstly, his definition of skill and of the process of de-skilling and, secondly, from his interpretation of the family and of the changes occurring within it.

As noted above, Bravermann argues that it is the progressive de-skilling involved in contemporary production that has created new employment opportunities for women. This argument is, however, predicated on a particular notion of skill—an 'old fashioned' notion (according to Bee-chey) and one which fails to recognise the creation of *new* skills and occupations that has accompanied the evolution of, for example, factory assembly lines. The oversimplification inherent in Bravermann's thesis ignores the fact that capitalism, while encouraging de-skilling in parts of the production process, has created new skills, for example technical and management occupations, in others. Notions of de-skilling in themselves fail to explain *why* it is women and not men that fill the new occupations and are best suited for unskilled work.

Bravermann has been accused of over-simplification in respect to his analysis of the family and, in particular, its evolution in relation to capitalism. This is due, Beechey (1987) suggests, to the fact that his work was based largely on the study of the farm family in which a much more direct relationship between production and consumption is discernable. In general the relationship between production in the domestic economy and in large-scale industry is more complicated than Bravermann concedes — some parts of the production process transferred at a very early stage to the factory while others took much longer. There are, moreover, jobs that continue to be performed in the domestic sphere (homeworking) for which wages are paid. Consequently, the family has not been "simply or instantly changed by the development of industrial capitalism" (Beechey, 1987, p. 78). Bravermann can also be criticised for suggesting that changes in the productive role of the family under capitalism mean that it only exists for the purposes of consumption. This argument ignores the important and continuing role of the family as an influence on social life and, moreover, fails to acknowledge the essential interconnections between production and consumption.

In developing his ideas Bravermann drew on the concept of the reserve army of labour. This concept has been widely used by Marxists in order to explain women's movement in and out of the labour force, although Marx himself only went as far as identifying it generally as important to the process of capital accumulation rather than specifically in the context of the gender division of labour. Broadly, it is argued that important to capital is a group of workers that can be brought into the workforce at times of growth and then easily released during periods of economic stagnation or contraction. This group, the reserve army, must, therefore, be readily available as parts of the economy expand and yet not in a position of total dependence on that employment. Proponents of the reserve army thesis (see, for example Bruegal, 1979 and Milkman, 1976) see the existence of such a group as critical to the process of capital accumulation since without it wages would continue to rise and surplus value would be squeezed (Bruegal, 1979).

Many of these theorists, like Bravermann, go on to argue that women, as a group, constitute an important part of the reserve army of labour and that the rise in women's participation in the labour market clearly "fits the picture of the continued expansion of the reserve army drawn by Marx"

(Bruegal, 1976 p. 41). Married women, in particular, conform to the description of a reserve since they can be 'supported' by their husbands and thus can 'disappear' back into the household at times of labour market contraction. It is this disposability that writers like Bravermann and Breugal have seen as the key to women's participation in paid work and to the recognition of women as a reserve army of labour.

Those who ascribe to the view of women as a labour reserve cite examples from history of incidents when women have been recruited into the workforce in response to a particular shortage or gap (for example women working in munitions factories during the Second World War or as part of the land army) and then released from the labour market when their labour is no longer required by capital. Other authors have, however, questioned the empirical validity of the concept, arguing that in many instances evidence has not actually supported the reserve army theory. This is particularly true in relation to women 'being let go' by capital once the labour market, or part of it, is contracting. As Walby (1990) points out, women did not leave the labour market at a greater rate than men in either the US depression of the 1930s or the recession that hit the western world in the 1970s. Moreover, during the 1980s in Britain the number of women's jobs has, overall, continued to increase, while the number of jobs done by men has declined during this time.

But criticism of the reserve army of labour thesis goes beyond its empirical validity. The theory has been seen as internally inconsistent in explaining women's involvement in waged work. *If* women's labour is so important or attractive to capital because it is cheap, surely capital is acting against its own interests in disposing of women's labour before men's? *Why*, moreover, are women concentrated in the more buoyant sectors of the economy while the declining areas are dominated by men? Again, it appears that while the reserve army of labour thesis may be useful in describing the movement in and out of the workforce of groups of workers, it does not adequately explain why it is that women constitute one such group.

This brief review of different theoretical approaches demonstrates that any analysis of women's entry into the labour market cannot be divorced from the *conditions* of their employment. Many of the theories that have been discussed have drawn attention to women's involvement in specific sectors of the labour market and while such theories have largely failed to *explain* the differential access of men and women to particular jobs or sectors, they have reinforced the importance of the links between labour market participation and employment segregation. In short it is clear that we cannot fully understand the circumstances that dictate women's involvement in waged work without some sort of appreciation of the characteristics of that involvement in terms of, for example, the type of work performed, the levels of pay and promotion etc. As briefly mentioned in the identification of trends in women's employment, this has become particularly apparent in recent feminist analyses of post-Fordism (see, McDowell, 1991; Massey, 1991). Some of the theories mentioned above touch on the fact that these characteristics do vary between men and women but, as noted, provide little insight as to why this variation exists. So, after examining, in the following section, some elements of employment segregation an attempt will be made to provide a theoretical underpinning which helps to explain the 'gendering' of jobs.

Occupational Segregation and Women's Employment

Any analysis of gender and the labour market quickly reveals a high degree of occupational segregation. Women and men are unevenly distributed in terms of both the type and level of work they perform. Horizontal segregation in the labour market operates to restrict both sexes to particular types of work, resulting in the emergence and reinforcement of 'men's jobs' and 'women's jobs', while vertical segregation means men and women have unequal access to different grades or quality of work. Considerable empirical evidence has been produced to demonstrate the extent of occupational segregation within the labour market (see Walby, 1988; Hearn and Perkins, 1987; Morgan and Knights, 1991). Central to such research has been the emerging links between occupational segregation and the quality of jobs available to women.

"Occupational segregation by sex is one of the most marked and persistent of the patterns that characterise our world... Women and men tend to cluster in separate industries, separate occupations, different departments and different rooms. We use different toilets, wear different overalls and different hats. At the industrial level men are about 86% of the labour force in the industrial group called 'mechanical engineering'. Conversely, women are about 67% of the labour force in retail distribution and repair of consumer goods" (Cockburn, 1988, p. 29).

In a major study of women's employment conducted in the early 1980s, Martin and Roberts (1984) confirmed the high levels of occupational segregation that characterise the contemporary labour market; 63% of women interviewed in their research claimed that they worked in 'women only' jobs. In certain professions segregation is extreme—it was revealed by the 1981 census, for example, that 98.3% of secretaries, typists and shorthand writers were women (Webster, 1990). Sectorally, women are disproportionately concentrated in service employment, while they are under represented in primary industry and manufacturing.

Occupational segregation does not appear to affect men and women equally. Women are concentrated into fewer jobs than men—men having made greater inroads into a wider range of professions, albeit in small numbers in some cases. There is, however, more consistency over time. Research by Hamkin (1979, 1981) shows little reduction in occupational segregation to have taken place this century, with the proportion of women working in female dominated industries *increasing* during the period 1971 to 1981 (Walby, 1990).

The labour market, then, is very clearly 'gendered'. Many jobs are seen as either men's work or women's work, requiring skills or attributes which are considered gender specific. Thus men are assigned jobs apparently requiring physical strength, technical competence or intellectual abilities (Cockburn, 1990), while women are associated with caring, clerical work and jobs requiring 'nimble fingers' (Foord *et al.*, 1986). Changes in work practices, and in particular the introduction of technology in the work-place, have on occasion initiated shifts in the gender identity of certain jobs—Cockburn cites the case of the clothing industry where the introduction of computerised systems have transformed pattern layout and cutting from male to female work. Another example is that of clerical work. As Walby (1988) points out, clerical work in the nineteenth century was seen as a skilled occupation carried out largely by men. Today, however, its is considered less skilled and is mainly undertaken by women.   It was noted above that as well as being concentrated within certain employment sectors, women are over represented in the lower levels of the labour market. They are clustered vertically as well as horizontally. Again, the research by Martin and Roberts (1984) provided evidence to demonstrate the uneven distribution of women in different grades or levels of employment. Other authors take up the point in relation to specific industries or professions, drawing attention to the poor promotion records of women and to the over representation of men in senior positions. Discussion of Greed's work on the professions involved in the building/planning industries has been incorporated in Chapter 4, while evidence has been recorded in Chapter 3 to demonstrate trends in planning departments. Even in female dominated sectors, men frequently monopolise the 'top jobs'—for example, over 80% of chief librarians in England and Wales are men, despite the fact that, overall, men constitute only 30% of public sector librarian staff (Lister, 1991).

The consequences of both horizontal and vertical employment segregation on women's participation in the labour market are very clear. The jobs into which women are concentrated are generally the less well paid, unskilled jobs—the boring and repetitive jobs providing little satisfaction or diversity. The conditions under which women work are frequently poor and they receive fewer employment related 'benefits' or bonuses (for example, sick pay, holiday entitlement, pensions etc.) than do men (see Martin and Roberts, 1984; Little *et al.*, 1991). Low pay for women is perhaps the most evident and immediate consequence of the gendering of jobs. Despite employment legislation (see below) requiring equal pay for equal work, women are consistently paid less than men. In 1988 it was calculated that women's wages were still only 75% of men's (Roberts, 1990) while in 1992 the gross hourly earnings for female industrial workers were 69% of men's (Morris, 1992).

This gap between women's and men's wages is not unique to Britain but occurs throughout the Western capitalist economy. As Walby (1990) notes, however, there are variations between different countries with the gap being largest in the USA and smallest in Scandinavia. While the wages gap has closed very little over time there has been a significant narrowing of the difference between the educational qualifications and skills of men and women.

A number of authors (McDowell, 1991a; Luck, 1991) have noted that conditions of employment are particularly bad for women engaged in part-time work. In 1989 women working part-time earned only 75% of the average rate for full-timers (McDowell, 1991a). Part-time workers' security of employment is generally lower than that for full-time workers as is their receipt of holliday and sickness pay.

As has been asserted above, conventional labour market theories do not provide an adequate explanation for the particular characteristics of women's employment. They make little attempt either to describe or to explain the variation between male and female labour in relation to, for example, issues such as wage rates or conditions of employment. Feminist theorists have sought to develop new approaches which do address the position of women in the labour market. In so doing they have argued that women's employment can only be properly understood through the inclusion of an analysis of patriarchy inside the workplace and in the working of the labour market more generally. Only by looking at the operation of patriarchy, they assert, can we fully appreciate the extent of inequality in the employment experiences of man and women or hope to move towards an adequate explanation of that inequality.

While feminist theorists may be agreed on the importance of incorporating patriarchal relations into the analysis of waged labour, there is considerable debate as to the relative role of patriarchy *vis a vis* capitalist social and economic relations. As Chapter 2 outlined, the inter-relationship between structures of class and gender and of the processes of patriarchy and capitalism in explaining women's position generally constitutes perhaps *the* central question within feminist discourse. The different perspectives on this general discussion have already been rehearsed and it is not the intention to repeat the points made here. This section is concerned not so much with the basic origins of patriarchy or with its relationship with the capitalist mode of production, but aims rather to demonstrate the way in which patriarchal processes are reflected in the labour market and to show how they influence the nature of women's access to and experiences within paid work.

Patriarchy At Work

One of the criticisms levelled at certain conventional theories is that they have attempted to explain women's involvement in employment almost entirely as a function of the operation of the labour market and of the needs of capitalism. Women's waged work has thus been separated from their domestic role and the essential relationship between production and reproduction neglected. Where women's domestic duties are acknowledged (for example, by the 'sociological approaches' mentioned) they are not questioned but simply accepted as part of women's 'natural' role. And yet the constraints of women's domestic role, the servicing of the household, the caring for children etc. have a profound influence on their ability to participate in paid work (a substantive literature has grown up around the role of women's domestic labour within the process of capital accumulation; see, for example, Delphy, 1984; Redclift and Mingione, 1985; Whatmore, 1991). Their entry into the labour market and consequently the composition of the workforce cannot be understood without an appreciation of the distribution of responsibilities within the household *and* a recognition of the power structures that lie at the root of that distribution.

Dual labour market and the reserve army of labour theories see women's movement in and out of the labour market in relation to the demands of the economy and in accordance with the needs of capital. But as noted above, there are some inconsistencies in this interpretation (particularly in relation to the disposability of women's labour). The theories do not explain why it is women as opposed to men who are so apparently disposable and who are best suited to the more 'peripheral' jobs. Feminists (for example, Beechey, 1987; Walby, 1986) have argued that such issues can only be fully understood by looking at the exercise of male power within the labour process. The control of women's productive (and reproductive) capacity by men is a fundamental aspect of contemporary social and economic relations and of the workings of the labour market. This control cannot be explained by reference to capitalism alone.

A number of first hand accounts of women's experiences of working in different industries now exist. See for example, Pollert's study of women in the tobacco industry in Bristol; *Girls, Wives, Factory Lives* (1981), Cavendish's account of women's unskilled work in a car components factory, *On the Line* (1982), Wajcman's study of co-operative working in Norfolk (1983) and Sarsby's work on women in the pottery industry (1985). These studies, and others of their type, provide graphic accounts of the conditions which characterise women's paid work and demonstrate the effects of occupational segregation within the workforce. Many of them attempt to look behind the immediate indications of segregation in an effort to explain the process. Such work has highlighted management strategies, trade union policy and practice, and sexual harassment as expressions of male power underlying occupational segregation.

Of these, perhaps the most obvious demonstration of the operation of patriarchy at work is the sexual harassment of women. Stanko (1988) defines sexual harassment as *unwanted* sexual attention noting that it can take many behavioural forms including visual and verbal abuse, unwanted pressure for sexual favours or dates as well as actual physical assault and rape. Often the form of harassment (e.g. sexual teasing or jokes or the displaying of 'girlie calenders') is so common in certain parts of the workplace that it is not recognised as anything but accepted (and expected) behaviour

> "men managers with women subordinates may use sexuality, sexual harassment, sexual joking and sexual abuse as a routine means of maintaining authority. This may be thoroughly embedded in the taken-for-granted culture of the organisation" (Hearn and Parkins, 1987, p. 93).

Research has indicated the regularity with which women have experienced sexual harassment at work—a study by the Alfred Marks Bureau, for example, found that "66% of employees and 86% of managers reported that they were aware of various forms of sexual harassment present in their office" (Stanko, 1988, p. 93).

Important links can be drawn between sexual harassment at work and occupational segregation. In extreme cases, harassment may cause women to leave their job, or it may restrict them to certain parts of the workforce. Abuse or sexual pressures may be used by men to defend their territory— harassment is particularly prevalent when women enter traditionally 'male' occupations. Sexual harassment not only acts to restrict women's access to certain occupations or grades but can also be used as a weapon, by men, to prevent women from improving their position — for example by requesting higher salaries or better working conditions. Fear of losing their jobs or of physical attack frequently prevents women resisting or speaking out against sexual harassment at work—as mentioned, certain forms are so insidious as to go unrecognised. Women may feel helpless as the harassment often comes from the very person (her boss) to whom she would have to make any complaint.

Management strategies within the workforce also demonstrate the operation of patriarchy—although, again, not always in an immediately obvious way. The restriction of women to parts of the labour process and certain grades of employment have become established policy in some industries—used, again, to protect areas of 'men's work'. In extreme cases 'patriarchal closure' may exist, precluding women almost entirely from certain fields.

"Gendered strategies of exclusionary closure serve to create women as a class of ineligibles and secure for men privileged access to rewards and opportunities accruing from activities in the sphere of paid work" (Witz, 1988, p. 76).

These strategies basically exclude women from "routes of access to resources such as skills, knowledge, entry credentials or technical competence." Since the majority of managers are men such strategies are relatively easy to put in place and sustain.

Women's ability to fight the process of discrimination arising from management strategies is further constrained by their weakness within another traditionally patriarchal workplace organisation, the trade union (TU). A healthy literature now exists on the experiences of women within (and outside) the trades union movement (see, for example, Charles, 1983, 1986; Coote and Pattullo, 1990; Ellis, 1988). Such work has clearly documented the discriminatory practices of the early TU movement and considered the extent to which the membership and policies of TUs have changed to reflect the growing role of women in the labour market. Ellis (1988) has argued that while the TUC has recently started to pay more attention to the needs of women—establishing in 1987, for example, an Equal Rights Department aimed at giving high priority to women's issues—the management structures of Trade Unions remain dominated by men. Moreover, the attitudes of individual TUs vary considerably with some retaining very traditional attitudes and structures.

Walby (1986) argues that some trade unions have undergone substantial changes in gender relations in the last few years. She cites examples of the various unions that have made positive steps towards encouraging equal opportunities through the appointment of an 'equal rights' officer or working party. In 1980 the Equal Opportunities Commission (EOC) undertook a survey of the practices of TUs. They established that, of 52 unions, 21 had made particular studies of their structures to identify barriers to women's membership and 13 had set up special committees to deal with equality issues. Walby does however add a note of caution with the comment that such "enlightened" policies are still practised by the *minority* of trade unions.

During the 1980s, in response to what were seen as the inadequacies of existing theoretical approaches in explaining the position of women in the labour market, new approaches were developed which focused on patriarchal gender relations. These approaches (championed by the Lancaster group of sociologists who were part of the ESRC Changing Urban and Regional Systems initiative) assumed, as McDowell (1991) notes, a socialist–feminist perspective based on the dual systems principle outlined in Chapter 2. Thus they argued for two related but theoretically separate systems of capitalism and patriarchy, and saw women's domestic labour as central to the operation of capitalism. Men and capital were seen as benefitting in a labour market that worked against women's interests.

McDowell (1991, p. 401) has argued, however, that in the context of contemporary economic re-structuring, the concept of a dual system in which women's interests are "theorised as being in opposition to those of men and of capital" is inadequate. While this particular conceptualisation of the relationship between patriarchy and capitalism was perhaps appropriate for the Fordist era of production, changes in household and family form together with a decline in the need (by capital) for domestic labour means that it is now much less useful. The process of economic re-structuring has, moreover, initiated new divisions in the workplace which cannot be interpreted simply in relation to male/female inequalities. As McDowell (1991, p. 408) writes:

> "While it is undeniable that the new gender order of post Fordist times has deepened the subordination of many women, trapping them in the increasingly casualised, part-time and peripheral labour market, it has also opened up opportunities for some women to join the core occupations and so increased class divisions **between** women. But what it has also succeeded in doing is turning upside down the gender divisions between large numbers of men and women. Increasing numbers of men are employed in the peripheral labour market too, on terms and conditions that traditionally were regarded as 'female'."

Clearly the process of economic re-structuring has considerable implications for both empirical observation and theoretical understanding of gender relations at work and women's entry into the labour market. There is no time here to prolong this discussion, simply to reinforce the need for greater attention to be paid to contemporary patterns in women's employment participation and for past assumptions regarding the relationship between 'production' and 'reproduction' to be reassessed in the context of changes in both social relations of the household and family and the 'needs' of capital. New divisions between groups of women must be incorporated into theoretical debate as well as existing divisions between men and women. It is important now that we turn to the policy/planning response, to the inequalities observed. As noted this analysis cannot hope to be comprehensive. It will, moreover, dwell on positive aspects of legislation and policy. This is to some extent unavoidable but it should be remembered that while legislation to improve women's employment position has been given a high profile by the government, at the same time, other initiatives have had an important, though less well publicised, negative impact on women's employment opportunities.

National Legislation and Policy Directions

The examination of national legislation in relation to women's employment in Britain is dominated quite understandably by two acts introduced in the 1970s; the Equal Pay Act and the Sex Discrimination Act. The Acts are remarkable in that they constitute, as Walby (1986, p. 213) remarks, "the first positive attempts to improve women's position in paid employment across the country as a whole by the state" and represent an "important change in the direction of state policy". While they may be the first examples of actual legislation, the Equal Pay and Sex Discrimination Acts have emerged from a background of protest and political activity which demonstrates the lengthy nature of women's fight for greater equality at work. The task of persuading first the trade unions and then Parliament of the justice and importance of their cause has not been an easy one and even when legislation finally reached the statute books it did not, many would argue, go far enough.

The history of women's demands for equal pay and equality at work generally, has been outlined by a number of authors (see, for example, Phillips, 1987; Walby, 1986). Key events and dates in this struggle include the first formal support, in 1888, by the TUC for the principle of equal pay—this public pledge was followed, it must be noted, by the subsequent side stepping by the General Council of the opportunity to push for legislation. Strong campaigns during the Second World War and later in the 1950s succeeded in raising the profile of women's demands but the lack of institutional support meant that they again resulted in no political action. In the 1960s mounting pressure from European communities (in the form of Article 119 of the Treaty of Rome which required legislation on equal pay if Britain were to join the Common Market) resulted in both Conservative and Labour parties declaring support for equal pay (Walby, 1986). But it was not until the late 1960s, with the culmination of a series of militant protests by women (see Snell, 1981) and the backing of the then Minister of State, Barbara Castle, that the Equal Pay Act (EPA) finally emerged, to be passed in 1970. This was followed relatively swiftly by the Sex Discrimination Act (SDA) of 1975.

Both the Equal Pay and the Sex Discrimination Acts were designed, self evidently, to eliminate discrimination against women in pay and in employment (Snell, 1979). The details of each are outlined very briefly here.

The Equal Pay Act

This act addresses the issue of equal pay, as Mandy Snell (1979, 1986) notes, on both an individual and a collective front, providing an opportunity for women to seek equality with men in relation to particular jobs or types of work, and establishing a framework for the negotiation of wage agreements and pay structures more generally. Guidelines from the Department of Employment specify that:

> "An individual woman has a right to equal treatment with men when she is employed on like work, i.e. work of the same or broadly similar nature to that of men, or in a job which different from those of men, has been given an equal value to men's jobs under a job evaluation exercise" (Department of Employment, 1973, quoted in Mallier and Rosser, 1987, p. 131).

At the beginning of 1984 an amendment to the EPA was introduced which "gives an employee the right to claim equal pay at an industrial tribunal for work which *he or she* considers to be of equal value to that done by a member of the opposite sex employed by the same or an associated employer" (Mallier and Rosser, 1987, p. 196, my emphasis).

The collective provisions stipulate that wage agreements applying either to men or to women only can be referred to the Central Arbitration Committee for amendment and the removal of discrimination. The Act also states that wage rates applying to women only should be amended to not less than the lowest male rate in the agreement. This clause means that all women covered by an agreement or pay structure should have their rates brought up to the male minimum, at least (Snell, 1979).

The Sex Discrimination Act

This act closely followed the Equal Pay Act and was again supported by Labour and Conservative parties. While both parties had expressed sympathy for the principle of making discrimination on the basis of sex illegal, it was the Conservative party, in 1973, who took the first *active* steps towards legislation in the form of a consultative document. The Labour Government of 1974 responded with a white paper which closely resembled this initial document in recommending that a law be introduced to remove sexual discrimination. The White Paper formed the basis of the Sex Discrimination Act of 1975, an act which made unlawful sex discrimination in education, training and related matters, in education and in the provision of goods and services and in management practices (Home Office, 1975).

The aims of the SDA are essentially negative, unlike those of the EPA. They seek to *prevent* discrimination on the basis of sex, outlawing existing practices, as necessary, rather than requiring employers to take positive action on attacking inequalities in access to employment and education. Perhaps the most important contribution of the Act was the setting up of the Equal Opportunities Commission with the power to issue a Code of Practice on the details and implementation of the SDA (EOC, 1986). Specifically in relation to employment (where, it can be argued, the SDA had greatest potential), the Code of Practice covers the following areas; training and recruitment, promotion, transfer and training, health and safety, disciplinary procedures and dismissal and terms of employment. The Code also provides advice on the establishment and implementation of an Equal Opportunities Policy, giving more positive guidelines on ensuring that discrimination on the grounds of sex or marriage does not take place. Again, however, it must be noted that these guidelines are advisory—the EOC can only try to promote them as follows:

"This section of the Code....gives information about the formulation and implementation of equal opportunities policies. While such policies are not required by law, their value has been recognised by a number of employers who have voluntarily adopted them. Others *may wish* to follow this example" (EOC, 1986, p. 14, my emphasis).

These then, constitute the basic provisions of the two major pieces of government legislation on sexual equality at work. Clearly, for the purposes of this book, it is the extent to which such legislation can be deemed to have been 'successful' in eliminating, or at least reducing, discrimination between men and women that is of most direct concern. This is briefly considered below.

The impact of legislation

The extent to which either the EPA or the SDA can be interpreted as 'successful' is, of course, a matter of debate to which there can be no precise or universally applicable answer. The perception as to whether or not there has been a move towards greater equality at work is dependent on factors such as the interpretation of 'equal opportunity', the type of job in question and the time period under observation. More useful, perhaps, than trying to come to any one 'conclusion' about either equal pay or sex discrimination is to consider particular instances or case studies.

Two articles published in Feminist Review relatively soon after the Equal Pay and Sex Discrimination Acts (Snell, 1979; Gregory, 1982) report findings of original research carried out to assess the impact of legislation on women in the workplace. Snell looked at 26 organisations over a period of 3 years from 1974 to 1977 to evaluate the immediate impact of the EPA and SDA on the levels of pay that women received and their access to employment opportunities. She found, during the course of this research, that the implementation of the EPA had indeed resulted in

"considerable and sometimes dramatic narrowing of the differentials between the basic rates of main groups of manual and white collar women and those of men" (Snell, 1979, p. 39)

and that this narrowing had been reflected, for some women, in significant pay rises. The affects of the legislation appear, Snell argues, more dramatic in the case of manual workers as many white collar women workers were already employed in organisations where equal pay had been implemented prior to the Act.

Examples were found of industries where the legislation was effectively being ignored. Non-compliance in the form of separate (lower) 'women's wage rates' was relatively rare. More common, however, were instances where there was evidence of less favourable treatment but that management *could* have argued that differences reflected 'genuine material differences' in the work.

Despite important wage gains on paper, however, Snell found that in some cases the differential between men and women was protected by alterations to other components of their earnings. In other words, men were being compensated for women's increased earnings. For example,

"instances were found of deliberate alterations to incentive schemes as part of or as result of equal pay implementation" (Snell, 1979, p. 41).

Cases are cited of particular changes that meant that the women concerned had to work harder and produce more (in one instance 40% more) to earn the same amount of incentive pay as before equal pay.

Overall, Snell argues that while the gap between men's wages and women's wages has been narrowed it is still large—particularly if overtime pay is included. The essence of the problem she sees as the lack of job opportunities available to women and their consequent concentration in less skilled and lower grade jobs, often in poorly paid industries. Where women are doing skilled work it is often not recognised as such (a problem referred to earlier) and this is reflected in wages.

Employers' response to the SDA has, so Snell concludes from her case study evidence, been more limited—possibly, as noted above, the legislation does not carry a positive requirement for employers to act. In the organisations that she studied, Snell found very little evidence of change to employment practices following the SDA. Most employers assumed that their policies and practices met the requirements of the law and only in recruitment practices, in the removal of sex as a criterion for appointment, was there any indication of employers revising policy. Some examples were found in Snell's study of women moving into traditionally male areas of employment (engineering, portering), but in general these were few and the occupational distribution of women remained 'almost unchanged'. Manager's attitudes were seen by Snell as central to the implementation and effectiveness of the SDA (more so than with the EPA). She identified a strong view amongst many managers that legislation had not and would not change discriminatory practices since such practices were totally justifiable.

Gregory (1982) carried out an investigation of the tribunal process as it is used in the context of the SDA. She focused specifically on the withdrawal of cases which are recorded but then 'settled' before a tribunal hearing. This, apparently, happened in one third of cases and Gregory was interested to explore how they were actually 'settled'—i.e. whether the outcome was the removal of discrimination and thus a victory for the legislation or whether they were dropped for some other reason. Of the 82 cases that Gregory examined, only about one quarter obtained settlements that approximated their original claim. The others, she writes:

"remained convinced that their complaint was justified, but they were subjected to a variety of pressures which caused them either to settle for less than they had hoped or to withdraw without getting anything at all" (Gregory, 1982, p. 88).

The research on both equal pay and sexual discrimination cited here is quite apparently limited in scale and as a result its 'representativeness' to women's experiences in employment more broadly might be questioned. General evidence of wage levels and of women's poor access to certain types and grades of employment do indicate, however, that the sorts of experiences encountered by the women identified in the surveys featured here are unlikely to be just isolated examples. Moreover, while the research quoted was undertaken after the legislation had been in place for only a relatively short space of time, the general conclusions are supported by more contemporary cases suggesting that many of the weaknesses initially identified have yet to be addressed.

As noted, the EPA and the SDA constitute the two most direct pieces of legislation aimed at improving the pay and conditions of women's employment. In assessing the contribution of policy, however, it is important that as well as examining these specific examples, we take into account aspects of employment legislation that, while not overtly aimed at women's employment have nevertheless had an important impact on the wage levels and conditions of women's work. Examples of such legislation include the Redundancy Payments Act of 1965 and the Employment Protection Acts of 1975 and 1978 which denied certain rights to workers employed for less than eight hours a week disproportionally disadvantaging women who constitute the majority of the part-time work force. Cases of employers altering the pattern of hours worked by women to bring them below this threshold are quoted by Mallier and Rosser (1987). These authors also draw attention to the discriminatory affects of the Income Tax and National Insurance schemes which operate in such a way as to make part-timers relatively cheaper to employ. National Insurance contributions by employers are not mandatory below certain levels of pay and hours worked. There is an incentive, therefore, for employers to limit workers' hours to reduce their own indirect wage costs (Robinson, 1988). Changes in NI rates introduced in 1985 preserved the threshold principle (but at the level of 17 as opposed to 14 hours) and also *reduced* the amount of employers contributions at the lower end of the scale.

On paper it would appear that national legislation has done relatively little to address the sorts of problems faced by women in the work force. The gains made in relation to equal pay and sexual discrimination at work have been offset by broader employment legislation that has generally served to disadvantage the lower paid, part-time workers, the vast majority of whom are women. Legislation can not be evaluated in isolation, however. Its use, especially in areas like equal opportunities which are wide open to differences in interpretation, is closely linked to broader government policy. The assessment of the role and scope of legislation must, therefore take place within an evaluation of both national and local policy directions. The next section provides a brief summary of what are considered to be the major examples of recent national policy of relevance to the employment position of women in Britain. Within this summary broad comparisons are made with other countries in Europe. This review is followed by an analysis of locally based policies, as developed within the context of contemporary planning.

National Policy

In October 1991 the Prime Minister, John Major, launched, in a stream of publicity, the government's 'Opportunity 2000' initiative designed to improve the position of women in the workforce. The initiative, aims to secure commitments from leading employers, both public and private sector, to promote the representation of women at all levels of employment. Sixty-one employers agreed to participate in the scheme on its announcement, including representatives form large companies such as Marks and Spencer, Sainsbury, the BBC, British Airways, Shell and British Petroleum, as well as major public sector employers such as the NHS and British Rail. In joining the initiative employers agree to adopt a strategy for the next two years to improve the job prospects of women. The exact scope of the agreement, however, varies form company to company in accordance with the wishes of managers—some employers

> "will declare strict numerical targets to promote more women while others limit their commitment to general goals such as flexible working practices" (Beavis and Weston, 1991).

Of the sixty-one companies who agreed to take part in the scheme, only eight set actual numerical targets for the employment/promotion of women. The rest preferred to restrict themselves to generating 'cultural change' rather than to any formal commitment to equal opportunity.

Opportunity 2000 was introduced by the government in response to a number of different factors. Firstly was the recognition of Britain's appalling record on equal opportunities in comparison to the rest of Europe. According to the European Commission, the pay gap between men and women in Britain is 8–10% greater than in any other European country (*The Guardian*, 1991). In other aspects; maternity leave, childcare and conditions for part-time workers, women's rights in Britain also lag behind those of women in the rest of Europe. Secondly, the realisation that demographic changes, skill shortages and the need to be internationally competitive mean that women's contribution to the workforce is vital to the British economy. A third factor encouraging government action was the pressure by employers and by women themselves—including the questioning of Major's commitment to EO given his early failure to appoint a woman to his cabinet—for some sort of government initiative on the issue of women's employment.

At the time of writing the Opportunity 2000 initiative has been in place for just one year, and its impact on women's employment has so far been seen as patchy. Supporters of the scheme point to the impressive growth in companies entering the scheme—from the initial 60 to 130—and to individual companies in which there has been an increase in the proportion of women managers. Others, however, argue that the campaign has done little for the employment prospects of 'ordinary' women. Labour MPs have described Opportunity 2000 as a 'smokescreen' designed to hide the lack of real Government action to help women— especially in the context of maternity benefits. Particular failings of the scheme are its voluntary nature and its dependence on vague goals. Summing up the first year of its operation, Morris (1992) argues that Opportunity 2000 helps women near the top to get higher but does little to help other women.

The campaign surrounding Opportunity 2000 has fuelled the debate concerning the appropriateness of legislating for equal opportunity. Again, an issue on which there is much disagreement. Since coming to power in 1979, the Conservative government have generally been unwilling to impose 'legislative constraints' on employers. The belief is that legislating for equal opportunities is inappropriate as well as ineffective and that greater opportunities for women will emerge automatically as businesses recognise the benefits of tapping into an eager and often skilled labour source, namely women. The opposing view is that without legislation women's position in the workplace will remain marginal and insecure—vulnerable to economic fluctuations and the whims of managers. This view maintains that Britain must follow the rest of Europe in legislating more widely to promote equality at work and that existing laws have been largely unsuccessful because they fail to go far enough.

What is quite obvious is that in order to evaluate government commitment to EO initiatives such as Opportunity 2000 they must be viewed in the context of other policy preferences. When this is done a much clearer measurement of concern for change is possible. One MP, commenting on the impact of Opportunity 2000, claimed that any benefits for women acheived by the initiative would be more than offset if the Government's planned abolition of the Wages Council were to go ahead. Moreover, women's participation in paid work is, as has already been pointed out, more dependent than men's on the existence of childcare and of a whole range of other social services and welfare provision. Consequently, it is women's employment that is most vulnerable to changing government priorities for funding and women's employment that is most at risk through the reduction or removal of public money for such services.

Throughout the 1980s and early 1990s state subsidised services in

Britain have, almost without exception, suffered from a reduction (and in some cases a total withdrawal) of financial support. Cuts in the provision of pre-school nurseries have perhaps had the greatest impact on the ability of women to take a paid job and while some major (and mostly private) companies have begun to take the issue seriously by providing workplace nurseries for staff, such provision is patchy and has not been sufficient to compensate for the lack of state services.

Reductions in revenue to other state services such as health-care and public transport have also had an impact on women's participation in employment, frequently compounding the difficulties of the 'dual role', as discussed in Chapter 3, and making paid work for some impossible.

In terms of other legislation, the debate surrounding the Governments plans for 'Care in the Community' provides an excellent example of the relationship between the Conservative Government's policy towards the funding of public services and women's involvement in paid work. The policy incorporates a shift from the provision of institutionalised, state-funded care for the elderly and disabled to the 'privatisation' of care for these people within the home. Implicit within the policy is the promotion of what are seen as 'traditional family values' — in other words that the family and not the state should be responsible for the care of its members. It goes without saying that the implications of a massive reduction in institutionalised care are for families, and especially for women, very serious. Under the burden of caring for sick and elderly relatives the majority of women will lack the time, freedom or physical energy to work outside the home.

The Government's commitment to 'freeing up' industry by removing financial, legal and political barriers to the operation of the private sector (which of course is one of the motives for Care in the Community) also has ramifications for the *conditions* of women's employment. As noted earlier, the growth of more flexible employment has been linked to reduced job security, awkward hours/shifts and in some cases lower rates of pay at the bottom end of the scale. Women's jobs have been disproportionally affected by government's attempts to 'de-regulate' the economy; for example, part-time employment in cleaning and other domestic services or in shop work continues to be poorly paid and frequently requires women to work unsociable hours so that companies can enhance profits. One pertinent example of the trend towards flexibilisation and the impact it can have on women's conditions of employment is that of 'Sunday Trading'. During the latter part of 1991 large retail outlets in Britain started opening for business on Sundays, blatantly ignoring the somewhat anachronistic 1950 Shops Act and cashing in (literally) on the Government's ambivalence towards the requirements of the Act (amongst them the requirement that shops should not, except under special circumstances, open on a

Sunday). Research by Kirby (1992) has identified the implication of Sunday trading for women employed by these retail outlets. He argues on the basis of this research that while many women do not want to work on Sundays, their vulnerable position in the labour market means that they may be obliged to do so in order to keep their job.

The links between Government policy and women's employment are, as has been shown above, not always immediately obvious and yet can be very profound. As such they cannot be overlooked. So far discussion in this second part of the chapter has concentrated on the relationship between policy and women's economic activity in a general and, at times, abstract way. The intention now is to turn more directly to the planning system, to consider the role of planning in contributing to women's current employment position and, more positively, in developing initiatives to address the identified problems. In examining planning in this way the focus will inevitably be on a more local level of policy generation and implementation.

Planning Policy and Women's Employment

Given the weight of constraints that operate on women's involvement in paid work, the nature of those constraints and the overall scope of the planning system, one can perhaps question the extent to which local planning policies have the ability to influence either the availability or character of employment opportunities for women. Have district-wide local plans or even strategic planning policies any scope for positive action on women and the labour market in the face of, for example, the inadequacy of sexual discrimination legislation or the appalling lack of state-funded childcare? Furthermore, since planning is restricted in terms of *direct* power to land use, design and the physical characteristics of development, how can it intervene in what are essentially social and economic processes? Are we expecting too much of the planning system if we continually criticise it for failing to address the employment needs of women?

Here we need perhaps to return briefly to the arguments raised in Chapter 1 and, indeed to the basic starting point of this book. It has been argued that planning can and does have a very profound influence on what are seen as 'social' issues and amongst them issues of inequality. By the same token, as will be shown below, planning can and does affect employment availability and an individual's access to that employment. This is true not only in terms of the direction of industrial location and the development of particular sites, but in more detailed and localised negotiations surrounding the scale, accessibility and type of activity generated. Planners are increasingly getting involved in agreements with developers in which some element of 'planning gain' can be obtained in return for planning permission. Such planning gain may be used very effectively to enhance employment opportunities and, moreover, to address the specific needs of women (see Greed, forthcoming).

Clearly, planning's role in influencing aspects such as housing design or environmental safety are more visual and in this sense more immediately obvious than its capacity for improving access to employment. Its role in tackling women's needs in relation to employment is, however, potentially far reaching, and while it can not seek to turn round national trends in policy decisions, it can profoundly influence the local conditions through which such trends and decisions are reproduced. For example, through strategic guidance and local plans, planners can strive to ensure that employment is accessible and conveniently sited in relation to other facilities (local shops and childcare). As already mentioned, agreements can be made with developers/employers for the provision of childcare in association with employment creation—indeed such provision may be included by planners as a requirement of planning permission. Planners can also look towards encouraging, perhaps in co-operation with other local authority departments or outside agencies, initiatives for the provision of training, information and advice and even funding for women's employment. In certain circumstances, design specifications may improve the access of disabled people (many of whom are women) to employment. Finally, returning to an issue introduced in Chapter 4, planners also have some responsibility, through exerting pressure internally, to contributing to improving women's employment opportunities *within* their own organisations.

These suggestions are simply illustrative of the ways in which planning can intervene to improve women's access to work outside the home. The following section discusses their use (and that of other initiatives) by local planning authorities, identifying the frequency of use and the relative popularity of different initiatives. The information discussed derives largely from the survey of planning authorities described in Chapter 4.

The survey questionnaire asked local planning authorities to specify details of any planning policies aimed at women's employment needs. Of the 270 returns, only 35 gave a positive reply to the question. This represents only 13% of responding authorities in England. The positive replies were distributed as follows:

   4 Counties (12.9% of county replies)
   9 Metropolitan Boroughs (42.9%)
   9 London Boroughs (40.9%)
  13 Districts (6.7%)

The results speak for themselves—a clear reflection of the very different levels of commitment to planning for women's needs shown by the different types of authority and already discussed in Chapter 4.

The sorts of policies/initiatives for women's employment outlined by the authorities are categorised in Table 5.1. As is clear from the table, they fell mainly into three broad areas; training (including the provision of courses for 'women returners') (20 authorities), childcare provision (15) and location/accessibility (7). Also included, though not mentioned by as many respondents, were policies on design and on grant provision/advice (3). Finally 6 authorities simply responded with a vague statement that they provided encouragement for the recruitment of women into the workforce.

Where authorities were involved in training initiatives, planning departments frequently worked in combination with Economic Development Units or other 'teams' (some of which were situated within the planning department). In Wolverhampton, for example, the planning department has had a direct input into the preparation and publication of a range of training initiatives. Courses are provided, for example, for women returners, women in business, women managers and advice is given on how to access information and apply for benefit. Interestingly, Wolverhampton also includes under the auspices of their Safer Cities Project (see Chapter 3), courses for women in dealing with violence and aggression in the workplace. In other cases it was more difficult to ascertain the exact nature of planning departments' input into training schemes. The fact that they are mentioned indicates some commitment although it seems likely that, in some cases at least, the schemes themselves are initiated outside the planning department, albeit with resources/ expertise from planning.

In the two other main areas—those of childcare provision and employment location, planning's role in the formation and implementation of policy appears more central and direct. Authorities varied in terms of the strength of policies—some requiring childcare be provided as a condition of new development for employment—other simply advising that it should be encouraged. Cambridge City Council's policy on employment related childcare appeared to be one of the strongest, the Draft Cambridge Local Plan stating that:

> "Proposals for development falling within use classes A1–A3, and B1–B8 will be *required* through planning agreements to provide adequate childcare facilities for the workforce in accordance with city council policy or alternatively to make a financial contribution towards the provision of such facilities either directly by the city council or by someone else" (Cambridge City Council, 1991, my emphasis).

Similarly, Gateshead Metropolitan Borough Council's Draft Urban Development Plan reads that:

> "On all business and industrial sites likely to generate more that 1000 employees a facility for childminding should be provided" (Gateshead MBC, 1991).

Of those authorities adopting a more advisory or negotiative stance on workplace childcare, Manchester City Council for example:

TABLE 5.1 *Local Authorities with Policies on Women and Employment*

Childcare	Training	Location	Design	Grant aid/advice	General
Cambridge	Burnley	Southampton	Southampton	Beds C.C.	M. Keynes
Bournemouth	Norwich	Oldham	Dudley	Wirral	Cornwall
Sheffield	Southampton	Manchester	Lambeth		Merton
Manchester	Nitts C. C.	Doncater			Lambeth
Gateshead	Cornwall C. C.	W. Forest			Greenwich
W. Forest	Wolverhampton	Leicester			Bristol
Newham	Manchester	Bristol			
Merton	Bolton				
Lambeth	W. Forest				
Kensington and Chelsea	Lambeth				
Islington	Islington				
Hounslow	Sheffield				
Harrow	Leicester				
Leicester	Allerdale				
Bristol	Copeland				
	Ashfield				
	Newark				
	Epping F.				
	Hounslow				
	Herts C. C.				
15	20	7	3	2	6

Source: Questionnaire survey of local authorities (1991).

"aims to *encourage* the provision of childcare facilities in major new commercial and industrial developments" (MCC, Draft UDP, 1991).

Bournemouth take a similar approach — their town centre local plan states that:

"Planning permission will normally be granted for the establishment of day nursery facilities in suitable premises close to places of employment within the town" (BDC, undated).

The same sort of division is evident in policies concerning the location of employment provision. The Leicester City Council Local Plan (1991) recognises the need for employment (especially in service industries) to be situated such that advantage can be taken of the untapped supplies of female labour. The plan recommends, to this end, that:

"employment opportunities are located in areas that can be made accessible by forms of transport which are accessible to disadvantaged people" (LCC, 1991, p. 67).

The Doncaster MBC Draft UDP is somewhat more vague containing a commitment to improving access to employment in the town centre and thereby benefitting a "wide range of less mobile people" (including women).

Linked to ideas about increasing women's access to employment, Bristol City Council include in their Draft Local Plan (1992) an acknowledgement of the need to encourage 'alternative' forms of employment. They argue the need for the City's proposed Economic and Community Development Strategy to explore the potential offered to a number of groups including women of such initiatives as:

(1) new enterprise workshops (sheltered)
(2) low cost unserviced small workspace
(3) co-operative development
(4) community business support
(5) business development funds
(6) specialist support for enterprise development by ethnic minorities, women and disabled workers.

To this effect policy EC22 of the Bristol Draft Local Plan states that

"the City Council will support, in principle, development involving small business, community co-operatives, community enterprises and voluntary groups that provide a clear benefit to the long term unemployed, people with disabilities, people of minority ethnic origin, women, or serves other specific community needs" (BCC, 1992, p. 184).

Of the 3 councils that incorporate policies for design in relation to women and employment, 2, Southampton CC and Dudley MBC are concerned with safety and 1, Lambeth, with access for disabled women. In all three cases, the policies are in the form of recommendations—encouraging awareness of the problems for women and the need to negotiate safe and accessible design with developers.

While all 35 Councils identified do at least recognise (and, to some degree, address) planning's role in improving employment opportunities for women, even this recognition extends, in virtually all cases, to just a sentence or two. A notable exception to this lack of coverage is Southampton DC whose excellent *Design Guidelines for Women and the Planned Environment* contains a separate section on employment. The points made in the Guidelines demonstrate a very comprehensive understanding of the issues and presumably provide a strong framework within which to construct policy and justify development decisions.

Southampton's guidelines are premised on two main arguments:

> "1. The location, design and management of many workplaces have an impact on women's safety. A high proportion of women have low paid jobs such as cleaning or hotel, bar or hospital work, and have to travel at night and in the early morning, generally by public transport.
> "2. Safety at work is an issue that has recently come to the fore and there are both managerial as well as design aspects which could improve safety for women at work."

On the basis of these points, various objectives for the improvement of physical design of industrial/commercial developments are listed. These include, firstly, stricter control over the layout of large sites in order to provide pedestrian routes, bus stops and parking areas that are well lit; secondly, careful landscaping so that employees can be seen from adjacent streets and thirdly, safe access points and internal site and building layouts.

In addition to features of design, the guidelines include specifications on the management of employment sites which stress the need for alarms and panic buttons, the employment of women security officers, staff training on awareness, assertiveness and self-defence and the removal of offensive or discriminatory graffiti.

It must be added, however, that impressively comprehensive though they are, Southampton's guidelines are just that—in other words they are advisory rather than obligatory. This was the pattern found in the majority of responses. Few authorities went beyond recommendation and included requirements of the sort contained in the Draft Cambridge Local Plan example quoted above. Bristol City Council mention the use of Section 106 agreements as a means of securing "planning advantages" in economic development but do not specify where and for what purpose such agreements would be used. It is difficult to know how to interpret the absence of planning requirements for women's employment. Should it be seen as a lack of awareness of the possibilities offered for addressing women's employment needs through planning policy, an absence of commitment on behalf of planning departments or an acknowledgement of the chances of defending a policy which includes the issue of 'equality' as a criterion for economic development?

Answering this questions is beyond the scope of present research and requires much more indepth analysis than is undertaken here. In reality, the answer is probably a combination of the three issues. Whatever the reasons for planning's neglect of women's employment needs they clearly stem from underlying assumptions about women's involvement in paid work and from a policy background that has consistently downgraded the issue of equality of opportunity. Inevitably this brings us back to the wider questions surrounding women's participation in decision making and their access to power to precipitate change.

This chapter has incorporated a wide range of material in an attempt to introduce theoretical debate on the nature of women's employment experiences and to apply this debate to the examination and interpretation of the policy process. While it may be difficult to comprehend the direct relationship between theories of women's entry into the labour market and the failure of policy and the planning system to prioritise women's employment needs, the argument here is that some sort of link is crucial. That link, it is asserted, is the operation of patriarchy. As has been shown, patriarchal structures are critical to the theoretical understanding of women's access to and experiences within paid work. They are also apparent in the operation of the policy process and the workings of the planning system. In the recognition of women's needs and in decisions surrounding the choices and priorities for employment related development, both the broad arena of strategic policy and the more detailed day-to-day implementation of decisions reflect dominent patriarchal gender relations. As recession deepens 'economic' needs consistently take priority within planning. This frequently means that policies to improve access to employment for 'minority' groups such as women are suspended or shelved, further reinforcing existing interests and the unequal power relations within the decision-making process.

6

Accessibility and Transport

Introduction

One of the central issues emerging from the study of women and the built environment is that of access. Whether it is access to employment, to services, to power or to planning decisions, the inequalities experienced by women play a fundamental part in shaping their lives. Such inequalities both reflect and create gender identities, exerting a major influence over our expectations of the differing behaviour patterns of men and women. And yet so entrenched are these inequalities that we frequently fail to recognise their existence or question their role in determining the availability of opportunities.

Chapter 3 has discussed at some length the relationship between land use planning and gender inequalities. It was argued that the siting of major uses within the city—particularly the separation of home and work, the sites of consumption and production—places important constraints on levels of access. These constraints are frequently felt most strongly by women as a result of the demands of their domestic role, their greater involvement in shift work and the requirement to travel more often between different spheres. Women's accessibility was shown here to be a function not only of the physical location of different activities and buildings but of the gender division of labour within the household and the expectations associated with their domestic role. The situation is aptly summed up by the Women and Transport Forum of the GLC:

"Urban motorways and urban trunk roads cut through women's lives, driving a noisy, polluting, dangerous wedge between their homes and workplaces, schools and health centres, causing them to walk roundabout routes, through hostile subways or over windy bridges, diverting and lengthening bus journeys and creating unsafe, no-go areas of blank walls and derelict spaces" (see WTF, 1988, p. 121).

In addition to access to physical spaces, previous chapters have considered women's access to decision making and to power. Whether this be in relation to land use planning, the siting of different functions and the design of buildings, or in relation to sectoral policies such as employment and housing, women have been shown to have very limited access to formal and informal power structures. Strong links were made, in this context, between the notion of women's access to power and the organisation of social relations and the operation of patriarchy. Women's inability to influence decisions around the siting of services and the distribution of resources is, it was argued, primarily a result of the unequal distribution of power between men and women and the social structures within which this distribution is grounded.

It is not the intention of this chapter to repeat these debates. Instead, the aim here is to concentrate on one particular aspect of accessibility, namely transport. Having made this point, however, it is clear that even in dealing with the provision of transport facilities and the organisation of transport services, we cannot ignore issues of power and control and the implications of gender inequality in these areas. Neither can we see transport as isolated from other aspects of women's lives—their use of and access to different forms of transport are very closely linked to wider characteristics of their roles.

Unlike the previous topic, employment, there does not exist a vast body of literature on the issue of women and accessibility. This is particularly true of more theoretical work for while there have been some empirical studies that have explored the extent and nature of constraints on women's mobility and access (see for example, Greico *et al.*, 1989; Hamilton *et al.*, 1991; Pickup, 1985, 1988), there has been little discussion of related theory. In particular, few studies have interpreted empirical findings in the context of feminist theory (exceptions include Oliver, 1988) or broader discussions of women's powerlessness and subordination. There is a clear need for further research on the practicalities of women's mobility problems but this research must be informed by theoretical discussions of women's inequality. Similarly, in considering solutions to the constraints experienced by women, the identification of practical responses must be accompanied by an understanding of the wider constraints on women's activities and on the basis of their inequality.

Having made this point the following section is mainly devoted to a review of existing work on women's mobility and consequently is restricted in its use of theory. However, many of the points made draw on more conceptual ideas raised in Chapter 3, relating to women's use of space and the origins of the relationship between gender divisions and the built environment. Later discussions on women's safety in the context of mobility are more explicitly underpinned by debates on power and women's subordination as is the review of policy initiatives.

Access to Transport

Over recent decades British society has become a car-borne society. Levels of car use and car ownership have risen astronomically. In 1989/90 there were almost 20 million private cars registered in Britain—368 per 1000 people (Department of Transport, 1992). For the majority of people almost everything we do—employment, leisure, domestic activities such as shopping—is planned around the use of transport, predominantly the private car. Decisions around car ownership and use profoundly influence our spending priorities as individuals and our use of space and treatment of the environment as a society. The car has become an indicator of wealth and status. Ownership of a private motor car and access to car use now represent important 'dividers' within contemporary British society.

Car ownership levels are generally calculated on the basis of households. So, for example, in 1989 it was estimated that 66% of households had access to a car—an increase of 8% on the figure for 1988 (Department of Transport, 1992). It cannot be assumed that all members of the household have equal access to the household car and there are important inequalities between different groups in relation to their access to private transport. Research (for example Pickup, 1983) has shown that it is frequently men who control the use of the household car; it is their needs that take priority and it is men who decide when and by whom the car is to be used. Thus, a study by Matrix (1984) demonstrated, while 60% of households in Milton Keynes own a car, 75% of unpaid women working at home do not have access to a car during the week. In purely practical terms, women are less likely to hold a current driving licence than are men. In 1975/6 29% of all women in Britain held a driving licence as opposed to 69% of all men. By 1989/90 the gap had narrowed with an increase in the percentage of women holding a driving licence to 48%—still significantly lower than the corresponding figure for men, however, which stood at 78%.

Decisions about car use are not, however, solely a function of licence ownership but relate to contemporary culture more broadly. The car has assumed an increasingly powerful role in our society in the construction of images of male and female sexuality. For men, in particular, cars are associated with power and status. Fast cars, and the ability to drive at excessive speed are part of the macho male image—in advertising, car ownership is frequently linked with other symbols of power and success—for example, smart clothes, big houses and beautiful women. Male control over the car extends to a monopoly over technical and mechanical knowledge. A man is assumed to be able to understand the mechanical workings of a car engine. Such knowledge, on the other hand, is denied to most women who are then left powerless by this defense of male 'expertise'. When it comes to actually driving, women are often ascribed a secondary role and assumed less competent than men. 'Jokes' about women drivers are used to undermine women's confidence and, again, to protect the dominant position of men.

Male control over the use of the private motor car means that even amongst car owning households, women are frequently dependent on *public* transport. In addition, women constitute the majority of single elderly households—one of the groups most reliant on public transport. Oliver (1985) discovered from research in Surrey that women comprise 68% of public transport users on Mondays to Fridays and 65% on Saturdays. It is women, therefore, who are most affected by the availability of public transport and by the quality of public transport services. One important feature of transport provision in this country is that while there has been a dramatic rise, noted above, in private car ownership, the level of *public* transport provision has shown a steady deterioration.

Public transport in Britain has long been underfunded in relation to private transport. The past 10–15 years in particular have witnessed a deliberate attack through government policy on public transport expenditure. A myth still exists, however, that public transport users are subsidised at the expense of the private motorist (via, for example, licence fees). But, as Kate Oliver (1988, p. 21) argues

> "the truth is that 36% of car journeys terminating in London are in company owned cars and 77% receive some form of assistance with their motoring costs, such as free parking, petrol allowances and running cost subsidies. The tax payer is subsidising these company cars to the tune of an estimated 150–190 million pounds per annum."

While some change to the tax paid by those driving company cars has recently taken place, the sentiments behind this quote still apply and private cars, and company cars in particular, are still heavily subsidised.

By contrast Oliver notes the decreasing value of subsidies to public transport—for example, "in 1979 the revenue subsidy for bus and underground trains run by London Regional Transport amounted to 110.7 million pounds. By 1986 it was only 79 million per annum" (Oliver, 1988, p. 21). Similarly, as Hamilton *et al.* (1991) note, TEST (1984) have shown that the *total* subsidy for public transport in 1984 was similar to the subsidy received by company cars—something in the order of £1.5 billion. The deregulation of public transport following the 1985 Transport Act has led to a further reduction in the extent of government funding to public transport. This has had the affect of reducing the level of provision— especially on routes where profits were traditionally low—for example in many rural areas (see Bell and Cloke, 1990).

Quality of provision

Much of the literature on women's public transport provision has looked not just at the actual frequency of services but also at the quality of service provided. Women's use of public transport, it is argued, is not simply a function of availability but is also determined by the broader characteristics of provision. The timing of services, for example, is crucial to women—especially where they are trying to balance the constraints of home and work. Bus timetabling frequently makes it difficult or impossible for women to organise childcare, shopping and employment even where fairly short journeys are concerned. A lack of sensitivity when planning routing and timing of public transport (especially where changes are involved) can increase the complexity of women's travel patterns— particularly where journeys are undertaken at 'off-peak' times. Existing routes tend to favour the traveller who wishes to travel from the suburbs to the town/city centre (usually before 9.30 am) and then back again after 4.30 pm. By contrast they rarely prioritise journeys between different suburbs or out of town locations. As Oliver again notes (1988, p. 23):

> "Orbital routes which serve suburban facilities and are well used by women have lower priority than the radial routes to and from the city centre used by commuters, who are more often men. While central business districts are well served by public transport, suburban, industrial and housing estates are often inadequately served."

Women's use of public transport is also affected by physical/practical considerations relating to the design of buses and trains. The characteristics of women's role means that when they travel they are often accompanied by small children and/or carrying shopping. The design of 'standard' buses or train carriages makes getting on and off under such circumstances difficult, if not impossible. There is often no organised assistance for women getting on and off public transport with children, pushchairs etc. Once on board there is frequently nowhere to put shopping and other paraphernalia, and no proper provision of child seats. These practical considerations extend beyond the actual vehicles. Women may experience difficulties in using public transport due to the location of bus stops and train stations. They may be deterred by the inadequate provision of seats and shelter at bus stops and by awkward steps and crossings at railway stations. Again, it is women with children who find such practical constraints so debilitating.

In some instances these 'constraints' and 'difficulties' can be positively dangerous. Women can be deterred from using public transport because of the risk to small children and to themselves. A study by Hillman *et al.* (1974), while dated, demonstrates the important links between children's age and frequency of travel identifying perception of the risks involved as an important influence on women's decision to undertake journeys on public transport. Their own health can also influence women's use of public transport. Disabled or infirm women clearly suffer difficulties in using conventional forms of public transport. Pregnant women may also be at risk; Pickup and Town (1983) cite evidence from French research that "pregnant women who had to commute daily by urban rail into central Paris suffered a high incidence of premature births due to a combination of the effort involved in climbing stairs and the prolonged vibration on the metro" (Pickup, 1988, p. 107). The whole issue of risk and women's mobility is taken up in the next section of the chapter which looks specifically at fear and safety in relation to women's travel.

Transport and Safety

The issue of safety is central to the debate on women's use of public transport and many studies (both from academics and practitioners) have taken this as their focus. Women can experience sexual harassment, physical assault and even rape while travelling on public transport and fear of violence imposes serious limitations on women's travel, especially after dark. Some forms of public transport are regarded by women as particularly dangerous. Buses are generally considered safer than trains—in the latter women can be more easily 'trapped' in a carriage alone and consequently more prone to abuse or attack—although, as discussed below, the safety of buses is believed to be much reduced with the switch to one person operated vehicles.

Much of the risk and the fear surrounding women's use of public transport is associated not so much with time spent actually on vehicles but with the associated waiting or changing between modes. Bus stops, train and metro stations and taxi ranks are all seen as dangerous places where women feel vulnerable to attack. Again the fear and reality of harassment increases at night. Many of these places are poorly lit and isolated; railway and underground stations are often unstaffed at night, increasing the likelihood of attacks. Subways, too (which frequently must be used to access stations and bus stops) are almost invariably dark, unwelcoming places, renowned for the dangers they pose.

Fear of attack while travelling is widespread amongst women and, as already noted, can make a real impact on their daily lives. A survey carried out by the GLC as part of their 'Women and Transport Study' (1983) discovered that 63% of women avoided going out on their own after dark—a figure backed up by studies undertaken elsewhere (see Chapter 2). While women regarded travelling on a bus as one of the safer options, over 70% believed that it was unsafe to wait for a bus after dark. Research in Bradford revealed that 59% of women questioned avoided using any form of public transport at night (Trench and Jones, 1990).

Although women who travel by private motor car escape many of the problems associated with violence that are experienced by women who use public transport, they are by no means free from danger. Two areas of particular danger for women are using car parks—particularly large, multi-storey car parks—and breaking down. The former again requires women to enter a hostile environment—often dark and dirty and poorly, if at all, policed. Women in cars that have broken down are vulnerable—trapped, sometimes in remote and strange places.

It is quite apparent, from the brief discussion here, that constraints on women's mobility, whether directly a function of provision or more indirectly related to the quality of provision or to fear, do have a serious impact on women's lives. Dependence on public transport may limit the choices women can make in terms of employment opportunities, leisure participation and even in undertaking more mundane domestic tasks. Research undertaken in Reading by Pickup (1983) (referred to earlier) demonstrated that women who do not have access to their own car are less likely to seek jobs located on the urban fringe or that require journeys across suburbs or between two urban centres. In the same context, research has also identified an important link between incomes earned and mobility, with mean incomes being higher amongst those women who can commute outside the local job market.

Fear of sexual harassment or attack places particular constraints on women's mobility after dark. Some parts of the city become virtual no-go zones while many women are scared to leave the house alone. Such fears again limit the number and variety of leisure opportunities accessible to women. They can also affect the type of employment women do— especially where shift work is involved.

As well as these major, easily identifiable, impacts, constraints on women's mobility are felt throughout their lives. They may be so common place and widely accepted, however, that they are not recognised as a particular handicap. Waiting for long periods of time for public transport, having to walk some distance to get to a bus stop or train station and being subjected to dirty, cramped and uncomfortable travelling conditions are simply an inevitable consequence of using public transport for many women. Adjustments to their daily routines and, perhaps more import- antly, their expectations and aspirations (for both themselves and their children), are made often automatically as a response to these conditions.

While many of the mobility constraints experienced by women are common to *all* women (especially those surrounding safety and fear of attack) the extent to which they affect the lives of individuals will vary considerably in relation to social class and ethnicity. In the GLC study referred to above it was argued that inadequate public transport disadvan- tages black and ethnic minority women in particular, since these women are most likely to live in areas of cheap housing where job opportunities are poor and there is a general under-resourcing of shops and other facilities (WTF, 1988). The greater access to private transport enjoyed by women of higher social classes means that their lives are far less constrained by public transport availability. They are, as a result, less restricted in terms of choices surrounding employment and leisure opportunities.

Women's Mobility and the Influence of Transport Policy

It has been argued above that the deregulation of bus services in Britain has had a detrimental affect on levels and quality of provision and, consequently, on women's mobility. Deregulation of public transport is, however, just one of a number of policy decisions that have operated to the disadvantage of women both as the major users of public transport and also as users with particular needs and characteristics. The Women and Transport Forum organised by the GLC argued that government priorities for traffic management lay at the centre of women's mobility problems. Consequently they looked at national policy in order to help explain the local difficulties encountered by women on a daily basis—they drew attention, in particular, to what they see as women's 'invisibility' in government policy and transport planning, questioning "how 'public' is public transport" (WTF, 1988).

The privatisation of public transport has been high on the political agenda since the Conservative Government came to power in 1979. In keeping with Conservative ideology, it has been the intention of successive Thatcher governments to promote a fully commercial public transport system in the UK. Such a policy has had a number of fairly well documented consequences—these are worth considering here as they impinge on women's needs.

Privatisation has resulted, in many areas, in an increase in public transport fares. This is particularly true in rural parts of the country where the 'competitive tendering' for routes which was envisaged by government has not materialised (see Bell and Cloke, 1990). Bus companies have been unwilling to operate routes which do not attract large numbers of customers—where the less competitive routes have remained, it has been at the cost of higher fares and a lower frequency of service. Privatisation has had a further affect on fare levels by reducing the possibility for integrated fares. Where different routes and different modes of transport are operated by different 'companies' the opportunities for introducing cheaper, integrated fares are severely reduced. Here women undertaking complex journeys (albeit locally) lose out, having to buy several tickets to cover the different parts of the trip.

Where transport services have remained 'public'—or at least funded directly by government (e.g. London Regional Transport (LRT), British Rail)—the reduction in subsidies and the attempts to make the system more 'commercial' have also resulted in higher fares. In relation to women's position, however, it is not simply the fact that bus and train fares *overall* have increased, it is rather that fare increases have disproportionately affected certain *types* of ticket/journey. Hence, as the Women and Transport Forum write:

> "In the 18 month period (July 1984 to January 1986) after the government took control from the GLC, LRT imposed fares increases totalling 16%. This average conceals that both children's and short-distance bus fares increased by 50%, [and] the maximum children's underground fare by a massive 200%..... All these costs fall most heavily on women who accompany children and other dependants" (WTF, 1988 p. 126).

It is, on average, *local* fares that have increased most as a result of government policy and, as has already been argued, it is women who undertake the majority of local journeys by public transport.

Another direct result of the government's privatisation of public transport in the UK has been the reduction in the frequency of services in some areas. Again, as with fares, the areas worst hit are those where the returns are more marginal and hence competition to run the service non-existent.

In attempting to reduce expenditure, public transport providers have introduced a range of cost cutting measures — the effects of which have been to reduce the quality of services in ways briefly touched upon above. Of major importance amongst such measures has been a severe reduction in staffing levels in parts of the system. An absence of staff in ticket offices, on platforms and actually on board buses and trains has led to an increase in attacks on women while travelling and in fear of attack. The GLC Women's Unit reported an increase in the number of attacks on women travelling on the underground — reported attacks rose from 752 in 1982 to 1254 in 1984. While such figures cannot be automatically linked to reduction in staffing levels, women questioned about the dangers of travelling on public transport felt very strongly that the presence of staff helped reduce likelihood of attack.

Violence against women is not the only consequence of the reduction in staffing levels. Difficulties in lifting buggies and shopping bags on and off buses and trains are exacerbated by an absence of staff. One person operated buses have received particular criticism in this respect. They are also criticised for causing delays and slower journeys — the Women's Transport Forum noted that "passengers take four times as long to board the (new) one-person operated buses than they do the doorless, crew-operated buses where a conductor and not the driver collects the fares" (WTF, 1988 p. 124).

The research unit of the Campaign to Improve London's Transport (CILT) published a report in 1987 entitled "*Free to Move*" in which they identified the transport needs of women in the London Borough of Southwark. In this report particular attention was drawn to the issue of staffing and to the staff-cutting policies of LRT and BR. The report identifies direct results of such a policy:

(1) more and more buses becoming driver only
(2) guards being removed from trains
(3) station staff being cut such that staff may now have a responsibility for a group of stations. In addition, some station cleaners are being brought in under different contracts.
(4) fewer job opportunities for women and black and ethnic minority people.

The report goes on to document the affect of such a policy on the experiences of passengers. As well as the safety issues already discussed above, the Southwark study drew attention, in particular, to the use of one person operated buses. Most women, it was felt, disliked these buses for the following reasons:

(1) the lack of assistance in boarding buses
(2) the problems of finding change while standing up (with children, shopping etc.)
(3) the difficulties in asking the driver for information—especially while the bus is moving
(4) the risk of disturbances—particularly upstairs—with no conductor to intervene
(5) the feeling that the driver cannot be in full control, driving and worrying about what is going on behind him/her.

In many instances staffing cuts on public transport have been made in reaction to the introduction of new technology. Automatic ticket machines and close-circuit television, for example, have been used as a means of *reducing* the physical presence of people on the ground. Clearly, while changes made in the name of technological 'progress' have allowed less staff involvement, they have not necessarily had the same beneficial impact on the experience of the transport user. Improvements here, it may be argued lie, very often, not in sophisticated technological innovation but in simple aids such as seating and lighting.

The experiences of privatisation demonstrate that as well as looking at individual policies that affect women's transport needs and experiences, we must be aware of other government priorities that have dictated the fundamental direction of transport policy. The introduction to this chapter noted that, despite widespread belief to the contrary, the private car user has consistently been subsidised at the expense of the public transport user. This favouring of private provision has been a key tenet of Conservative government policy and is clearly illustrated in the priority (in terms of funding and political attention) that has been given to road building. It is commonly the case, not only in Britain, but in other western countries, that major transport projects (particularly those deemed to be national show pieces) receive far greater degrees of government support than do local bus and train services. Surely questions must be asked as to the extent that projects such as Concorde, the TGV and the Channel Tunnel really address the day-to-day needs of women transport users! (Oliver, 1988).

National policies together with broad assumptions about transport use have, it would appear, failed to adequately recognise the needs of women and have exacerbated or at least reinforced existing inequalities. Women's lack of power within the decision-making process, as discussed in Chapter 4, has left them badly placed to challenge the basic direction of policy at either a national or a local level. Sylvia Trench, in an article in *Town and*

Country Planning (1991), describes attempts made by the Institute of Planning Studies at Nottingham University to bring together transport operators, transport planners and women in workshops to discuss the 'special needs' of women public transport users. The workshops elicited a disappointing response from both transport operators and local authority planners. Designed specifically to demonstrate to *male* policy makers the strength of women's feelings (especially on the issue of safety) the workshops succeeded in attracting only women planners and no male transport operators, prompting Trench to question the commitment of planners and transport providers to taking the needs of women seriously.

Contrary to the general direction of transport planning in Britain, initiatives aimed specifically at women's needs do exist. Some of these have been developed by local authorities but the majority have been either partly or wholly initiated by voluntary groups. Such projects provide important examples of the way in which women have sought to challenge established practices and polices and, in some cases, bypassed existing channels of decision making.

Planners, while (in local authorities at least) not necessarily responsible for broad transport policy, do provide an important input into the transport system. As noted earlier, there are a number of areas where planning can intervene to influence the efficiency and safety of both private and public transport use. Encouraging 'unconventional' forms of transport provision in recognition of the particular needs of different groups, for example, is certainly within the remit of strategic and local planning and arguably as important as the facilitation of traffic circulation and the provision and siting of car parking. In many towns and cities planners have begun to pay considerable attention to reducing traffic in city centres and providing better conditions for cyclists and pedestrians. Again, such measures can be seen to benefit many different groups in society—one of the largest of these is women.

The following section considers the role of local authority planning departments in transport initiatives for women. Using original information from the questionnaire (as in the chapters on housing and employment) the *extent* of planning's involvement in the development of policies and initiatives aimed at women's needs will be identified. The section will then continue with a detailed look at the type of policies that are proposed by local authorities identifying a range of responses to the difficulties faced by women. In the final part of the chapter attention will turn to a number of selected schemes that have been developed to try to alleviate women's transport problems. These schemes have been implemented with varying levels of commitment and support from planners but demonstrate the *potential* role of planning departments in contributing to greater equality in transport use and access.

TABLE 6.1 *Planning Authorities with Transport Initiatives for Women*

Cambridge (DC)	Lewisham (LB)
Hartlepool (DC)	Merton (LB)
Southampton (DC)	Newham (LB)
Hereford (DC)	Sutton (LB)
Leicester (DC)	Waltham Forest (LB)
Norwich (DC)	Hammersmith and Fulham (LB)
Thamesdown (DC)	Richmond Upon Thames (LB)
Birmingham (MC)	Lambeth (LB)
Gloucestershire (CC)	Doncaster (MC)
Wiltshire (CC)	Dudley (MC)
Barking and Dagenham (LB)	Manchester (MC)
Barnet (LB)	Oldham (MC)
Bexley (LB)	S. Tyneside (MC)
Enfield (LB)	Sheffield (MC)
Greenwich (LB)	Wolverhampton (MC)
Hounslow (LB)	Bradford (MC)
	Islington (LB)

Source: Questionnaire survey to local planning authorities (1991).

Transport Planning Initiatives for Women

Of the 270 local authority planning departments who responded to the questionnaire survey, 33 (12.2%) claimed to have specific initiatives aimed at women in the area of transport policy. Table 6.1 provides a list of these authorities broken down by type. As in other policy areas, it is apparent that those authorities most likely to have introduced women's initiatives in their transport policies are the London boroughs and the Metropolitan councils. Fifteen of the London boroughs (62.5% of those responding) and 9 of the Metropolitan councils (38.1%) were among the 35 authorities with women's transport initiatives, as opposed to 7 district councils (3.6% of those responding) and 2 counties (6.5%). Not surprisingly those authorities listed in Table 6.1 demonstrate a considerable overlap with those in which policy initiatives aimed at women's needs in either employment or housing have been identified.

The form and content of the different local authority initiatives varies significantly, ranging from the simple recognition of women's particular needs as transport users to detailed recommendations and specifications over a wide range of transport issues. Policies are mainly concentrated in two areas—transport supply/provision and safety, with a greater emphasis on the latter—possibly reflecting assumptions about the boundaries of appropriate and effective planning involvement. Considerable variation is apparent in the commitment of different authorities to addressing women's transport needs—many simply including a passing reference to women as one of a number of disadvantaged groups. Other authorities have clearly made considerable effort to identify and understand the extent of women's mobility problems and to work towards effective, appropriate action.

Looking initially at the 33 authorities who claim to have implemented (or are in the process of implementing) women's transport initiatives, it is apparent that in at least a third of the case's policies are of a very generalised nature. These cases refer to the access difficulties experienced by 'less mobile' or 'disadvantaged' groups registering an awareness of the needs of these groups and, in some instances, a commitment to addressing these needs. There is, amongst these authorities, little reference to the problems of *women* or any acknowledgement that the access constraints experienced by women may be different from those of other disadvantaged groups such as the elderly or the disabled.

The London Borough of Sutton, for example, incorporates in its draft Unitary Development Plan the need for improved public transport to increase the accessibility of those with mobility problems, while South Tyneside refers to the preparation of a policy within their UDP for 'mobility disadvantaged people'. Similarly, Barnet, in their adopted UDP, seek to improve access to public transport facilities, comfort while waiting for services and interchange between transport modes and routes. These factors, they stress, are of particular importance to those who rely on public transport, *including* women (my emphasis).

The Cambridge Draft Local Plan chapter on transport contains policies which generally aim at increasing accessibility within the city for *all* the population through encouraging public transport, cycling and walking. The issues section of this chapter refers to the problems faced by women as amongst those less likely to have access to a car.

Other authorities include much more explicit reference to the particular problems experienced by women and go into far greater detail in relation to the formulation and implementation of specific policy initiatives. More emphasis is placed by these authorities on the links between the constraints experienced by women in the context of employment and leisure opportunities and their low levels of mobility. The London Borough of Lambeth, for example, in Chapter 4 of their Local Plan (soon to be succeeded by the UDP) which considers a range of women's issues, in stressing the importance of public transport to women write:

> "Women's opportunities and access to jobs show they are curtailed due to lack of safe and good public transport, geared to women's needs. More buses running between housing and shopping areas, catering for off-peak journeys, the majority of which are made by women and elderly, are crucial (Policy T22).
> "The Council is committed to pressing London Regional Transport on certain matters. These include matters of particular relevance to women, e.g. the need for more bus shelters and measures to improve the safety and access of buses and tubes. The Council can provide better lighting and seating at bus stops" (Policy T24).

Southampton City, in the introduction to policies on transportation in their guidelines on Women and the Planned Environment, recognise the complexity of women's transport needs together with their greater dependence on public transport. The document puts forward a range of proposals concerning the provision of different forms of public transport and the design of transport networks and the environment within which people travel. Importantly, Southampton City Council does recognise, in its proposals for transport provision, the role of other influences—transport operators, national policies etc. on their own ability to respond to the identified problems. They acknowledge common interests, however, that can be addressed jointly by the local authority and transport operators.

As noted, the most detailed proposals put forward by local authorities in dealing with women's transport needs relate to safety issues. Safety both in the context of the design and operation of different modes of transport and more generally within the planning of the built environment is seen as critical to women's mobility and to their access to particular functions of urban areas. Other chapters have already reviewed the dangers and difficulties posed by aspects of the design of public spaces and residential environments, and considered the role of design solutions as a response to women's fear. It is not the intention here to repeat these debates. It is perhaps appropriate, however, to look at some of the specific proposals to encourage the development of 'safe environments' that have been put forward by different authorities in the context of transport planning.

Explicit reference to the importance of providing safe public transport and/or encouraging safety in the built environment in the planning of transport facilities was made by 20 local authorities in their responses to the questionnaire survey (with a further 2 providing vague and ambiguous references to women's fear). Again, there is considerable variation between authorities in the degree of detail provided in either the recognition of design problems or their responses to them. The most comprehensive proposals were put forward by three authorities, Manchester Metropolitan Borough, Southampton City and Leicester City, as part of extensive documents on planning for women and safety in the environment. Thus Manchester, for example, as well as providing guidelines for the design and siting of footpaths, car parks and subways and the provision of street lighting, also include a number of specifications relating to specific forms of transport (although they recognise the limited influence of planning *per se* within this sphere). The following proposals, they believe, deal with some of the main areas of concern:

Buses
 (1) Bus stops should be located in places where visibility is good, and in well used locations, but away from likely trouble stops.

(2) Landscaping at bus stops should not screen people waiting from other uses of the area and should not create shadows at night.

(3) Bus stops and pedestrian routes should be well lit.

(4) The frequency of off-peak services should be increased and it should be ensured that services run to time, so that waiting time is minimised.

(5) The possibility of allowing people to hail buses at night, and to disembark wherever they chose should be investigated.

(6) The feasibility of providing different bus routes or sites for bus stops at night and at weekends, when sites which are well used during the working day may be fairly quiet, should be looked at.

(7) The reduction of fares at off-peak times.

(8) Extending service on routes that women have to visit, e.g. between residential areas and schools, shopping centres and clinics.

(9) Further support of dial-a-ride schemes, especially for the elderly and disabled women, and women's taxi services.

(10) The re-introduction of bus conductors, especially at night.

(11) Providing alarms on buses, especially on the top deck.

(12) The investigation of women's travel patterns in Manchester by travel diary services.

(13) Ensuring that no sexist advertising is allowed on advertising hoardings sites on council-owned land adjacent to bus stops.

Trains

(1) In stations which are staffed, the regularity with which platforms are controlled should be increased, particularly at night.

(2) In unstaffed stations closed-circuit T.V. should be installed with the intention of improving security. The location of waiting rooms, toilets etc. should also be carefully checked to ensure that they are close to the main entrance.

(3) Women only waiting rooms should be re-introduced.

(4) The platform, and access to it, should be well lit.

Taxis

(1) The location of taxi ranks should be reviewed to ensure they are positioned so that women do not have to walk far to reach them.

(2) Lighting and landscaping at taxi ranks should be checked to ensure that they do not reduce safety.

(3) At night, taxis within the city centre should be willing to stop for women away from established taxi ranks.

(4) Taxis should display identification so that it can be seen before people get in.

(Manchester City Council Planning Department, 1987).

These are quite clearly extensive guidelines that cover a wide range of concerns in relation to women's safe use of public transport. Although not all are within the control of the planning department, it is important that these proposals have been specified by planners not simply to acknowledge their awareness of the problems faced by women but to provide very concrete advice in areas which do interact very closely with the planning process. The implicit recognition here is of a need for planners to work together with other actors in the provision of transport to ensure a broad based and consistent approach to minimising danger to women.

Some councils incorporate a safety dimension into their planning for private as well as for public transport. Most frequent are proposals for the design and maintenance of car parks. Again, some discussion of the dangers posed to women and the possible responses to these dangers was included in Chapter 3 in a more general discussion of the planning of 'safe' environments.

The Southampton City questionnaire response included, under details of transport initiatives for women, copies of correspondence with British Rail (BR) which form part of a dialogue between BR and planning officers (on behalf of the Women's Sub-Committee) aimed at seeking improvements for women on trains and at stations in the city. The dialogue demonstrates the importance of co-ordinated effort by those with responsibility for transport planning and provision. It also shows something of the frustrations experienced by planners in attempting to introduce improvements in areas beyond their immediate control. Following the publication by Southampton City Council of the Safety Guidelines for Women (already referred to), a meeting was held between representatives of the Council and BR to discuss the particular implications of the report for BR's women passengers. Certain areas had been highlighted by the Council as being of primary concern. These were summarised as "dark lonely stations, quiet trains and threatening or disturbing incidents" (Policy and Resources (Women) Sub-Committee, Southampton City Council, 1989). A BR representative was questioned about BR's intended response to these areas of concern.

On the issue of lighting the BR representative argued that lighting had in fact been substantially upgraded over the past two years. There were currently no plans to extend this upgrading to the stations where no programme had been undertaken. Similarly, no change was anticipated by BR in the staffing arrangements on trains. They claimed rather that:

"Staffing decisions were taken by BR on a *business* basis and that staffing levels will only be improved if there is a net economic benefit to BR. It is not anticipated by BR that staffing levels (at the stations specified) will be increased in the foreseeable future" (SCC, 1989, my emphasis).

A similarly negative answer to the Council's request that the policing of stations be increased was received—the current 'over stretching' of the

British Transport Police service meant that a continuous presence at stations is not possible. BR did agree to review the provision of video cameras at stations but added that extra provision could only be entertained where there was 'a problem'. At present, they claimed, the Council's survey on women's safety and claims about fear of attack did not correlate with evidence from BR who had received no reports of incidents within the city 'for several years'. Clearly, BR did not count the unrecorded fears and threats experienced daily by women passengers.

On the issue of reporting violence, BR did not support the Council's suggestion of a card system through which passengers could record the occurrence of threatening incidents. They argued that such incidents should be reported to BR staff or to the police. More positively, BR claimed that their policy was to increase the number of women staff in all aspects of BR services, including their employment as guards and train drivers. Such a policy might help to encourage the reporting of violent and threatening behaviour.

Finally, the report of the meeting between the Council and BR concludes with the following statement:

> "Whilst BR and the City Council have together achieved much to improve the general quality of the environment in and around railway stations in the City in physical terms, it is doubtful whether this alone will alleviate the real fears which many women in the Southampton area experience as passengers of BR. The real measure of a 'quality' environment is the level of well-being which users feel within it, which often involves satisfying a basic human need to know that other sympathetic people are close at hand or at least that help can be summoned quickly if needed".

While the report itself recognises the importance of maintaining the dialogue between the Council and BR, noting the common awareness that was established and the possibilities for future action subsequent correspondence does not appear to bear out this optimism. When asked to report progress on the areas agreed by the meeting, BR's Area Customer Services Manager replied in an extremely negative fashion, denying either the possibility of or the need for future action.

This example not only further illuminates the areas of possible action on behalf of public transport providers and the opportunities that exist (in theory) for planners to work with such agencies, but it also demonstrates very well the difficulties of achieving real co-operation and a unity of purpose. The economic priorities driving BR's arguments together with their blinkered approach are very clearly apparent, and while the report of the liaison meeting is couched in very positive terms in relation to the possibilities for future action, the end result shows no real or practical progress. The planner's lack of power in this area is aptly demonstrated, despite careful research and a commitment to achieving change through advice and information exchange.

Returning to the survey of planning authorities, a small number of local authorities—8 in all—recorded the existence in their area of a safe women's transport scheme[7]. One authority, Wolverhampton, claimed to be negotiating the setting up of a safe women's transport initiative while another, Lewisham, said that they used to have such a scheme but that it had to be abandoned due to lack of funding. The level and type of involvement of different planning authorities again varied. Some authorities such as Cheshire County Council acknowledge the operation of a scheme in their area but register no formal planning department or local authority input—the scheme being financed and run by a voluntary organisation. Other authorities note the involvement of planning in supporting safe women's transport schemes; such support normally taking the form of advice or funding. Other authorities have their own, council funded scheme. The London Borough of Newham provides support for their safe women's transport scheme within the planning department's policies. Moreover, they note that from 1992/3 the scheme will be funded through the Urban Programme.

Safe women's transport schemes, while not necessarily very numerous, have attracted some mention in the literature (see Pickup, 1988; Trench, 1991; WTF, 1988). Work has identified the different forms that safe transport schemes have taken. Trench (1991) describes the Bradford 'homerunner' service which provided door-to-door evening transport in mini-buses which have been adapted for wheelchair users. The flat rate fare of 90p covers about one-third of the running costs of the scheme and compares favourably with local taxi rates.

The Bristol Safe Women's Transport scheme was among the first to be set up and was modelled on the scheme already mentioned operating in the London Borough of Lewisham. It was established in 1987 following a number of attacks on women in the city. Early in the year a women's conference had identified the dangers facing women living in and visiting Bristol and had made a commitment to positive action. Certain groups were seen as particularly 'at risk'—ethnic minorities, elderly women and young girls. Following the conference, women started a very effective lobbying campaign which resulted in the introduction of the Safe Women's Transport scheme with a grant of £110,000 from the BCC Women's Committee.

The Bristol scheme was run on a non-profit making basis by a women's co-operative and was staffed by 6 women. Users were charged an annual membership fee (initially £6.00 rising more recently to £10.00) after which all lifts were free. The scheme was ostensibly open to all women wishing to travel within the city although it was recognised that limited resources meant that priority had to be given to certain groups (those identified

---

[7] Not all these authorities are included in the list in Table 6.1 as not all the schemes identified had planning department or even local authority involvement.

above as particularly 'at risk'). While the Safe Women's Transport service was aimed primarily at women who have suffered from and/or are scared of travelling, it also provided a resource for women who could not afford 'ordinary' transport fares. In addition, disabled women were encouraged to join the scheme—the scheme's two vehicles being adapted for wheel chair use.

The Bristol Safe Women's Transport scheme ran until the beginning of 1992. Following an auditing exercise criticising the running of the scheme, however, grants were frozen and the service suspended. It was claimed that the Safe Women's Transport scheme was used by only 178 women and consequently did not justify the £300,000 of tax payer's money that had been spent on it. It was estimated that each individual trip made by the service was costing about £26. Tory and Labour councillors clashed over the benefits and value of the scheme—the Tories seeing it as wasteful and ridiculous and Labour as vital to the needs of women.

In discussions over the longterm fate of safe transport for women in Bristol the Labour Party remained committed to providing some sort of service. The chair of the Equalities Committee argued that while the service may not have been used by many women, its problems were essentially management problems. A number of women, it was claimed, were dependent on the Safe Women's Transport scheme before it closed down, these women subsequently found it much more difficult (or impossible) to get about—especially at night. Labour councillors looked into ways of re-starting a Safe Women's Transport scheme—exploring different management structures and the possibility of sponsorship from business.

The view expressed by the Tory members of the council, however, was very different. The party declared an intention to fight any proposals to establish a similar kind of scheme saying that it would only accept a service that was 'self-financing (and) available to everybody' (Goul, *Evening Post*, 5/3/92). Tory councillors argued that it was a waste of public money to fund a scheme of the sort that had existed when there were taxi companies available to offer a safe service.

Comments by the Tory councillors demonstrate a very poor understanding of the nature of the dangers and fears faced by women. As noted earlier, waiting for taxis and travelling alone with male cab drivers are high on the list of dangers experienced and perceived by women. The arguments about finance illustrate the way in which the reduction in local government spending is having a very direct and profound effect on public services, and in particular on less 'conventional' and more 'controversial' women's initiatives.

Very recent developments at the time of writing show an interesting turn round of events. The Equalities Committee of BCC have agreed to support the setting up of a replacement Safe Transport scheme for women in the city. According to one councillor, the new scheme was accepted 'without a murmur' from those previously opposed to SWT. This acceptance he puts down to the fact that the replacement scheme was introduced under an *Equalities* Committee rather than the Women's Committee that had previously supported the SWT service. The case demonstrates the wider political acceptability of 'Equalities' Committees, as was noted in Chapter 4, as well as the negative reactions automatically engendered by women's initiatives—especially those aimed specifically and exclusively at women.

Safe women's transport schemes, while clearly meeting a genuine need, do highlight the issue of segregation as an appropriate response to women's mobility constraints. As Trench (1991, p. 236) notes, women only transport initiatives—be they safe women's transport schemes, women only waiting rooms or railway carriages or segregated car parks— perpetuate the "notion that women are only safe under some kind of curfew". Such schemes do not confront or challenge the problem of male violence but simply serve to bypass it. In some circumstances the segre-gation of women can even increase women's vulnerability, presenting would-be attackers with 'sitting targets'. Safe women's transport schemes can, it is also argued, help to reduce women's use of conventional forms of public transport still further, reinforcing the dangers for those women who continue to use it. In response to these arguments, however, it must be stressed that the evidence is that safe women's transport schemes *are* a popular and successful response to the principle problem of women's safety. The fact that they address the manifestation of male violence rather than its cause is hardly surprising and should not serve to detract from their importance. They should, however, be supported as one of *a number* of responses to the dangers that constrain women's mobility and used in conjunction with design and land use measures, such as improved lighting and sensitive street patterns and use etc. not as a replacement for such initiatives.

Conclusion

The issue of women's accessibility is clearly one which cannot be seen in isolation but must be examined in the much broader context of both daily activity patterns and basic life chances and expectations. Accessibility is often the key to employment opportunities, to social activities and even to the ease and 'efficiency' of domestic tasks. The purpose of this chapter has been to review the constraints on accessibility experienced by women in the context of the availability and use of transport. As noted, transport is just one part of the 'access jigsaw'; women's accessibility, and indeed their mobility, is very closely influenced by a range of physical and social characteristics that govern not only the physical layout of the built environment but also the nature of women's travel requirements. These 'other issues' have been partly addressed elsewhere in discussions surrounding the evolution of the planned environment and the expectations of past and contemporary gender role stereotypes.

Transport policy and provision is clearly an area in which local government planners have a relatively limited input. Many of the issues raised here have concerned the availability of, in particular, public transport where the preferences and suggestions of planners are not necessarily given priority (especially given the privatisation of transport services). The example of the negotiations between BR and Southampton City Council bears witness to the powerlessness of the local planner in issues surrounding the extent and quality of transport provision.

In other areas, however, planners may have a more direct input. In the debate surrounding the prioritisation of the private motor car, and the resulting damaging effects this has had for the physical environment and the health and safety of those living and working in the city, planners do have a greater role to play. Issues concerning the welfare of the pedestrian may not be 'women's issues' *per se* but as has been shown here, the distribution of private transport together with the gender division of labour, has traditionally meant that women constitute a majority of pedestrians. Consequently, a transport policy which increases safety and prioritises public transport use over that of the private car will find greatest support amongst women.

This chapter has also demonstrated that there are other areas of transport planning in which change is both influential to women's use and possible to effect. Relatively minor changes to the safety and comfort of railway and bus stations, for example, can transform women's experience of public transport. Similarly, the re-design of car parks to address the issue of women's safety can enhance their use of private cars. Planning may also have a role to play in supporting the development of alternative transport 'solutions' to the mobility constraints experienced by women.

Finally, although little has been said so far about the distribution of women planners *within* planning departments/employment, it is pertinent to note the absence of women from transport planning. Again, the priorities that have characterised transport planning—the emphasis on the private car, on road building and major engineering projects (as identified earlier) has meant that few women acquire a special interest in transport planning. The lack of women in this important field is noticeable also in planning education where few women elect to specialise in transport planning. As Chapter 4 has argued, the recognition of women's needs in planning and the commitment to addressing those needs is influenced, to a considerable extent, by the presence of women in the decision-making process. This is not only true of the planning profession in general but is equally important to particular sectors and even issues within planning.

7

Gender and Housing

Introduction

Certain important aspects of the planning and provision of housing have already featured in earlier chapters of this book. Chapter 3 in particular has examined the location of housing in relation to other city functions and drawn attention to the spatial separation of the home from the workplace. Reference has also been made to safety issues and the relationship between the layout and upkeep of housing estates and the fear and reality of violence against women. Elsewhere in the book discussion has touched briefly on the ideological/emotional meaning of the home and its importance in shaping and reflecting gender roles and relations.

These are issues that are clearly of fundamental importance to the construction of a feminist approach to housing provision and to the basic understanding of gender and housing policy. While not wishing to repeat the arguments already rehearsed, it is inevitable that these topics be included within a wider discussion of housing as contained in this chapter. In addition, there are several other issues not so far considered that play a key role in the debates surrounding gender and housing. As has been the pattern for the proceeding chapters on employment and transport, the intention here is to provide an overview of the main areas of interest incorporated within a feminist approach to housing planning/policy. Again, the range of relevant issues and the lack of space will preclude a very detailed or comprehensive examination of any one particular aspect. Discussion of the various topics will be followed in the second part of the chapter by an analysis of planning responses to some of the issues outlined through the use of examples drawn from both secondary and original sources.

Housing Studies

Before looking at more practical policies surrounding housing provision, it is useful to consider very briefly how the issue of women and housing has been approached in academic studies. Academic debates are important in helping to identify and interpret housing problems and consequently highly relevant in devising policy responses. The significance of housing not only to peoples' daily existence but also to their long term life strategies has made it a focus for researchers from a wide range of academic disciplines. Geographers, sociologists, historians, economists and planners (to name only the most obvious) have incorporated debates on housing — its cost, supply, quality, cultural meaning etc. etc. — as a part of their mainstream work, while the interest generated in housing has been significant enough for a separate sub-discipline, housing studies, to be created.

Since the 1970s there has been a growing recognition within housing studies/research of the debates surrounding gender issues and of their relevance to housing provision and policy. As in other areas of the social sciences, this recognition has been manifest in two distinct foci within the broad research agenda. Firstly, there are what Watson refers to as "women and" studies (Watson, 1988) in which researchers have sought to make explicit the particular circumstances of women in relation to aspects of housing and homelessness. As Chapter 1 has pointed out, these studies serve primarily to identify women's roles and, while important as a first step towards an analysis and explanation of basic gender inequalities, cannot be interpreted as necessarily feminist in either their approach or purpose. They consequently leave unchallenged a whole host of values and assumptions surrounding resource use and allocation that have characterised traditional approaches. The second 'category' of housing study in which gender has been included are those which attempt to *explain* the inequalities experienced by women in terms of the operation of gender relations and the influence of patriarchy. Such studies generally adopt a feminist approach to housing provision and consumption and, in so doing, draw attention to the unequal access to power and decision making that lies at the root of women's housing problems.

The majority of work on gender and housing has conformed to the first of these approaches, essentially 'adding in' women to existing research questions. Studies have remained largely silent on the ways in which gender relations and the operation of male power have been reproduced within key areas of the production and consumption of housing. Exceptions to this general rule include Austerberry and Watson (1985); Munro and Smith (1989); Watson (1988); Madigan *et al.* (1990). In what is essentially a critique of current research agendas, the latter draw attention to three specific areas from which explicitly feminist research can (and should) widen our understanding of gender differentiated housing environments. These areas, the design of housing, the relations of exchange and the variation in meanings of the home, are elaborated on below, not only as important questions for feminist researchers but also as offering potential focal points for planning responses to women's inequality.

Housing Design

In concentrating on issues of production rather than consumption existing housing studies have marginalised women's interests. There is, however, one area of the production of housing that *is* particularly significant to women and which has been consistently neglected in relation to gender issues, namely that of housing design. Questions of design incorporate a number of issues of importance to a feminist interpretation of housing provision—some of these are examined below. The section will adopt a broad interpretation of 'design', looking not only at discussions of housing interiors, room layouts etc. but also at trends in housing style and type. In considering the latter, we will return to some of the arguments raised in earlier chapters concerning the assumptions behind, in particular, suburban style housing.

In her book, *Living in a Man-Made World*, Marion Roberts provides an informative and original interpretation of the gender assumptions that lie behind trends in modern housing provision (Roberts, 1991). Setting the background to her more contemporary analysis she looks briefly at patterns of development from the beginning of the nineteenth century, drawing attention to the relationship between new housing styles and public welfare legislation and to the underlying social and moral expectations that accompanied housing provision. Roberts' arguments demonstrate the extent to which attitudes about family life and gender roles, so influential in the location of new housing during the nineteenth and early twentieth centuries (see Chapter 3), were also manifest in the *style* of housing adopted and in its interior constitution/layout. What is clear in following Roberts' examples is that no attempt to understand the objectives behind housing policy and production can ignore the influence of and implications for prevailing gender ideologies.

The ubiquitous nineteenth century bylaw housing consisting of terraced dwellings intended for a single family provides an early and very apt example. Strict regulations laid down in covenants were attached to the building plots on which such housing was built. These regulations varied from area to area but generally covered aspects of design and appearance and also prohibited occupants from using the dwelling for certain trades. The bylaws, together with the high rents which such houses commanded were explicitly intended to regulate the social class of the occupants. They also carried firm implications for the division of labour between men and women and for associated gender relations. Implicit in the conditions of occupancy was the

> "notion that an ideal family consisted of a male wage earner with a dependant wife and children. Rents of whole terraced houses were such that single women, with or without dependants could not afford them" (Roberts, 1991, p. 25).

As the nineteenth century progressed and suburban growth spread outwards, the implications of occupancy conditions were reinforced by the geographical distance that separated housing from centres of employment.

Roberts illustrates the ways in which assumptions about gender roles and women's use of space were reflected in the internal design of bylaw houses. One of the key features of design was the firm division between the 'public' space in the form of a front parlour and the 'private' space of the kitchen and living room. The domestic functions of the household were kept strictly separate from formal entertaining and special family occasions. This division was reproduced in the actual quality of the spaces with the front parlour being large and elaborately decorated by comparison with the rear domestic rooms. Tacked on to the back of the house was generally a small (and frequently dark) scullery in which the heavier domestic work would be carried out. To Roberts

"the use of the by-law housing combined with its design shows a concern for the appearances of domesticity but with little regard for the conditions under which housework was carried out in the late nineteenth and early twentieth centuries" (p. 27).

She goes on to suggest that the emphasis on formality and order in the public sphere combined with meanness and squalor in the private sphere symbolised, quite simply, the subordination of women to men.

In addition to the bylaw housing, several philanthropic societies became involved in housing provision in Britain during the late nineteenth century. The majority were inspired by the need to improve the squalid conditions under which many poorer people lived, but incorporated, as did the bylaw housing, an underlying concern for standards of decency. The scale of the rents, however, meant that, again, it was the 'deserving poor', the working man and his family, who benefitted from the work of such societies and little was done to relieve the slum conditions facing the very poor. Attempts were made to provide affordable accommodation in inner city areas in the form of flats—experiments in reducing costs further by including shared facilities were not particularly successful in that they conflicted with prevailing aspirations for privacy.

This desire to protect the private space of households in the design and provision of housing also influenced the Garden City movement of the early twentieth century (see Wilson, 1991). As Madigan *et al.* (1990) point out, this period saw a "convergence of housing types" with a decline in the size of middle class dwellings and an increase in the space standards for working class housing. Garden cities were planned to lower densities than had characterised earlier development, houses were built in larger plots emphasising the privacy of the single family. Changing views on domestic work and family life styles meant that, internally, the strict separation between the formal 'public' room (the front parlour) and the 'private' family/domestic quarters began to break down. As noted in Chapter 3, however, domestic functions were still kept firmly within the individual unit—radical attempts to provide communal facilities in Letchworth, for example, were strongly resisted—and the gender division of labour *within* the household protected.

Following the First World War Britain entered a new phase of housing provision which, although prompted primarily by the growing unrest of the working classes, was not unaffected by demands voiced by feminists concerning the health and welfare of women and children. It was clear by this time that the housing needs of the poorer sections of society were not being (or able to be) met by either the owner-occupied or the private-rented sectors. The Addison Act, introduced in 1919, required all local authorities to identify housing needs in their area and to build council houses using money from local rates. It was the first time that the Government had got involved, on a large scale, in the subsidising, financing and building of housing (Matrix, 1984).

Women from groups such as the Women's Co-operative Guild and the Women's Labour League (both considered in Chapter 4 in the context of women's changing political power/activity) expressed concern not only over the actual provision of housing for working class women, but also over the design of such housing. In response the Government set up a Women's Housing Sub-Committee to look at the 'housewife's needs' in the design of the new state-built houses (Matrix, 1984). The committee, composed of many women who were well informed about the conditions under which working class women lived, demanded that all local authority housing should contain:

> "a separate work room for cooking and food preparation; a separate bathroom; a front parlour; labour saving devices (such as hot and cold running water, a kitchen range that did not involve stooping, with easy clean finishes); and play spaces for both older and younger children" (Matrix, 1984, p. 29).

The actual committee itself was very interested in exploring radical forms of housing design that would facilitate a new kind of life-style and domestic organisation. Research was conducted on the benefits of co-operative arrangements involving communal domestic provision of the sort mentioned previously. Their final report, however, reflected the more traditional views and preferences of the working class women they had interviewed.

The views expressed advocated an improvement of the conditions under which housework was carried out in terms of the provision and design of space within the house. They failed, however, to challenge or even question the idea that it was women who were responsible for the domestic servicing of the household and consequently reinforced the "dominant patriarchal ideas about the role of the women in the nuclear family" (Matrix, 1984, p. 31).

More influential in terms of the actual building of local authority housing at the time was the report of another government advisory group—the Tudor Walters Committee, set up in 1917 and consisting entirely of male housing 'experts'. Although driven by the need to keep costs to a minimum, the report became important in terms of establishing a set of space standards and design qualities which were adhered to not only in the construction of state housing but also by speculative builders. Insufficient local authority resources meant that state housing programmes put forward under the Addison Act could not be completed and, in any case, were not sufficient to meet needs. Owner occupation and private house building were encouraged with the help of local authority grants to would-be buyers for deposits and repairs. The typical plan conformed to by speculative builders, as recommended by the Tudor Walters Report

> "was a combination of by-law house formality and [a] concern with sunlight and fresh air....houses were built with rudimentary damp-proof courses, electricity and fitted bathrooms....running hot water was available for the kitchen sink, bath and wash basin" (Roberts, 1991, p. 39).

In the design of inter-war housing, the encouragement of owner occupation and the suburban location of development, women's domestic role and their dependency on their husbands was reinforced. Madigan *et al.* (1990, p. 630) have argued that although the new housing did not reflect more radical feminist and Utopian solutions, "what shines through the Tudor Walters Report ... is a profound respect for domestic labour" which had not previously existed in housing design. But what must be remembered here is that while internal standards and facilities *had* been improved, the increasing cost of housing meant that, as noted in Chapter 3, in order for the family to survive, women were required to have a paid job. So although housing policy supported the idea of the nuclear family with the dependent woman at home in the domestic sphere, the realities of housing provision meant only the comparatively well-off could sustain such a life style.

Traditional assumptions concerning the role of women in the family continued to influence housing policy in Britain following the Second World War. A series of Government reports (including the Barlow Report, the Scott Report and the Uthwatt Report) on planning and housing incorporated the main priorities for post-war reconstruction reflecting a deep concern for the maintenance of family life and the stability of the home. The reports emphasised the need for government intervention in the distribution of industry, the development of the agricultural industry and the containment of urban sprawl. While support was expressed for the building of communities containing a mix of land uses, housing and industry, the need to provide housing again encouraged the provision of flats within central city areas. Opinion as to the suitability of flats either for meeting the housing needs of the population or for encouraging family life and increasing the birth rate were divided. They were, however, supported by planners such as Abercrombie who argued that a mixture of decentralised and inner city development was required.

As Watson (1986) points out it was very much the idea of the *nuclear* family that was sustained by post-war housing policy in Britain. This ideal family form could be housed in the suburbs, the outlying estates and the new and expanded towns. Little provision was made, by comparison, for single people, young or old, and unmarried mothers except in the form of flats. So,

> "despite the fact that 11% of private households in England and Wales in 1951 were one-person units only 6.3% of dwellings built by local authorities in 1953 were one-bedroomed units" (Watson, 1986, p. 49).

The neglect of single person or non-nuclear family households, also referred to by other writers (see, for example, McCarthy and Simpson, 1991; Bull and Stone, 1990), is a feature of government housing policy that has continued to the present day, demonstrating a lasting support for the conservative ideology of the traditional family form.

Post-war housing provision certainly meant an improvement for many families in the actual *quality* of housing conditions. By the early 1950s a substantial proportion of the housing stock in Britain was dilapidated, squalid and lacked basic amenities such as hot water and an internal W.C. The new estates clearly compared favourably with much existing provision. As in the past, poor housing conditions and, indeed their alleviation, were closely linked in policy prescriptions to ideas about standards of women's behaviour and morality. The belief was that re-housing people in new estates led to a change in attitudes and behaviour—a change that enhanced family life, encouraging mothers to take a keener interest in the health and welfare of their husbands and children and in the well-being of the local community.

Notions of community spirit were also important in designing the physical form of new housing estates. Architects drew heavily on rural imagery in, for example, the design of the London County Council estates (see Roberts, 1991; Davidoff *et al.*, 1976).

> "Just as the eighteenth century landowner would look out at the view from the loggia of his country seat, so the tenants of the LCC's new council estates could gaze at the 'pleasing prospects' of their estate from the windows of their flats. Just as intrusive elements, such as farm labourers, ploughs and barns were cleared from the park, so were the clutter of domesticity, rabbit hutches, dustbins and working life banished from council housing estates" (Roberts, 1991, p. 114).

Despite attempts to engender feelings of community in the layout of some housing estates, the way of life, reinforced by, for example, housing tenure and internal design, stressed the importance of privacy. More recently, the lack of resources going into the upkeep of 'public' spaces on local authority housing estates has undermined the use of communal areas and re-asserted the importance of protecting the private spaces of individual dwellings.

Internally, the same assumptions about the gender division of labour within the household/nuclear family continued to dominate the design of space in post-war housing. Immediately after the Second World War the government's desire to improve living conditions led to the setting up of the Dudley Committee whose brief was to look into ways of alleviating the difficulties faced by women in carrying out their domestic tasks. This report recommended an increase in space standards for council housing together with the provision of certain domestic appliances. As previously, the implementation of these standards led inevitably to higher rents and consequently to married women taking up paid work.

Matrix (1984) show how the various design guides, to which the majority of state and privately built houses conform, assume stereotypical views of the family and of the roles of individuals within it. These design guides (such as *Housing and the Family* and *Space in the Home*) have been compiled by groups of so-called experts, whose aim is to

"improve both the convenience and the use of space and to promote higher standards and better value for money" (Matrix, 1984, p. 83).

The use of space in these guides is seen as something of a scientific problem. The activities and expectations of various members of the household go unquestioned and no recognition is given to the fact that design reinforces accepted 'norms' of behaviour.

Gender assumptions are clearly apparent in the design guides' approach to providing for privacy in the home. It is generally accepted that, when he comes home from work, the male partner will want somewhere to relax away from the main domestic activity of the family. In larger houses he may, in addition, command sole (or possibly principal) use of a study or work room which affords a degree of privacy. Madigan *et al.* (1990) comment on the increasing tendency, since the 1950s, for *children* to have their own rooms—more recently often furnished with their own TVs, stereos etc. Yet women rarely have their own private space within the house. As Katherine Whitehorn observes:

"Women have real difficulty in knowing what if anything is their own exact territory. In one sense a woman controls the whole house; but in another she may feel she owns nothing personally but her side of the wardrobe" (quoted in Madigan *et al.*, 1990, p. 632).

Clearly, Whitehorn's quote introduces the issue of ownership of space in the house beyond simply that of design. Women may feel that they have less right to their own space since they have less direct (i.e. financial) control over the ownership of the house. We will return to this important question in the discussion of housing tenure that follows.

Internal design of contemporary housing does little to break down existing gender role stereotypes. 'High tech' kitchens and labour saving devices are provided with the aim of reducing the burden of domestic labour and can be seen, in part, as a response to the growing involvement of women in work outside the home. Hence, design may improve the conditions within which domestic work takes place but fails, in itself, to recognise the unequal division of labour associated with such work. It may be argued that to criticise housing design in this way is to attach false expectations to what it can be expected to achieve—expectations which tend in some ways towards a dangerous degree of physical determinism. Chapter 2 has been at pains to argue that gender roles and relations are socially constructed. They are not, therefore, a direct result of the physical arrangement of space. Design *does*, however, have the capacity to trap people in existing roles and make it difficult for those roles to be challenged. So while the physical layout of a house may not, in isolation, make it obligatory for women to do the washing-up and meal preparation, in conforming generally to traditional patterns of room size and distribution, design practices may reinforce conventional household structures and relations and hence a greater acceptance of traditional gender roles.

In identifying the absence of feminist perspectives, or, indeed, of any recognition of the importance of gender divisions in housing design, some commentators have drawn attention to the lack of female architects within the profession (see Greed's study of the membership of professional bodies in planning related fields already referred to in Chapter 4—Greed, 1992). Others have stressed, however, that women's needs will not necessarily be addressed simply by an increase in the numbers of women involved in the practice of housing design. They argue that it is not (primarily) the absence of women as *architects* that is responsible for the neglect of gender issues but rather their invisibility in terms of positions of authority. While a growth in the numbers of women architects is clearly desirable to offset a huge gender imbalance in the profession, as in other areas of planning already considered, if women are to have a greater influence on the details of contemporary housing design they need to increase their access to political power and to decision making.

Housing Exchange

A second important focus for feminist research on the production and consumption of housing concerns, as was outlined in the introduction to this chapter is housing exchange—and, in particular, the conditions surrounding owner occupation. The following section will briefly outline the position of women in the housing market. It will demonstrate the existence of clear gender divisions in terms of both access to owner occupation and to control over the benefits which accrue from the private housing market. Both issues are extremely significant to the identification of housing inequality and to the evaluation of housing policy.

The growing importance of owner occupation within the housing market has been outlined by a number of researchers. McCarthy and Simpson (1991), for example, note the increase in home ownership from just 10% of all dwellings before the First World War to almost 70% in 1989. A recent focus has been the relative increase in home ownership in Britain since the start of the Thatcher government. Studies have also considered the significance of changes in the composition of housing tenure in terms of wealth accumulation and political ideology. While some of these studies have identified the different levels of home ownership amongst men and women, few have taken this analysis any further in the recognition or examination of gender divisions in other aspects of the relations of housing exchange. Consequently, many of the disadvantages experienced by women through the operation of the housing market in Britain have gone unnoticed. The essentially sexist nature of housing exchange for not only women's immediate living conditions but also their wider experience of access to and control over housing as a resource and as a form of financial gain has been considerably under-emphasised in conventional research, and the inequalities women have experienced as a result, down graded in policy terms.

Owner occupation and women's representation

Women, it is clear, experience more difficulty than men in becoming owner occupiers in their own right. Female-headed households (either women living alone or single mothers) are generally poorer than male-headed households (Brion and Tinker, 1980; Watson, 1988) since women continue to earn, on average, significantly less than men (see Chapter 5 for details) and are frequently employed on a part-time basis—especially when they have child-rearing commitments. Women living alone as a result of divorce often do not have the skills to compete in the job market as they have generally spent their married lives managing a home and family—too busy to gain the formal qualifications and skills required for well paid jobs. Moreover, women form a higher proportion than men of other tradition-ally low-income groups such as the elderly.

Single women find difficulty not only in raising a deposit and meeting monthly mortgage repayment, but also in paying for the everyday upkeep of a house. As a result, fewer women own (or are buying) their own houses (Watson (1988) notes the reliance of non-nuclear family households—particularly women under 40—on the private rented sector) and fewer, as we shall see later, experience the benefits of home ownership as single women living alone or with children. Where women *can* afford to enter owner occupation, they tend to buy cheaper, older properties—often without amenities such as central heating. In 1985, 36% of new female purchasers in Britain bought pre-1919 properties compared with 23% of males (Bristol City Council (BCC), 1988).

But even women living as part of a couple or nuclear family in a house that is owner occupied, may not enjoy ownership rights over that house.

They may gain the 'benefits' of 'living in their own home' (perceived as greater security, a freedom to control the use of their own space and an escape from the financial disadvantages of renting—although the 'crisis' in the housing market in Britain in the early 1990s may throw this latter into some doubt) but do not experience a variety of other exchange rights that come with home ownership.

An appreciation of the problems experienced by women in becoming owner occupiers (either in their own right or jointly) serves to highlight their essential dependency on men in terms of housing consumption. Watson (1988) stresses how the operation of the housing market in capitalist economies such as Britain reinforces that dependency and, indeed, the position of the nuclear family. She notes that housing provision in Britain:

"assumes and is structured around the patriarchal family form. This structuring acts to create and reinforce women's dependent economic status and domestic role. Intricately related to this dominance of the family model is the marginalisation in the housing system of households that do not fit this traditional model. Many of these households .... are headed by women. Further, this process of marginalisation of women in housing terms reinforces women's inferior status, both within the labour market and within society more generally" (Watson, 1988, pp. 21–22).

Until relatively recently women's dependency on male partners was also reinforced by the way in which mortgages for house purchase have been allocated. Single women or women co-habiting have experienced relative difficulty in the past in obtaining a mortgage—their access to owner occupation impeded by the discriminatory practices of building societies and banks. These practices, as Brion and Tinker (1980) point out, were very common prior to the 1980s, with some societies asking for a male guarantor when a woman applied for a mortgage alone or with other women. Pressure exerted on lending institutions has helped to reduce the inequalities experienced by women although some building societies and banks were, even in the early 1980s, still looking on 'unconventional households' as "dubious mortgage risks" (Brion and Tinker, 1980). Even if these inequalities are gradually being ironed out, however, arranging housing finance still involves dealing with professionals such as estate agents, solicitors and building society managers and coming into contact with complex procedures and bureaucracy. Many women will have had little experience in such activities in what is still essentially a male dominated world.

In an analysis of housing policy in Britain and Australia, Watson (1986) argues that despite the passing of Sex Discrimination Acts in both countries, many forms of direct and indirect discrimination operate towards women applying for loans on their own. In a study of applicants for loan finance in Australia, it was claimed that:

"women interviewed complained of being confronted by chauvinistic and patronising attitudes expressed by the staff of financial institutions. Likewise women applying for loans with male partners reported that their income was not taken into account, assumptions were made about their future employment prospects, the likelihood of future pregnancy and child-bearing in their lives, and assumed automatic withdrawal from the labour force during motherhood" (Watson, 1986, p. 5).

Madigan *et al.* argue that women are disadvantaged not only in terms of their access to home ownership but also as a result of being denied other benefits associated with and accruing directly from housing exchange. The most obvious of these is the access to capital gain acquired from buying and selling the house (where a profit has been made[8]). Although, as these authors stress, little firm evidence exists on the organisation of household finances, it is clear that men are more likely to hold greater power in decisions over household spending. Control over budgeting is likely to extend to control over capital gains from the house—especially when the house may not be owned jointly by the male and female partners but be only in the man's name (research undertaken in the 1970s demonstrated that in 42% of cases the 'family home' was owned in the name of the husband alone (Brion and Tinker, 1980s). This is thought less likely to be the case today but no recent evidence can be found to support this assumption).

Evidence that women do not share equally in the accumulation of wealth from housing is seen in the fact that, on divorce, women are less likely than men to remain as owner occupiers and more likely to see a real decline in their standard of accommodation (Madigan *et al.*, 1990). A number of studies have pointed to the growing importance of relationship breakdown to housing. Questions surrounding changes in housing tenure and quality experienced by couples who split up, together with policy responses to divorce/relationship termination, are discussed by McCarthy and Simpson (1991) and by Symon (1990). There is not time for an extensive review of their findings here. It is important to note, however, that among the conclusions reached in relation to housing and divorce was the fact that patterns of resource distribution which result form divorce "often reflect patterns of inequality which existed within the marriage with men being the main controllers and beneficiaries of resources" (McCarthy and Simpson, 1991, p. 126). Economic deprivation resulting from divorce is therefore most acutely felt by single person households headed by women. Housing costs constitute a major factor in such patterns of deprivation.

Women's lack of control over wealth accumulated from the exchange of housing means that they are less likely to benefit from the status attached

---

[8]The particular state of the housing market in the early 1990s with house prices declining dramatically has highlighted the issue of *negative* equity—a house being worth less (and frequently substantially less) than the purchase price. In such a situation women (and men) may be trapped within a relationship against their wishes due to an inability to actually sell the property and to finance an alternative situation.

to property ownership. As noted earlier, home ownership is perceived to carry with it a number of benefits—it is also, importantly, seen as an *achievement* on the part of the individual 'owner'. Where men are more dominant in terms of housing finance and capital gains then the status of home ownership will be more directly experienced by them. Moreover, for a man the status of home ownership is reinforced through ideas about dependency of women and children and the assumption that, in buying a house, he has provided for the family.

There are a number of other aspects of house purchase and ownership where clear gender differences operate in decision making and control. As well as housing finance (including fundamental decisions as to whether to rent or to buy), men are more likely to control housing mobility, playing a more dominant role in decisions surrounding the timing and location of moves. Madigan *et al.* (1990, p. 636) cite various examples of research on household mobility which lend weight to the view that, even amongst two career households, moves are "almost never made to benefit the women's career alone, although they may be for the benefit of the man's". Women are more likely to control decisions relating to the *type* of property which is bought or rented and to details of the interior decoration and furnishing of the house. Both of these, however, may still be determined at a broad level by the male partner's control of overall household income and expenditure.

Women and the rented sector

The fact that a significant number of women are marginalised through low incomes from the process of home ownership means that they are dependent on the rented sector. Since women, moreover, constitute the majority of single parents, they are relatively more reliant than men on *public* housing. The shortage of council housing, however, together with growing numbers of single mothers has meant that the public housing offered to women is often in a poor state of repair, on a rundown estate or in a high-rise block (Watson, 1986). Single women living on their own are unlikely to be considered eligible for council accommodation, and while some attempt was made during the 1970s to respond to the housing problems of single people by making available 'hard to let' dwellings on a short-life basis, government policy and the workings of the housing rental system continues to favour families over single people (McCarthy and Simpson, 1991).

In research published in 1986, Watson and Austerberry examined the housing problems experienced by single women. They draw attention to the growing demand for single person accommodation and link a reluctance to provide for one person households on behalf of the government and housing industry to the issue of homelessness. Difficulties surrounding definition make homelessness hard to quantify — this is particularly true as far as women are concerned. Watson and Austerberry (1986) argue that the lack of hostel accommodation for women tends to mean that women's need for housing is concealed. 'Homeless' women are more likely to end up staying with friends on a temporary basis or perhaps returning to the family home. Accepted 'formal' calculations of the number of homeless people tend to depend on the figures held by local authorities.

The National Cyrenians believe that, despite the difficulties of quantifying hidden or concealed homelessness, it is possible to identify a significant growth in the numbers of homeless women. They write, in a report published in 1988 that:

> "The 1981 National Census shows 30% of hostel and common lodging residents to be women. The number of women, 10447, had more than doubled in a decade. Statistics from the Housing Advice Switchboard in 1981 revealed 52% of callers needing accommodation to be women" (quoted by Bristol City Council, 1988, p. 2).

On a more local level, a report by BCC adds weight to this argument, concluding that within the general growth in homelessness in Bristol (an estimated increase of 112% between 1983/4 and 1986/7), women represent an expanding group. This report attempts, as do others (see, for example, Levison and Atkins, 1987) to account for women's homelessness. 'Social Reasons' are seen as the primary causal factor — women losing their home following a dispute with a partner or with family. The fact that a higher percentage of single women than single men (52.8% against 35.9%) cite social reasons as the main cause of their homelessness reveals, BCC claim, women's dependency on family, friends or partner for housing and underlines their particular vulnerability to homelessness during domestic disputes. The evidence produced by BCC

> "explodes the myth that women keep the home following relationship breakdown, and supports the findings of previous research that single women are just as likely as men, if not more so, to lose the home following separation" (BCC, 1988, p. 23).

Other important reasons for women's homelessness stem from problems relating to the security or quality of their previous housing. The loss of tied housing, for example, illegal eviction or unhealthy and unsanitary conditions.

The provision of temporary accommodation in, for example, hostels or bed and breakfast, is the subject of a number of publications (see, for example, BCC, 1988; Watson and Austerberry, 1986; Institute of Housing, 1987; Pahl, 1985). Such studies demonstrate the real vulnerability of women to exploitation when homeless and link this vulnerability to the serious lack of provision made by local authorities. Particularly at risk are those women who have suffered violence and have been forced to leave their homes in search of safety. These issues will be looked at again in the context of housing policy. Here it is sufficient to acknowledge the extent of homelessness as a very real consequence of women's general vulnerability and inequality within the broader scope of housing tenure and access (see Russell, 1991).

It is clear from the preceding sections that a feminist analysis of the production and consumption of housing must incorporate explicit recognition of the gender divisions in the meaning of the home. As was pointed out above, the principles which have guided not only housing type but also its interior and exterior design have both emerged from and adhered to the notion of the home as a place of security and tranquillity—a refuge from the problems of the 'world outside'. This view has been further reinforced by an ideology which celebrates and elevates the nuclear family and supports owner occupation above other forms of housing tenure. Sophie Watson (1988) argues that it is the continuation of an assumed separation between production and reproduction that has sustained this common notion. Her belief, however, is that, for women, the constant merging (and, indeed the inseparability) of 'productive' and 'reproductive' tasks denies the reality of the home as a 'private' sphere. For women the home is the site of work (mainly the unpaid 'reproductive' work of servicing the domestic household, but possibly 'productive' activity) and represents, very often, the place of oppression and even violence.

Unequal access, between women and men, to home ownership and to decisions surrounding housing investment (as discussed above) means that women do not have the same experience of security within the home as do men. Again, the widely accepted notion of the home as a safe haven from the outside world—and within this of owner occupation as the *most* secure form of tenancy is one which may be experienced differently by men and women. There is no space here to undertake a detailed or comprehensive analysis of the ways in which gender divisions are relevant to people's experience of the home. It is important, however, to recognise that many of the common images of the home may be more readily applicable to a male experience than to a female experience.

The gender relations that operate to ensure the different meanings of housing consumption between men and women are reinforced, so Madigan *et al.* (1990) argue, by aspects of social policy. As stressed elsewhere in this book, the 1980s and early 1990s have laid claim to a range of measures designed to strengthen the importance of the family and to re-assert women's role within it. Legislation, albeit introduced within a supposedly liberal framework of equal opportunities, has done much to push women back into the home, to take (unpaid) responsibility for a host of services from which the state has chosen, both financially and ideologically, to distance itself. The theme is one which has emerged repeatedly throughout this book—its importance here, in the context of the different meanings of the home, is essentially that policy reinforces a set of gender relations that ensure that men and women experience the notion and reality of the home in different ways.

Gender and Housing Policy

In the course of the previous sections references have been made to aspects of government policy on housing provision. These references have been fairly general, drawing attention, for example to the setting up of legislation for the building of council housing or the influence of by-laws on the design of nineteenth century suburban dwellings. The next part of the chapter will include a more sustained examination of housing policy; the primary aims being to assess the gender implications of both public and private sector policy in Britain and to determine the extent to which planners and policy makers have reacted to the inequalities experienced by women in relation to either the production or consumption of housing. The focus of the section will be largely contemporary and, as with the previous themes, will inevitably entail crossing boundaries between strictly 'housing' policies and other policy areas which have a direct and important bearing on women's housing experience. The intention is not to attempt a comprehensive critique but rather to select key trends in housing policy as well as examples of legislation that together illustrate the dominant attitudes of governments and the resulting constraints imposed on policy makers and local implementors.

National policy

In examining the development of housing design and the background to housing provision in this country, one of the key observations of early sections of this chapter has been the enduring support that has been shown, through legislation and policy, for the notion of the nuclear family. Attention has been drawn, repeatedly, to the assumptions that have been made concerning household size, space requirements and gender roles in the building and allocation of housing and, similarly, to the ways in which accepted priorities (whether these be in the size, location, tenure and affordability of those houses that *are* provided, or in the neglect of the needs of other consumers) have reinforced conventional patterns of household structure and divisions of labour. Late nineteenth century and early mid-twentieth century housing policies concentrated primarily on the provision of *family* accommodation and incorporated an ideology which stressed the nuclear family as the principal form of household organisation. Together with a range of social welfare reforms (discussed in Chapters 3 and 4), housing policy generally, as well as specific plans (see, for example,

Roberts' (1991) description of post-war housing provision and planning by London County Council), have promoted motherhood as the 'natural' role of women and the domestic sphere as their 'proper' place. Improvements in the quality of housing and in the internal provisioning of individual units important only in that they increased the efficiency of women's domestic work.

By the same token, policy has neglected the position of women and men *outside* the traditional family. Throughout the twentieth century (and before) in the allocation of public housing and in the priorities of state and private sector building programmes, single households have been neglected. Moreover, government legislation concerning the private rented sector has, arguably, reinforced the problems of people living alone. These issues are returned to later in this section.

The provision and allocation of public sector housing clearly demonstrates dominant government attitudes and policy directions, both past and present. While divisions as to the appropriateness or necessity of a large stock of state housing for rent to meet the needs of the poor and the homeless currently exist between different political parties, there has traditionally been less of a gulf over standards of council housing and policies of allocation. Early public sector housing, built following the Addison Act of 1919 and in response, as noted earlier, to a lack of decent accommodation in many towns and cities, was aimed primarily at the family and demanded rents too high for the majority of working class households and, of course, single women. The unwritten assumption was that such housing go to the 'deserving' families whose hard work and decent standards of living made most suitable. Roberts (1991) in a study of a 1950s local authority estate also notes the emphasis that was placed by residents and management on the 'respectability' of tenants—the preference for 'nice', 'decent' people. She draws particular attention to the regulation governing behaviour on the estate and to the belief that privacy and isolation reflected a basic decency amongst residents.

More recently the character of local authority estates has changed significantly. Following the 1977 Homeless Persons Act, since incorporated into the 1985 Housing Act, local authorities have had a duty to re-house households with dependent children who are homeless. This has meant that single mothers have been prioritised in the allocation of council houses. As numbers of dwellings decline, however, the proportion of single mothers and other claimants who are tenants has grown. Morris and Winn (1990) suggest that some local authorities have a policy of allocating such 'stigmatised groups' to particular estates where the quality of accommodation and surrounding environment is particularly low. Better-off families, encouraged by government support for owner occupation and by the availability of mortgages, have tended to move away from the worst local authority estates, helping to reinforce existing stigma.

The commitment of successive governments to investment in local authority housing has consistently fallen foul of 'economic' pressures and priorities. The building of council flats with their associated poor environments to re-house inner city dwellers, for example, was partly a response to increasing land values following the war. More recently there has been a drastic reduction in local authority building programmes and a disinvestment in the maintenance and upkeep of existing estates. Such trends have not only limited the availability of council housing, discriminating against 'non-priority' groups such as single women, but have contributed significantly to the problems of squalor, vandalism and violence that are frequently associated with local authority estates.

The 'Right to Buy', introduced by the Conservative Government in the 1980 Housing Act and giving sitting tenants generous discounts, has further compounded problems of council house availability and quality of stock. The effects of the 1980s housing legislation, together with the implications of the general encouragement that both Tory and Labour governments have given to home ownership, on housing inequality have been well documented in the literature (see, for example, Forrest and Murie, 1988; Malpass, 1989; Morris and Winn, 1990). It is not the intention to repeat the conclusion of such authors in detail here, simply to point out that changes in subsidy have succeeded in increasing housing costs for those in rented accommodation at the expense of subsidising owner occupiers. As Morris and Winn (1990, pp. 29–30) write:

> "There has been a general shift from subsidy at the point of provision of housing .... to subsidy at the point of consumption.... More and more public money is going into subsidising housing, yet homelessness is increasing, poor housing conditions remain a major problem, and housing is becoming more expensive".

It is also important to note that the sale of council houses has reinforced many of the problems experienced by women already noted above. A dwindling stock of local authority dwellings has denied access to some and increased social stigma for others. Perhaps most significant has been the deterioration in living conditions, particularly the lack of safety for women and children, that has accompanied the government's withdrawal, financial and ideological, from council house provision.

Conservative government policies during the 1980s and the early 1990s, the so called 'rolling back the state', have not only served to increase the difficulties of those in rented accommodation, but have steadily eroded the provision for those unable to afford even housing at the bottom end of the rented market (among them single parents and students). Funding for hostel accommodation for homeless people has deteriorated as a function of general cuts in public spending, despite the growing numbers of homeless people. Although, in general, the effects of government policy have been felt by both women and men, the vulnerability of women in the housing market; their low wages, poorer access to owner occupation and greater dependence on the rented sector means that women have been particularly disadvantaged by recent policy.

Within this general framework of central government legislation and policy there is, so many would argue, little scope for individual authorities to address the housing needs of women at the local level. With the government dictating not only the terms of council house sales but also the re-investment of any profits made by the authority, there is little that can be done to directly increase the availability of rented accommodation. The power of the private sector (as determined largely by the favourable conditions produced by the government) frequently leaves little scope for positive control or intervention to help particular groups. Debates recently, especially in rural locations, have centred on the provision of affordable housing and the involvement of housing associations to address the problems of those with 'special needs'. Initiatives in these areas may have received a fair amount of publicity but have not, as yet, been widely implemented. Moreover, they *may* single out women specifically but are more frequently directed towards the elderly and people with disabilities.

Having said this there is evidence that attempts are being made by some local planning authorities to confront directly the housing needs of women. The following section focuses on some of these attempts, drawing largely on material collected in the questionnaire survey of local planning departments that has already been referred to. The questionnaire asked whether the particular planning department had any written policies specifically aimed at the needs of women.

Housing policy clearly falls largely within the responsibility, at the local authority level, of the housing department. The allocation and management of council housing, for example, as well as the administration of subsidies and grants fall *outside* the remit of planning. There are, however, a number of very important areas where planning departments can and do influence housing provision. Both in determining individual planning applications and in producing strategic and local plans, planners can intervene positively in decisions regarding the characteristics of the housing stock and the availability of housing of different types. It is apparent from the questionnaire responses that planning authorities respond very differently to these opportunities in relation to the particular needs of women.

Housing and Local Planning Initiatives

In total, just 12 of the 270 authorities who responded to the questionnaire claimed to have written planning policies which specifically addressed the housing needs of women. The 12 included 4 of the London Boroughs (Greenwich, Harrow, Merton and Waltham Forest), 4 Metropolitan Councils (Dudley, Manchester, Oldham and Wolverhampton) and 4

Districts (Thamesdown, Cambridge City, Southampton and Cleethorps). In addition 1 other, Hartlepool, said that although the planning department as such had no policies in women's needs in this area, authority-wide schemes—in Hartlepool's case the sponsoring of a women's aid refuge—did incorporate an element of 'planning' input.

Where local planning authorities have included positive policies on women and housing they have fallen into three main areas. These are: housing provision (for rent and owner occupation), the design of housing and the provision of hostel accommodation for homeless and battered women. Each is looked at in more detail below.

Housing provision

Six planning departments incorporated statements on the importance of increasing housing provision generally to meet the needs of women living in their areas. Included here were commitments to ensuring that the stock of residential accommodation was protected and that dwellings were not converted to other uses. All six authorities stressed the importance of encouraging a mix of housing type where new development was planned or envisaged and, in relation to this point, the need to provide *affordable* housing for women and those on low incomes.

Three of the six authorities (Harrow, Greenwich and Waltham Forest) stressed the importance of giving priority to the needs of single women who are disadvantaged within the housing market.

Only one authority, particularly mentioned the need to increase council housing to make greater provision for women.

There was a general recognition amongst authorities of the difficulties of formulating and implementing policies on housing provision directed specifically at women. Manchester City Council was typical in declaring a commitment to:

> "seek to ensure that a wide range of housing types exist to meet different housing needs including the availability of low cost housing for sale or rent."

At the same time it recognised that:

> "Though not specifically targeted at women many (women) have to exist on benefits or low incomes and/or are single parents, and this policy should help meet their housing needs." (Manchester City Council, draft Unitary Development Plan, 1991).

Housing design

Incorporated in the housing policies of six of the planning authorities was explicit reference to the need to design for women. Two authorities in

TABLE 7.1 *Women's Needs in the Design of the Neighbourhood and the Home*

Wanted
 (1) Overlooked streets and pedestrian ways not 'hemmed in' by high walls, fences or high planting
 (2) Planting and landscape features which create or enhance the character of an area creating workable, attractive and safe spaces for public use
 (3) Readily accessible communal open spaces located close to high use areas such as housing or main roads
 (4) Easily accessible, direct pedestrian links to all community facilities
 (5) Main footpaths should allow clear views for some distance ahead (long curves not zig-zags)
 (6) Where possible alternative routes should be made available to provide choices for the user
 (7) Drop kerbs to all road junctions in residential areas to improve mobility of people with pushchairs and in wheelchairs
 (8) Easily accessible, well-lit garages, preferably within the territory of the house. Where possible parking should be directly visible from the house
 (9) Car parking space to serve every home, preferably a lockup garage within the curtilage of every home
 (10) Children's play areas overlooked by housing
 (11) Clear visual or physical definition of public and private spaces and, where appropriate, transition zones of semi-private space, which clearly 'belongs to' and is overlooked by housing and within which the presence of outsiders would be readily noticed
 (12) Private clothes drying areas
 (13) Back gardens designed to discourage intruders
 (14) Individual gardens wherever possible
 (15) Low rise housing preferred

Not Wanted
 (1) Blind corners, hiding places along pedestrian paths
 (2) Main footpaths passing through open spaces which are physically or visually isolated from areas of human activity
 (3) Footways positioned so that objects can be thrown on pedestrians
 (4) Poorly designed deck access with no alternative route
 (5) Long corridors
 (6) Thick, dense undergrowth close to paths that could conceal attackers
 (7) Isolated derelict land, degraded due to lack of maintenance
 (8) Underground garages and passages. If unavoidable these areas should be well-lit and ventilated with views in and out

Source: Southampton City Council (1991).

particular, Manchester City and Southampton, have produced quite extensive design specifications intended to act as guidelines in the planning of both the internal space in the home and the external environment surrounding new and existing developments.

All six authorities stressed the need to address, through design, the issue of women's safety in and around the home. Manchester City provide a detailed list of measures which, it is claimed, are currently being proposed by 'researchers' to improve security for women within the home. They stipulate that these measures should be considered in "all new-build and refurbishment schemes, in both public and private sector". They follow these specifications with a comprehensive review of design around the dwelling, again suggesting ways in which, through careful planning, women's safety can be improved.

Examples of the measures specified by Manchester include designing new houses in simple street patterns or cul-de-sacs so as not to create hiding places for muggers, avoiding the provision of rear lanes as access points for houses and providing waist high walls or hedges in the front of houses and an enclosed private parking area. A special set of recommendations are incorporated for multi-storey blocks. These include designing entrances and corridors so that the number of access points is kept to a minimum, adequate lighting in stairwells and corridors and on landings, the use of entry phones and the replacement of large separate garage courts with smaller parking areas within the private or semi-private areas.

As a result of recent research (involving their Women and Planning Officers Working Group), Southampton City Council have produced a list of factors concerning the physical design of the built environment which either contribute to or detract from women's safety and feelings of security (Southampton City Council, 1991). Points are categorised in terms of three sections; the design of neighbourhoods and home, 'fixtures and fittings' and 'management', as shown in Table 7.1, and provide a comprehensive list of what women themselves 'want' or 'do not want' from their home environment. They illustrate the importance of safety in the neighbourhood to women's feeling of security in the home and stress the essential interconnectivity between the dwelling and the immediate environment. A key point noted in the report is that measures taken to increase safety for women must be *comprehensive* and therefore need to recognise the links between surveillance, territoriality and security.

The majority, if not all, the design suggestions made in the Southampton report are realistic and relatively inexpensive to implement. They involve modification to existing practices and design specifications rather than the imposition of a totally new form or style of built environment. This being the case, one might perhaps legitimately question the likely effectiveness of such policies in increasing women's safety. However, the writers of the report are clearly aiming first and foremost for acceptability. As a first step towards incorporating a greater sympathy towards women's needs in planning new developments and managing and maintaining existing houses and neighbourhoods, the points raised in the report are clearly valuable. The design specifications included will, it is envisaged, be incorporated in schemes through Planning Briefs, in the operation of Development Control and in the negotiation of legal agreements. As such, it is recognised, they must at least be *potentially* acceptable to developers and must strive to raise awareness of the problems faced by women (and others) in their use of the built environment. Such awareness, the report would appear to argue, is more effectively gained through minor adjustments and non-contentious suggestions than through radical and rigorous planning requirements. This is, of course, a debate that has surfaced in various forms throughout this book and one which is impossible to resolve. We nevertheless will return to it in the final chapter.

Hostels and the Provision of Women's Refuges

The third policy area included within planning for women's housing need was the provision of hostels and other temporary accommodation for homeless and/or battered women. Six authorities mentioned such provision as a priority. None of the authorities appeared to develop the issue in depth but simply noted the shortage of hostel accommodation and the need to increase the availability of emergency, 'safe' housing for women. Lambeth stress the urgency of finding accommodation for women who have been forced to leave their homes because of violence and/or sexual harassment. They note that women are being turned away from existing women's aid centres daily because of a lack of space. Only one authority, Greenwich, specifies a need for increased hostel provision to meet the needs of lesbians and gays who have been evicted from existing accommodation because of their sexuality.

While the preceding section summarises the main policies for women and housing as highlighted by those authorities responding to the questionnaire survey, they clearly do not represent an exhaustive list of either the practices of all planning authorities or, perhaps more importantly, the policy options available to planners in this field. The survey has, however, drawn attention to two key points. Firstly it is clear how few authorities currently have specific policies for addressing women's housing needs. Secondly, most well developed are initiatives on designing for women's needs and, in particular, designing for safety in and around the home. Neither of these conclusions are particularly surprising. The general absence of direct policy initiatives is arguably a function of a broader reluctance to plan for women as a group as has been discussed in earlier chapters of this book. The emphasis on design, similarly, reflects the known limitations and scope of planning—a desire to work within the 'art of the possible', in ways that do little to threaten existing priorities and yet do elicit tangible and, in some cases, important results. Again, the debate cannot be conducted without a broad understanding of the constraints within which planning operates—including, crucially, its relationship with the development industry.

In addition to the actual policies which already exist in written form within local planning authorities, it is important to look at the advice/ recommendations coming forward from different agencies, both formal and voluntary, with an interest and expertise in planning for women's housing needs. Such advice will (hopefully) play a valuable role in informing authorities of the potential for positive action and alerting them to problems and issues which may have gone unrecognised. Groups such as the London Women and Planning Group, the Women's Design Service and Cities for People as well as individuals in practice and academics, have highlighted some important considerations for planning authorities both in terms of the formulation and the implementation of practical policies.

The recommendations of these groups fall largely within the areas already discussed. The London Women and Planning Group (LWPG), for example, stress the importance of affordability in terms of housing provision for women. In a report entitled *Shaping our Borough: Women and Unitary Development Plans*, the group recommends that a proportion of all new housing be reserved as low-cost or social housing. They also argue that houses in multiple occupation should be protected since they provide a source of cheap housing for small households without children. At the same time they do warn of the danger of losing family houses as a result of conversion to single bedsits.

As with the policies already examined, emphasis is placed by groups such as the Women's Design Service on good design. The WDS report, *Women's Safety on Housing Estates*, referred to in Chapter 3, incorporates a number of important recommendations concerning, in particular, the provision of lighting in corridors and stairways, the use of entry phones and the careful planning and siting of playing areas. The LWPG's report also draws attention to the issue of play space and recommends that both public *and* private playing areas be included in new family-sized housing.

An important point not explicitly raised in the local authority questionnaire responses but included by the LWPG is the need to plan new housing within mixed development schemes. It is, of course, likely that many authorities will favour mixed development. It is interesting, however, that none should include such a policy within the context of planning for women's needs. As noted by the LWPG, women frequently need to live near their place of employment. The separation of different uses serves to increase women's isolation in the home (again, this was noted in Chapter 3).

Finally, a number of reports (for example, Manchester City Council, 1987; LWPG, 1991; WDS, 1988) in making policy recommendations on the issue of women and housing, highlight the importance of women's involvement in the decision-making process. Many of the points they raise—for example, the alienation women feel from the powers of the decision making and the need for women themselves to express their own requirements—have been discussed elsewhere in terms of the wider involvement of women in the planning process. There are some, however, that relate specifically to housing.

The involvement of women in the internal design of housing (for example, in the guise of the Women and Housing Sub-Committee and the contribution by women to the drawing up of the Parker Morris Standards) has already been referred to, as has the short comings of this involvement.

Alison Ravetz (1984, p. 16) aptly sums up the situation by arguing that women were only really "commenting in what was already there, or what was about to become a *fait accompli*". In her paper, *The Home of Women: A View from the Interior*, Ravetz identifies three women who can be seen as particularly influential in the production of housing in the nineteenth century. These women, Angela Burdett-Coutts, Henrietta Barnett and Octavia Hill, worked largely to improve the living conditions of the poor. Their ambitions were not feminist and, indeed, many of the recommendations (of Octavia Hill in particular) reflected the paternalism of male designers, housebuilders and policy makers. But while they did not succeed in challenging women's traditional role within the household, and consequently their influence over housing production and consumption, they did, nevertheless, so Ravetz claims, lay the roots of women's involvement as housing managers.

Women's participation in the process surrounding housing provision has, during the twentieth century, remained marginal, whether as architects, surveyors, construction workers, building society managers or estate agents. One area where women have successfully infiltrated is in the management of housing stock.

As consumers, women in Britain have been particularly silent. Ravetz talks of women's 'acceptance' of the inappropriate design of housing generally but quotes a Mass Observation Survey, undertaken in 1943, to demonstrate the underlying (but unquestioning) interest women had in the internal and external design of housing.

In the USA and Canada this interest has found a much greater public expression. Dolores Hayden (1981) writes of the co-operative, feminist inspired settlements with their Utopian kitchenless houses as portrayed in the plans of Marie Stevens Howland and Alice Constance Austin. The ideas of these women, and others like them, encouraged women to get involved in the creation of new socialist settlements which challenged the traditional organisation of domestic life and with it male power within the household, confronting accepted notions of housing/community design as well as the gender division of labour. In a more contemporary context, Gerde Wekerle (1988) describes the attempts by Canadian women, frustrated by accepted ways of delivering and managing housing which has resulted in their becoming victims of the housing market, to take charge of their own housing in a number of co-operative schemes.

Wekerle's study focuses on ten women's housing projects in eight Canadian cities and examines the development of each programme through the various stages of decision making and construction. The work also documents women's experiences as residents living in housing co-operatives. There is no space here to go into the details of the projects—in her conclusions, however, Wekerle does include some points about the projects in general that are valuable to our understanding of women's participation in the decision-making process and in the provision and construction of housing. She notes, for example, the value to women of the opportunity of getting involved in decision making and learning the new skills that this demands. The projects, while small-scale in terms of their impact on the supply of housing, have succeeded in drawing attention to women's homelessness and to the housing problems experienced by different groups of women, giving them the strength to campaign specifically for women's needs. Having said this, Wekerle does make the point that the Canadian women's housing co-operatives can not be seen as demonstrations of distinctly feminist design solutions. While some incorporate a multi-dimensional view of housing that includes communal space for economic activity and childcare facilities, the guidelines of institutions such as the Canada Mortgage and Housing Corporation preclude the design of residential units for home-based occupations. The continuing power of such organisations demonstrates the relatively weak position of women in the decision-making process even in the context of co-operative projects.

Conclusion

This chapter has demonstrated the broad scope of a feminist analysis of housing. It has considered a number of issues relating to the design and provision of housing in Britain, identifying within this analysis some of the key questions of relevance to a feminist perspective. Women's inequality in relation to both the production and consumption of housing has been examined, particularly in relation to dominant assumptions about gender roles and the importance of the nuclear family. Having identified the major characteristics of women's inequality, the chapter went on to explore the contribution of planning policy to the maintenance of this inequality. It was argued that policy, at a national and a local level, has tended to reinforce women's housing needs by adhering strongly to the traditional assumptions surrounding household structure that have characterised past policy responses.

Many planners argue that they are unable to dictate conditions for the provision of housing given the financial and political power of the development industry. Consequently, they maintain, they are unable to do anything about the inequalities experienced by women in terms of access to housing. This, however, is to side-step the issue. It has been shown here that there *are* ways, even in the contemporary climate, in which planners can attempt, in re-defining their priorities, to address the needs of women. Unfortunately, the evidence presented here suggests that few planning departments are exploring these opportunities. As a result women remain disadvantaged not only in overall access to housing but in the quality of available alternatives.

8

Conclusions—A Future for Women's Initiatives in Planning

Introduction

This book has sought to provide a feminist interpretation of planning, offering an introduction to key theoretical debates on women's inequality and linking these to areas of practical planning policy. The massive scope of such a study has been apparent from the start and it has been necessary to leave many relevant issues unexplored. In some ways a book which focused on one particular area of planning—say transport or housing— would have allowed a more comprehensive analysis of gender inequality and policy both from a theoretical and a practical perspective. But, as has been maintained all along, what is more urgently needed is an overview of the planning system which demonstrates the perpetuation of women's subordination in the policy process and interprets this within the framework of patriarchal gender relations and the scope and influence of planning. The use of practical examples has been only partly to increase understanding of women's needs and planning policy in that *particular* area. Equally important has been the wider identification of the commitment (or lack of it) of planning to addressing women's inequality and its ability to effect real change through existing channels of power.

Problems of sheer scale have been reinforced by the difficulties in establishing boundaries—both in terms of issues affecting/reflecting gender inequality and the influence and remit of planning policy. The fact that tight lines cannot be drawn around either 'gender issues' or the limits of planning responsibilities has added further support to a broad-based approach which highlights gender issues in the context of the function of the planning system generally as well as in relation to specific policy areas.

Although one of the main motivations behind the book was the incorporation of 'live' practical planning policies, the intention was not to be prescriptive. The focus on specific policy areas aimed to give the reader an understanding of the nature of gender inequalities and of women's

174

experience in relation to chosen topics, and to provide insights into existing planning responses together with potential planning opportunities for the future. Hopefully, by identifying ways in which planning currently encourages and alleviates women's inequality in the built environment and by highlighting where improvements could be made in the future, the book will provide an impetus (however small) for those involved in planning/ decision making on the ground. It is acknowledged that the examples and suggestions made here are not necessarily appropriate in all instances, and that each situation demands a thorough understanding of local needs and circumstances as well as a knowledge of potential areas of action. By simply drawing attention to some of the responses that have been tried (as well as others that have yet to emerge from the drawing board), however, it is hoped that encouragement may be provided to those in appropriate positions of power.

Having concentrated to some considerable degree on the nature of women's inequality and the widespread reluctance and impotence of planning's response, this final chapter will consider the possibility of future change. This will entail looking at the practicalities involved in introducing initiatives for women — and will in this sense inevitably draw, as with the thematic chapters, on those authorities where attempts *have* been made to explore and implement policies to alleviate women's needs. It also demands that we consider the attitudes of authorities where *no* specific concessions have been made to either the acknowledgement of women's needs or the introduction of policy changes. In keeping with the central argument of this book — that women's inequality in the context of planning and the use of the built environment is related to their wider subordination and the operation of a system of patriarchal gender relations which maintains male power — it must be acknowledged that whatever potential exists, in terms of ideas and responsibilities, for future planning responses to women's inequality, those responses are themselves dependent on the commitment and will of those in control. This issue was raised in Chapter 4 in discussions of women's access to political power and to positions of influence in the planning system. Here the focus is, in an extension of this debate, on the attitudes and beliefs of key actors concerning existing and future commitment to pursuing gender equality. In this way, the hope is to make a broad but realistic assessment of the overall contribution of existing initiatives to the general position of women as interpreted and as dictated by the planning system.

The Adoption of Women's Initiatives

The questionnaire returns indicated that fifty two authorities in total had introduced policy initiatives within the sectors studied aimed specifically at women's needs. Subsequent chapters have discussed, in more detail, the distribution of initiatives over the different policy areas studied. The detailed analysis covers only three main policy areas, however, and as the *total* figures indicate, does not account for the full range of women's policy initiatives. In particular, no mention has been made, as yet, of what has proved to be a widely supported area, that of childcare.

It was decided, in setting out the structure of the book, that there should be no separate chapter on childcare policies as a form of 'women's initiative'. This was partly because the need for childcare is an issue which, in terms of women's position, is commonly dealt with (as has been acknowledged here) in relation to other policy areas such as employment and transport. Moreover, childcare *per se*, some would argue, should not be classed as a 'women's issue' and to see childcare initiatives automatically as *women's* initiatives is to perpetuate the gender stereotyping which plays such an important part in women's inequality. It must be recognised, however, that while we might fight for basic changes in gender roles and challenge the primacy of women's child-caring responsibilities, the reality of the situation is that the opportunities available to women within the built environment do increase considerably in many instances, with better childcare provision (see Bowlby, 1990). There is seemingly no doubt in the minds of local authority planners that childcare initiatives play a central role in addressing women's needs. Indeed, as will be demonstrated below, policies on childcare provision frequently constituted the *only* form of 'women's initiative' referred to in the questionnaire returns.

Of particular interest here is the extent to which childcare initiatives can be taken as representing a recognition by planners of the needs of women and a commitment to facilitating changes in gender roles. Care must be taken in interpreting the nature of childcare policies since not all can be seen as steps towards ensuring greater equality for women. Some may form part of (or an initial step towards) a broader strategy for addressing women's inequality, devised and implemented in the context of a comprehensive programme of initiatives. Others, however, may be seen as an end in themselves, sufficient alone to meet, or give the impression of meeting, the needs of women.

Childcare policies

Fortytwo of the two hundred and seven planning authorities responding to the questionnaire reported the development of childcare initiatives under policies for women. While this is just 15.5% of the total it is a higher rate than for any of the other policy areas considered—partly because, as noted earlier, childcare cross-cuts the other sectors (although where this happens the initiative has generally been also recorded under that section). The

TABLE 8.1 *Local Authorities With Planning*
Policies on Childcare Provision

Milton Keynes	Dudley
Cambridge	Gateshead
Hartlepool	N. Tyneside
South Lakeland	Sheffield
Plymouth	Wolverhampton
Bournemouth	Barking and Dagenham
Weymouth and Portland	Barnet
Braintree	Bexley
Chelmsford	Harrow
Southampton	Hounslow
Dartford	Islington
Shepway	Kensington and Chelsea
Leicester	Lewisham
Broadland	Merton
Norwich	Newham
Crawley	Sutton
West Wiltshire	Waltham Forest
Thamesdown	Hammersmith and Fulham
Birmingham	Richmond
Bolton	Lambeth
Manchester	Greenwich

breakdown of initiatives by authorities (see Table 8.1), as compared with other policy areas, shows a relatively more favourable response from the districts and London boroughs (18 (9.3%) and 18 (75%) respectively) but less support from the Metropolitan and County councils (6 (28.6%) and 0). The total absence of county council initiatives on childcare reflects what appeared to be a relatively common pattern, namely that policies on childcare tended to be linked to development control procedures rather than to broader strategic planning. Clearly, county planning departments perceive no role for childcare within the framework of strategic planning but rather see childcare as an issue outside their remit and more appropriately addressed in local plans and development control. This may be the case in terms of the implementation of detailed criteria for childcare facilities in the context of, for example, major retail development, but indicates a lack of commitment to the development of childcare provision as part of a broader strategy for addressing women's needs. Such a strategy would surely constitute an appropriate focus for those concerned with long term strategic planning.

The content of childcare initiatives within the local authorities where they had found support, demonstrated the same degree of variation that characterised other policy sectors, with some authorities simply registering a need to encourage the provision of childcare and others providing quite detailed guidelines and specifications. Many of the policies quoted linked the adoption of childcare initiatives to new employment development, suggesting, as part of local plan or UDP policy, the need for crèches and nurseries at places of work to allow women greater access to employ-ment. Others incorporated childcare initiatives into retailing policies stressing the importance of play areas, crèches and baby changing facilities as part of new retail developments.

Within these areas there was a considerable range in terms of the apparent strength of written policies. Most commonly, authorities dec-lared an intention to *encourage* the provision of childcare facilities, some elaborating on this statement by saying that they would look sympatheti-cally on those planning applications that incorporated nursery or baby changing facilities. Two London boroughs, Lambeth and Richmond, identified policies which advocated the use of planning agreements under Section 106 of the 1991 Planning and Compensation Act to ensure childcare facilities were included in new employment and retail develop-ment (a further borough, Islington, quoted an example where such an agreement had been used). Only one authority, however, The London Borough of Merton,[9] in responding to the questionnaire, stipulated that childcare facilities would be a *condition* of development of, in this case, retail sites. Policy S.17 of the Merton UDP states that:

> "In all new retail proposals exceeding 2,000 sq.metres gross floor space, the council will require the following facilities:
> (a) Conveniently located, wide parking spaces for the vehicles of people with disabilities;
> (b) Sheltered, lockable space for push-chairs and buggies;
> (c) Provision for customer and wheel-chair accessible toilets, seating, nappy-changing and baby feeding areas." (London Borough of Merton UDP, 1991, p. 85).

In addition to individual initiatives to encourage the provision of childcare facilities, three authorities; Birmingham, Bolton and Islington, mentioned that their planning departments were involved in the production of authority or city-wide childcare strategies. In each case these strategies incorporated at least one other council department with planners provid-ing specialist advice on the location and design of facilities together with a commitment to push for change as part of the development process. *Islington's Women's News* described their childcare strategy at its launch as follows:

> "'*Childcare: A Guide for Employers in Islington*' advises employers on a range of childcare options. The guide also highlights help the council gives to local employers who are considering childcare provision to recruit and keep staff, particularly women returners. The guide was produced by the Women and Childcare Coordinator in the Women's Equality Unit in liaison with the Economic Development Unit and the Planning and Education Departments. It is part of the Council's overall strategy of working in partnership with private employers to increase the range of childcare facilities for women with children who live and work in Islington" (*Islington Women's News*, 1991).

---

[9]Other UDps, not available at the time of writing, may also include similar statements in the final version.

TABLE 8.2 *Local Authorities with
Internal Childcare Arrangements*

Slough	Lichfield
N.E. Derbyshire	Stoke on Trent
E. Dorset	Bedfordshire
Wealdon	Gloucestershire
Tewkesbury	Hertfordshire
Reddich	Nottingham
Wychavon	Somerset
Maidstone	

They claim to be the first London Borough to produce such a guide, seeing it as essential to the provision of adequate childcare facilities for women in the Borough.

Leicester City Council provide a good example of the extent to which planning *can* get involved in the provision of childcare facilities. They supplement their policy to encourage nursery and crèche facilities with a set of guidelines on planning policies for private day nurseries. This outlines in a very simple and positive way the steps that need to be taken by people wishing to set up nurseries or become childminders. The guidelines are particularly useful in spelling out planning procedures and explaining the processing of planning applications. The Leicester guidelines deal with issues that are not solely the responsibility of planning departments and in doing so demonstrate a commitment and concern for the provision of childcare facilities that goes beyond a narrow interpretation of planning's role and influence.

In addition to outlining the existence (or not) of planning policies concerned with the external provision of childcare facilities, a number of authorities identified *internal* council arrangements for childcare which could be used by women employed by the authority. This is an issue which clearly relates to equal opportunities for women employees and to the argument that the inclusion of women's initiatives in planning is dependent on greater involvement of women in the planning profession. It is not possible to say exactly how widespread such initiatives are since the questionnaire did not ask specifically about such arrangements. Those authorities that identified the availability of council nurseries, crèches, childcare allowances etc. and there were fifteen of them in all (see Table 8.2), were generally those where no other formal *planning* initiatives existed. Interestingly, five County Councils claimed to have council organised childcare schemes—a contrast to the total lack of planning based initiatives from the counties. The availability of internal childcare to planners is taken up again briefly below in discussions around equality of opportunities in planning departments generally.

In attempting to reach conclusions on the depth and comprehensiveness of policies for women's needs it is important that, having commented quite extensively, on individual sectors, we look across the policy areas. Chapter 4 has compared the adoption of women's initiatives with the existence of a council women's committee or equality unit. So far, however, no comparison has been made between the uptake of initiatives in different policy areas. Yet such a comparison is important if we are to make any realistic assessment of the general direction of planning strategies for reducing women's inequality and of planning departments' commitment to such strategies.

The spread of planning authorities aimed at women's needs is relatively large. In all a total of 52 authorities recorded policies in the 3 areas discussed (35 in employment, 12 in housing and 33 in transport) a further 11 authorities had *only* childcare initiatives. Only 7 of these — Manchester, Merton, Waltham Forest, Cambridge, Southampton, Wolverhampton and Dudley included policies in all the sectors discussed. 12 authorities listed policies in 2 of the sectors discussed. By far the largest group of authorities, 33, however, claimed to have introduced planning policies in just 1 of the sectors.

The distribution of initiatives indicates that the recognition of women's inequality and the introduction of policies to alleviate women's disadvantages have generally taken place in a piecemeal fashion. The fact that there is a wide spread of initiatives may be seen as preferable to the concentration of policies into very few authorities — showing a broader awareness of women's needs than might otherwise have been the case. Yet the thinly distributed introduction of policies for women suggests an absence of comprehensive strategies by planners for reducing women's inequality. Where 'one-off' initiatives have been supported they represent possibly the commitment of an individual or sub-group with responsibility for a particular area rather than a department-wide acknowledgement of the importance of meeting women's needs.

Mention has already been made in Chapter 4 of the greater levels of support for policies on women's needs from the London Boroughs and Metropolitan Councils. Such authorities not only demonstrated greater numbers of initiatives but were more likely to have adopted policies in two or more sectors. The new Unitary Development Plans being prepared or recently adopted by these authorities clearly incorporate a greater commitment to devising a broad strategy on women's needs than do the vast majority of structure and local plans (see work by Greed, forthcoming, for further discussion of this point). One London borough, Lewisham, did, however, note that the now outdated Local Plan for the borough did have a separate chapter on 'women' which had been lost from the new UDP, although this in itself doesn't necessarily imply a downgrading of policy initiatives aimed at women (the debate over separatism versus integration will be looked at later). What is clear is that where women's initiatives have been supported by *districts and counties* they are much more likely, with notable exceptions, to represent 'one-off' policies than to appear as part of a broad programme directed at the alleviation of women's disadvantage.

Another interesting facet of the spatial unevenness in the adoption of women's initiatives was an apparent (although not general) urban/rural divide. A number of questionnaire respondents gave the rural character of their authority as the *reason* for the absence of planning policies for meeting women's needs. As one replied:

> "There is no specific attention given to women's issues. The department is small and the district is rural".

The respondents who made this link tend to see the sparcity of the population and the lack of resources as key factors in the poor responses of rural authorities. Exploring their comments more thoroughly and talking to other planners employed in rural areas, however, suggests that the more conservative attitudes of both officers and councillors is crucial to the status and uptake of women's initiatives. There is insufficient time here to explore this discrepancy. It does, however, serve to reinforce the importance of the attitudes of key personnel in the authority—a point to which we return at some length later in this chapter.

It is impossible here to come to any more than very general conclusions about the *content* of the policies for women that have been supported by planning departments. The level of detail and some measure of strength of particular policies has been discussed in relation to the different policy areas. Perhaps the most important observation to make on the policies as a whole is their tendency to adopt an advisory or encouraging stance. Only in a very few cases were initiatives *required* or even strongly recommended as part of the development process.

There is obviously, as shown below, a need for planners to win the support of their colleagues, councillors and the public in attempting to address what are seen as politically sensitive issues. Many of the initiatives as they currently stand, however, represent little more than a passing gesture to women's needs. One must question, in such instances, whether political acceptability has all but rendered the policies useless or whether their inclusion, however insipid, is important in at least drawing attention to the issue. On balance, the majority of planners involved in pushing for women's initiatives would support the latter argument, acknowledging that securing any gains is, in the vast majority of councils (if not all) an uphill struggle. The accusation of tokenism has been frequently used in cases where policies become so watered down as to become useless—in such cases there is a real danger of women's needs overall being actively damaged—the casual mention of equality between men and women being used to pre-empt the adoption of effective policies in a sustained strategy, policies which challenge the status quo and threaten the established power base.

The lack of strength behind many of the initiatives discussed in this book goes back in part to the question of boundaries again. As noted in Chapter 1, the scope of planning and the legitimacy with which it enters into 'social welfare' issues such as women's needs is still a matter of much disagreement both outside and inside the planning profession. The claim that planning does not have the right, the power or the resources (or all three!) to involve itself in 'women's issues' is a well-voiced argument although, hopefully, one that is, amongst the planning profession at least, more true of the past than the present. It does provide a convenient excuse, however, for those who are ignorant of the problems that women face or simply opposed to greater equality. Those councils who *have* succeeded in devising and implementing policy initiatives aimed at women's needs, demonstrate how far planning can effectively and justifiably go in supporting equality in the use of the built environment.

One area in which the intervention of planning is perhaps seen as more appropriate in the context of policies for women, and, consequently, one that finds considerable support amongst the authorities who have adopted women's initiatives, is that of design—in particular the design of safe environments. As noted in the context of specific sectors, many of the authorities who identified policies aimed at women's needs focused in those policies on issues of design. The adoption of certain design specifications are seen as important in two areas in particular—women's mobility and safety. In many instances these two are interlinked since women's fear of violence and attack may, as was discussed in Chapter 3, limit their mobility. As well as individual policies advocating planning's encouragement of the design of 'safe' environments—providing street lighting, avoiding subways and the creation of dark street corners etc.— three authorities, Southampton, Leicester and Manchester, had produced more comprehensive strategies on the contribution of design 'solutions' to women's safety. Details of these strategies have been included elsewhere and it is not the purpose of this section to repeat the comments that have been made. What is important here is to note that in no other policy sector has such a comprehensive strategic approach been adopted. Clearly, a particular role is perceived for planning in designing for women's safety, a role that derives essentially from the easily identifiable nature of problems and anticipated solutions and the fact that they fall very obviously into an area of key responsibility for planners.

There can be no denying the importance of planning's role in promoting women's safety within the built environment, nor indeed of the need to address male violence against women as part of any strategy to promote gender equality. Chapter 2 has argued the centrality of male violence to the subordination of women and any attempt, through planning policies, to reduce violence against women must be supported. Design 'solutions', however comprehensive, can provide only part of the answer. As noted in

Chapter 3 and argued by various authors (see for example Valentine, 1991; Trench, 1991) planning policies put forward to improve the safety of women on the street and in other public places can only hope to address the manifestations of male violence and not its cause. While planners must do whatever is in their power to reduce the dangers faced by women in their use of the built environment, they must recognise the limitations of design solutions as an end in themselves.

Planning for equality within the built environment is more than simply reducing the physical dangers experienced by women. It is concerned with the provision of equal opportunities for women throughout their lives. It is only through achieving greater equality in areas of employment, mobility, housing etc. that the majority of women will gain the power to fight the underlying causes of their oppression. Planning is quite clearly only *one* influence on women's overall situation but it can nevertheless, in ways that have been outlined in this book, play a part in promoting gender equality. Yet it is clear from the research undertaken in the course of writing this book—from interviews with planners and from questionnaire replies— that the planning system, as it has been defined and analysed here, is largely failing to respond to this opportunity.

Planning's reluctance to fight for women's equality is certainly a complex issue. It includes, as noted above, an uncertainty, not only amongst planners but also other decision makers and the general public, over the role of the planning process in addressing the question of equal opportunity. What is rarely recognised is that where planning fails to act positively in promoting the needs of women it frequently, almost by default, reinforces their *in*equality. Lack of finance is another factor often raised to account for planning's neglect of women's initiatives. As Chapter 4 has argued, however, it is impossible to explain the absence of planning policies aimed at women's needs without also looking at the role of women in the planning process and more broadly at the attitudes to equality of those in positions of power. We have already noted the low numbers of women who reach senior positions within the planning system. This is hardly surprising when we look at some of the attitudes that perpetuate within the planning profession. The following section considers the importance of such attitudes in undermining the general recognition of and response to women's inequality stressing the links that exist between the experiences of women *within* planning departments and the development of women's initiatives.

Women's Initiatives and the Attitudes of Planners

Despite the commitment of the RTPI to promoting equal opportunity (see the RTPI document *Planning for Choice and Opportunity*, 1989) and to the inclusion of equality issues (especially gender, race and class) in the syllabi of planning courses, the questionnaire revealed the endurance of a considerable degree of ignorance in relation to the nature of women's needs and how planning may be used in response to problems experienced by women. Perhaps more disturbing than this ignorance was the hostility expressed by more than a few respondents to the inclusion of women's initiatives.

Most common in the questionnaire responses was a surprised indignation on behalf of the respondent over the (perceived) implication that the policies of their department were in some way unequal. Several stressed that their authority was an equal opportunities employer and consequently did not discriminate either positively or negatively against *any* group. Similarly, others reported that the needs of *all* people were considered in the formulating and implementation of planning policies and that women therefore suffered no disadvantage. Such replies were accompanied by the following sorts of statements:

> "There are no formal (written) or informal policies promoting or discriminating against opportunities for women in this department. The council promotes equal opportunities and promotes/appoints on personal merit regardless of sex, race or creed."
>
> "Both men and women are regarded as people, just as all races are. We do not discriminate positively or negatively."
>
> "Having worked in the planning department for many years, I can honestly say that there is no positive discrimination either for or against women, either in the workplace or in the wider environment."
>
> "We don't discriminate between any separate groups in our policies."
>
> "I do not feel it necessary to exercise positive discrimination. All staff are treated as people—weak or strong, fat or thin, black or white. Maybe I am missing something but I regard ability and personality as dominant traits. I don't regard 'women's needs' as being any different than mens."

The attitudes of one County Council were summed up succinctly by their respondent who claimed that:

> "Your questions are irrelevant to a strategic authority."

The questionnaire also yielded a number of replies from women who are fighting a long and (often) losing battle against male sexism and the general refusal amongst colleagues to take women's issues seriously. Many replies, obviously written by women, drew attention to the absence of positive responses to the questions about policies for women generally commenting on the lack of awareness of such issues within the department. Others remarked that 'women's issues' did not feature at all in the work of the department, or were not given enough coverage and treated as a secondary issue. As one respondent from a district council wrote:

> "There is very little appreciation of how planning, especially development control, can influence life for women in the community. (There are) only two women DC officers and little encouragement to undertake initiatives to aid women. Major development where crèche/pram parks could be incorporated tends to be dealt with by senior male officers."

while another respondent from a London Borough claimed that:

> "They (women's needs) are not considered an issue; either by councillors or senior officers. With some difficulty we secured agreement to accessibility policies in the draft UDP, which will have particular relevance for women."

Many of the questionnaire replies were from planning officers who believed that the lack of concern for women's needs could be blamed on the absence of women from senior posts in the department. They saw the entrenched (usually male) attitudes of those in the upper echelons as a very real barrier to the acknowledgement of women's inequality and to the adoption of positive responses.

> "There is definitely a bias towards men in senior and principal roles, and at times the salaries are not comparable. Management expects women to be grateful for their wages but a man can ask for, and get, more."

> "(Women's issues) are not considered and it is very difficult to put pressure on when there are so few senior women and no strategy guidelines to follow."

> "I could just say, what women's issues?! but to be more constructive I still think that women are viewed as less reliable and likely to leave for family reasons. No proper provision for women with families or hoping to start a family are made. No encouragement to retrain or progress is given but then I suppose its not in the authority's interest to train clerical staff since they'd have to pay them more and at the end of the day good intentions give way to financial considerations in most authorities *unfortunately*."

One County Council respondent summed up the situation in her authority in the following way:

> "I am sure there are too few women councillors—reflecting the bias throughout the planning system. If there's no support from politicians or from senior management its difficult to implement new policies aimed at women."

In similar vein a couple of respondents noted that women always seemed to be fighting in a minority for their needs to be taken seriously. They referred to the work of one or two women as crucial in promoting women's initiatives but regretted that such initiatives were dependent on this sort of minority commitment rather than being accepted departmental practice. One of these respondents, a woman planner working in Essex, wrote:

> "I wish your forthcoming book could be made compulsory reading for all the upper levels of local authorities! As you can see (the council's) record on women's issues is pretty pathetic. Whilst recognising, in some quarters, that women can actually make quite good planners, women's different needs in the social and physical environment and the ability of women to fill the top officer positions has not quite penetrated. Makes you wonder if we've come out of the Middle Ages yet? Nevertheless, one of my (single female) colleagues is trying extremely hard to push through the barriers. For me, as a working mum, its virtually impossible to attend evening meetings so ambitions have to be suitably pegged."

The importance of attitudes 'at the top' is aptly demonstrated by the response of Bristol City Council to the questionnaire used in this research. Bristol City was sent a copy of the questionnaire in 1991 in common with all other authorities in England. The questionnaire was not returned despite a reminder being sent some weeks later. Inside information from planning officers working in the City Council revealed that the questionnaire had indeed been circulated to relevant officers—some of whom had made substantial comments—and that it had been returned to the chief planning officer. Despite internal requests for the questionnaire to be returned the CPO failed to release it. While this ommission could be put down to chance or incompetence, one interpretation is that a certain commitment to addressing women's issues further down the hierarchy was being thwarted by senior management. Interestingly, the then CPO has now been replaced by a woman. She has not, at the time of writing, yet taken up the post but there is hope that her appointment could initiate a change in approach and a greater sympathy towards 'women's issues'. The chair of the planning committee has identified a more progressive attitude emerging on the planning committee but what will happen 'on the ground' remains to be seen.

Returning to the questionnaire it should be stressed that not all comments on the attitudes to and take up of women's issues were negative. A few respondents (not surprisingly all from either London Boroughs or Metropolitan Councils) remarked that while their own authority may have some way to go in terms of the commitment to addressing women's needs, they were better than many. As one respondent from a Metropolitan borough remarked on the attitudes in her department:

> "Not perfect but a lot better in comparison to many other councils I know of."

while another noted:

> "The situation is improving as a corporate women's network has been established which will help female employees. I am hoping to produce a statistical base for the department looking at women. This will feed into the UDP review."

There was a hope amongst women from the London and Metropolitan councils that the new UDPs might provide an opportunity for greater priority to be given to women's issues. This hope is echoed in the document *Shaping our Borough: Women and Unitary Development Plans* produced by the London Women and Planning Group and referred to in Chapter 7. The document outlines the kinds of policies and proposals that could be included in UDPs, providing examples of what are seen to be 'good policies' and making a number of suggestions for their future use. It makes few suggestions, however, concerning ways in which attitudes can be changed. It is important but not sufficient, as the experience of the GLC's 'Women in London' proposals show us, to simply highlight the potential for action. There seems to be little in the 'Shaping our Borough' document that wasn't said by the GLC – why should we expect the response to be any better? As a letter published in *The Planner* (4/9/92) aptly puts it:

> "I do not share (the) optimism that the current crop of UDPs make adequate provision for gender issues. Most of them, at least in London, simply confine their equal opportunity statements to introductory chapters, which have only limited significance in a policy or implementation context."

The question of implementation is obviously of great relevance. This book has tended to concentrate on the formulation and adoption of what are seen as appropriate policies. Little has been said specifically on the implementation of policy—other than to raise the point above that commitment is required to translate policy statements into action. Several planning departments also drew attention to this issue—one London borough suggesting that it was an important stumbling block in addressing women's needs.

> "The 'Policy' side is quite well developed. The gap (as recognised) is the implementation of policy by Development Control officers and the need to develop liaison and expertise on 'nitty gritty' details about safety, childcare requirements etc."

There is insufficient time for a major focus on implementation here. It does open up a related issue, however, that requires some attention—namely how (in an organisational sense) women's issues are dealt with by departments. So far we have looked at the presence or absence of women's initiatives and questioned the level of commitment to the adoption of policies. Also important is the way in which departments approach women's issues—in particular are they seen as a separate focus of activity or are they regarded as implicit in the work of planners generally.

Separation or Integration?

Whether or not women's needs and our response to them should be seen as separate from or integral to other social issues is a complex and long standing political question that has always vexed feminists and been the source of division between feminist groups. The roots of this debate lie in the theoretical arguments discussed in Chapter 2 and concern the discrete nature of patriarchy as against other forms of social relations. Theoretical divisions have been reflected in political activism with often fierce battles between those who advocate the total separation of women in terms of political organisation and those who believe women's interests are best served 'from within' existing groups in a broad attack on inequality. This is obviously something of an extreme interpretation—in reality many groups and individuals remain somewhere between these two positions— recognising the importance of women organising separately from men and mixed groups but also acknowledging the limitations implicit in an approach that totally divorces them from existing power bases within society.

In some authorities, mostly the London boroughs, the debate over the separate organisation of women has been important in terms of the overall commitment to women's issues within the council. More often than not this has been tied up with internal disagreements within political parties (generally the Labour Party) and has been further complicated by class and racial divisions. Chapter 4 has outlined what are seen to be some of the key issues here—drawing attention to Halford's study of the relationship between the London Borough of Camden's Women's Unit and the Council's ruling Labour Party and to the history of the Bristol City Council Women's Committee. In the majority of local authorities the priority afforded to women's issues is insufficiently great as to evoke such political tensions and the debate over separation or incorporation irrelevant at a general level. Within planning departments, so the questionnaire revealed, there is some difference of opinion concerning the extent to which 'women's issues' should be dealt with separately or incorporated more broadly into the work of the department. The debate is felt, by some, to be important to the adoption of policies to address women's needs.

In many authorities it is clear that what are perceived as 'women's issues' are compartmentalised and 'hived off' from the day-to-day work of the planning department. Women's needs are therefore seen as the responsibility of one (or more if they are lucky) member of the department and all matters seen as relevant passed on to her (hardly ever him). This point was well illustrated by the fact that the vast majority of questionnaires were handed to a woman member of staff for completion. One respondent noted how this pigeon holing of women's issues resulted in their marginalisation and reinforced the need for commitment by those seen as responsible for this area.

> "Unfortunately anything that comes in about it is handed to a women to sort out; there are no women on the council's management team and women's issues are at best marginalised but generally not addressed, managed or anything else—perhaps filed!"

Another respondent talked of women's needs being seen as a 'specialist interest'—again an excuse for marginalisation and for the majority of planners to avoid getting involved.

> "Most planners (women and men) don't consciously think of 'women's issues' as relevant to their work. It is something that someone else deals with. I would prefer it if 'women's issues' were taken more seriously by senior managers—ensuring that they are taken into consideration in the preparation of *all* work in the department, e.g. reports, planning applications, briefs etc. and not just marginalised into 'women and planning' type documents which should only be the basis for further integrated action on all areas of work."

One London borough did, however, raise the benefits of at least having a named officer 'in charge' of women's issues although the point was justified by a somewhat contradictory statement:

> "It would be useful to have a specific officer dealing with women's issues in planning and the design division. Awareness of women's issues in planning and design could be more extensive and a requirement for all officers."

This issue is clearly related to the question of the links between council women's initiatives and the planning department (see Chapter 4 for discussion). If, as in the case of the example quoted above, there is no formal channel of activity for the exchange of information and ideas, then the appointment of a specific officer to provide that role may seem attractive. In general, however, the questionnaire responses were much more strongly of the view that women's issues should *not* be compartmentalised and seen as one person's (or group's) responsibility. All planners should be aware of women's needs and should ensure that they are considered, automatically, as part of the mainstream planning process. It goes without saying that some areas of planning as well as some particular topics and issues, will demand that closer attention is paid to the problems of women in particular and will lend themselves to more obvious solutions. But this does not mean that those concerned with other areas of planning can ignore the responsibility of maintaining an awareness of gender inequality and a commitment to addressing its manifestation in the built environment.

To return to the central question of this chapter — what potential exists for change? Having arrived at a number of rather depressing conclusions concerning the commitment that currently exists to the identification of women's needs and the adoption of policies aimed at alleviating those needs, we are left to speculate on the direction of future trends. Despite a few pieces of legislation (for example the Equal Pay and Sex Discrimination Acts) and the higher profile of 'equal opportunities' within local authorities generally, there appear to be very few signs of change in either levels of awareness or in the takeup of women's issues in planning. Talking to women working in planning offices it seems that the last decade or so has seen perhaps a growing acceptance of the idea that men and women have different needs within the built environment but very little evidence of that acceptance working its way through to policy adoption and implementation in anything other than a sporadic fashion.

There are, as has been shown by the research for this book, a number of examples of 'good practice' where departments have shown a real understanding of the needs of women and sustained a strong commitment to developing policies to meet those needs. But such councils continue to remain a *small* minority. Other departments have apparently learned little from those more committed councils and there has been no indication of progressive understanding or action. It is clear that some departments remain blind to women's inequality and to the potential that exists for planning to address that inequality. Evidence from the research carried out here reveals that such departments tend to represent the norm rather than an exception.

In looking to the likelihood of future change in this situation, the questionnaire sought to identify what attempts are being made by planning departments (either in isolation or as part of wider council initiatives) to encourage awareness of women's problems and needs. It identified, in particular where departments had made a commitment to education and training as a means of raising staff consciousness and encouraging positive action on 'women's issues'. Fifty one authorities claimed to run or to support staff participation in relevant courses or training events. The type of initiative supported ranged from general courses on equal opportunities to much more specialised events such as seminars or discussion groups on women and planning issues. The generalised EO courses—usually run centrally by personnel or by union representatives (NALGO) were most common (21 authorities). While such courses are clearly important in terms of promoting an understanding of equality issues and helping to ensure that gender divisions and the needs of women make it onto the agenda within local authorities, they tend not to be aimed specifically at planners or the planning profession. They may be helpful in drawing attention to 'women's issues' inside the authority—issues relating to promotion and conditions of working etc.—but less geared up to the discussion of inequality within the built environment more widely or to the identification of 'planning' solutions.

A further 16 authorities stated that they run courses on assertiveness for women and provide awareness training on violence/safety. These courses were seen as particularly important for women planners involved in site visits and presumably help to promote awareness amongst both men and women on the possible dangers facing women in their use of the built environment. From brief descriptions of such courses it would appear, however, that any responses offered to the dangers faced by women were of a self defense rather than a planning nature. Interestingly, a total of 7 authorities noted that they had recently issued women members of staff with rape alarms or mobile phones as a response to the increasing dangers which are seen to exist for women in carrying out their responsibilities as planners. These essentially short-term measures are no doubt comforting to women and indicate an important recognition on behalf of the local authority of the special dangers faced by female planners. They are, however, reactive measures that will do little if anything to promote equality of mobility within the built environment.

In 13 of the 51 authorities the courses or training events cited were specifically 'women and planning' orientated. These included events that were run outside the department/council—for example attendance at the

RTPI Women and Planning conferences and at the London Women and Planning meetings were both identified as 'Continuing Professional Development' (CPD) training of importance to women. Of the 13 departments 8 organised 'in house' women and planning seminars or training courses. These appear to represent the most important form of internal commitment to increasing awareness of planning for women's needs and the form of initiative most likely to facilitate the uptake of positive responses to gender inequality through the planning process.

Looking at the distribution of relevant 'women and planning' training initiatives between authorities, it is not possible to identify any definite relationship between the support of courses and training on women's needs and the adoption of policy initiatives in planning. This having been said, there is a concentration of the more specifically 'planning' orientated courses within the London boroughs and Metropolitan councils where women's initiatives, as we have seen, are more common. It is impossible to say whether the more enlightened approach to training has helped in creating an awareness of the needs of women and a commitment to planning responses, or whether the greater apparent sympathy towards women's issues has ensured that courses, seminars, discussion groups etc. are supported. Probably both. It is interesting that training courses for women are supported by counties and districts—many of whom have not adopted planning initiatives aimed at women's needs and some of whom appear positively antagnostic towards the suggestion. Clearly, while we could anticipate that current attitudes towards training will help to promote an appreciation of women's needs we must be wary of assuming that this will necessarily be translated into planning initiatives.

The questionnaire produced only two respondents, both London boroughs, where training on gender issues has been made compulsory for all planning staff. Presumably, in other authorities, attendance at courses is partly or wholly a matter of choice. Under such arrangements, it is unlikely that those with the most entrenched and 'traditional' attitudes towards women's needs, will be first on the list of participants. Courses are likely to remain best supported by 'the converted' and while their attendance at such events will help them to gain knowledge and confidence, it will do little to persuade those holding the sort of views quoted above of the importance or scope of planning's role in addressing women's needs.

The struggle to get gender inequalities and, in particular, women's needs recognised within the local government planning process has been, and continues to be long and painful. From the adoption of women's committees to the uptake of individual initiatives and the organisation of training, women have fought, often in very small numbers, to challenge attitudes and promote change. Some support has been provided by the RTPI—both centrally and at the branch level—and while this has provided important inspiration to many women, it has done little to stir the more entrenched views within the discipline. One questionnaire respondent identified a need for central government action suggesting that:

> "If a government circular or policy guidance were to be produced it would certainly 'concentrate' our and other LPA minds".

Given current government attitudes towards the appropriate role of planning, such a move would appear unlikely in the near future.

A lack of initiatives for women, together with the persistence of priorities which result in the creation of hostile, dangerous or simply inaccessible spaces, has encouraged women to try to influence the planning process from outside. As noted in Chapter 4, women are frequently excluded from conventional channels of decision making—especially in areas like major commercial or industrial development or road building programmes. Their way into this process has generally been through 'community' based groups, within which women often play a leading role (see above). Some of these groups are *women's* groups fighting specifically for the needs of women (and often children) and for the sorts of positive policies that have been discussed in the preceding chapters. A number of the respondents to the local authority questionnaire noted the importance of women's participation within the public consultation process—especially in relation to what are described as 'community issues'.

While women's participation in planning is generally small-scale, informal and issue specific, there are instances where their involvement represents a more broad-based challenge to the traditional priorities and assumptions of much land use planning practice. One key example is the Birmingham Cities for People Women's Group work on the re-development of Birmingham City Centre. This work, which has already been referred to in Chapter 3 above, included the production of a report, *Women in the Centre* (BCP, 1989), and is considered briefly below as one example of local women's participation in proposals for the re-development of a city centre. It identifies women's views on existing planning responses to the problems of Birmingham and suggests some alternative proposals favoured by women. The short case study also looks at the *way* in which women organised their opposition to the scheme put forward by planners and developers.

The Re-Development of Birmingham City Centre: The Involvement of Women in the Community

Plans by owners, London and Edinburgh Trust (LET) to re-develop the Bull Ring site in the centre of Birmingham in 1989 prompted the Cities for People Group[10] to launch a campaign to find out what kind of Birmingham

[10] A non-party political group which arose from a national initiative launched by Friends of the Earth and the Greater London Council to advocate the planning of cities "round people not cars."

local people wanted. From this central campaign a special focus on women emerged, reflecting a particular concern that although the proposed development included a huge retail facility, no attempts had been made to consult women in drawing up the plans. Women felt isolated from the planning process and feared that if the development by LET went ahead in its proposed form, it would result in a city centre that was disliked by and dangerous for the majority of women.

The women's group of BCP decided to organise their own questionnaire to find out more about the particular needs and preferences of women in relation to city centre re-development. They felt that a questionnaire was necessary "to give women a chance to air their views on what *they* felt about the city centre". From this questionnaire it became obvious that, in the words of BCP Women's Group:

> "women have a different geography of the city to men.....Public life is seen as male and the female geography of the city is far from the minds of those who plan and design it" (BCP, 1989, p. 7).

The research demonstrated that many women felt the city centre to be an unpleasant and alienating environment; they were dissatisfied with the shops and amenities, anxious about using subways and public transport and annoyed that the needs of the car consistently took precedence over those of the pedestrian. It is not the purpose of this analysis to discuss the detail of women's concerns about Birmingham City Centre and its re-development—they very closely mirror the sorts of anxieties reported in earlier chapters. More important here is the actual *process* of women's participation in the identification of problems and the nature of the proposed solutions.

The first step in the process of incorporating a separate focus on women's needs in the analysis of what sort of city centre the people of Birmingham want, came when a core of five or six friends (and members of BCP) produced a leaflet for distribution at a women's festival in the city. This leaflet introduced the issues and asked for further involvement from any women interested. A further five women came forward in response. Between them this core group produced a questionnaire—seeing this as essential to the identification of women's needs and to the broader process of consultation. One thousand questionnaires were circulated to known women's groups and organisations and from an initial mailing, just over two hundred responses were received.

The questionnaire generated a considerable amount of information on the needs and priorities of women in the context of city centre re-development and planning. The information is incorporated in a report, *Women in the Centre*, published by BCP. In addition to the questionnaire a public meeting was also organised by the women's group with the purpose of bringing women together to discuss their views about the city centre. This meeting, held in June 1989, was attended by over 50 women and was

addressed by Clare Short, the MP for Birmingham Ladywood, representatives from the Rape Crisis Centre and from Birmingham City Women's
Unit.

Like the majority of public meetings of a voluntary, political/pressure
group nature, the Women's Group meeting attracted mainly middle class,
white, well educated young or middle aged women. While most were
clearly interested in the issues discussed at the public meeting, few came
forward to get involved with the group more broadly or to push for the
issues which emerged as central concerns for women to be taken any
further. There remained an active core of less than 10 women who, by their
own admission, were cliquey, and organised their meetings on a social
basis which made them difficult for outsiders to participate in.

At this point the women's group of BCP had reached a critical stage.
The main concerns of women had been identified and researched. It was
now a case of trying to persuade LET to consider (and hopefully adopt) the
proposals as they had emerged. The impetus from the early meetings was
proving difficult to sustain and although members of the group held a
number of meetings with LET they could only acheive quite minor
adjustments to the proposals. The pattern of events over the next couple of
years demonstrate very clearly the powerlessness of small voluntary based
community initiatives within the development process and the almost total
refusal to look beyond or to start to question *economic* gains.

At the time of writing the LET proposals are awaiting the outcome of a
public local inquiry. Considerable changes have been made to the original
scheme and yet they are unlikely, according to the CPO of Birmingham
City Council, to come close to satisfying the concerns that were raised by
the women's group. One example of LET's insensitivity to the demands of
women as the inclusion, in the scheme, of a 3,000 space *underground* car
park — hardly in sympathy with the conclusions of the *Women in the Centre*
report.

Yet the fact that LET are, in the current economic climate, proposing to
undertake what is seen as a very ambitious scheme, is likely to appear
attractive to those wishing to bring development into the city. The BCP
women's group draw attention to the final paragraph of a report from LET
to the Planning Committee. They claim that their proposals will:

> "provide a new pedestrian environment which is attractive, interesting, safe, comfor-
> table and memorable. This will bring an additional benefit to the City in the form of
> enhanced values of property adjacent to new attractive urban spaces thus acting as
> another catalyst for further private sector investment" (BCP, 1989, p. 12).

The Women's Group believe that such statements, together with references to 'prestige addresses' for business are responding to the Council's
wish to attract business and investment to the city — a wish that is likely to
conflict with and take precedence over the needs of Birmingham people. As
the final outcome of the planning application for the LET scheme is still

not known it is impossible to say with what degree of 'success' BCP have drawn attention to women's needs. While the conclusion of the *Women in the Centre* report is hopeful concerning the willingness of the City Council to take on board many of the proposals that have come forward, they are cautious in predicting the extent to which such proposals will take precedence over possible economic gains.

On the more general level, the BCP women's group have formally disbanded, the lack of finance making it impossible for them to continue as an organisation. They were, however, successful in securing money for a 'one-off' project—the production of a video on women and planning. At the current time the women involved are intent on searching for finance so that they can continue to fight for greater equality in the built environment.

Earlier in the discussion of policy adoption it was suggested that the lack of women's initiaives in the formal planning process is frequently put down to the legal, negotiative and financial limitations of planning powers. From the position of the local government planning officer this assessment may hold some truth. One of the purposes of this book, however, has been to demonstrate how, even in the current economic and political context, this need not and indeed should not be the case. The examples given here, limited though they are, have shown the potential that does exist for the formulation and implementation of policy initiatives which aim specifically to address the needs of women. Such initiatives, it is argued, will not work in isolation but require the development of a strong framework in which equality and gender issues are prioritised. At present, opportunities and mechanisms do exist for planners to develop strategies in which women's needs are prioritised but it must be recognised that this involves challenging traditional assumptions about planning's responsibilities.

It cannot be assumed that initiatives for women can simply be 'added in' to existing policies. Commitment to meeting women's needs means a commitment to the critical examination of planning's role in the creation and maintenance of inequalities. Only through understanding how planning has contributed to the subordination of women within the built environment can we hope to devise planning strategies to overcome women's disadvantage. Of course, as has been argued all along, planning is not soley responsible for women's position within the built environment and the underlying power relations that shape the essential character of gender inequality must be acknowledged. An understanding of gender relations, however, must itself help to inform planners of the specific contribution of planning to women's inequality.

In undertaking this research it was impossible not to feel discouraged by the realisation of just how far there is to go in changing attitudes and priorities within planning. 'Women and Planning' has been on the broad agenda (in terms of recognition within the profession) now for at least seven or eight years and yet the acceptability of planning's responsibilities in meeting women's needs appears (in many areas) not to have penetrated very deeply. At the same time it was also clear that *in specific* instances progress had been made both in changing attitudes and in devising positive initiatives for women.

Local government planning is currently in a state of some uncertainty with cuts in public spending and the re-organisation of authorities taking a toll on job supply and security. Traditionally times of change have seen a movement away from less conventional, more radical initiatives and the retrenchment of existing priorities (particularly those seen as 'economic'). This must not be allowed to happen in the area of planning for women. The fragile gains that have been made must be protected. The interest and enthusiasm shown by many participants in the research for this book shows that support does exist for using the planning system to achieve a more equitable built environment. It can only be hoped that such support will be effective in overturning opposition to women's initiatives at both the local and the strategic levels, to use change positively and to work towards greater gender equality in the built environment.

References

ADAMS, R. (1985) How all men benefit from rape. In Rhodes, D. and McNeill, S. *Women Against Violence Against Women*, Onlywomen Press, London.

ARBER, S. and GILBERT, N. (eds) (1992) Women and Working Lives: Divisions and Change, *Explorations in Sociology* 39, British Sociological Association.

ASHTON, F. and WITTING, G. (eds) (1987) Feminist theory and practical policies: shifting the agenda in the 1980s, *Occasional Paper* 29, School for Advanced Urban Studies, University of Bristol.

ATKINS, S. (1989) Women, travel and personal security. In Greico, M., Pickup, L. and Whipp, R. (eds) *Gender, Transport and Employment*, Avebury, Aldershot.

AUSTERBERRY, H. and WATSON, S. (1985) A women's place: a feminist approach to housing in Britain. In Campling, J. (ed.) *Women and Social Policy*, Macmillan, London.

BARRETT, M. (1980) *Women's Oppression Today. Problems in Marxist Feminist Analysis*, Verso, London.

BARRON, R. and NORRIS, E. (1976) Sexual Divisions and the Dual Labour Market. In Barker, D. and Allen, S. (eds) *Dependence and Exploitation in Work and Marriage*, Longman, London.

BEAVIS, S. and WESTON, C. (1991) Employers pledge to reward talent, *The Guardian* 29/10/91.

BEECHEY, V. (1987) *Unequal Work*, Verso, London.

BELL, D. (1991) Insignificant others: lesbian and gay geographies, *AREA*, 23, 323–329.

BELL, P. and CLOKE, P. (1990) *Deregulation and Transport: Market Forces in the Modern World.*

Be-Ro (undated) Book of Home Recipes, Thomas Bell and Sons Ltd.

Birmingham Cities For People Women's Group (1989) *Women in the Centre*, BCFP, Birmingham.

BONDI, L. (1990) Feminism, postmodernism and geography: space for women? *Antipode* 22, 156–167.

BONDI, L. (1991) Gender divisions and gentrification: a critique, *Transactions of the Institute of British Geographers* 16(2), 190–198.

BONDI, L. and PEAKE, L. (1988) Gender and the city: urban politics revisited. In Little, J., Peake, L. and Richardson, L. (eds) *Women and Cities: Gender and the Urban Environment*, Macmillan, London.

BOWLBY, S. (1990) Mixed blessings, *Women and the Built Environment* 15/16, 7–10.

BOWLBY, S. (1990a) Women, work and the family: control and constraints, *Geography* 17–26.

BOWLBY, S., LEWIS, J., McDOWELL, L. and FOORD, J. (1989) The geography of gender. In Peet, R. and Thrift, N. (eds) *New Models in Geography* 2, Unwin Hyman, London.

BRAVERMAN, H. (1974) *Labour and Monopoly Capital: the Degradation of Work in the Twentieth Century*, Monthly Review Press, New York.

BRION, M. and TINKER, A. (1980) *Women in Housing: Access and Influence*, The Housing Centre Trust, London.

Bristol City Council (1988) *Single Women and Homelessness in Bristol*, Department of Housing, Bristol City Council, Bristol.

Bristol City Council (1992) *Draft Bristol Local Plan*, Bristol City Council, Bristol.

BROWN, R. (1992) World war, women's work and the gender division of paid labour. In Arber, S. and Gilbert, N. (eds) Women and working lives: divisions and change. *Explorations in Sociology* 39, British Sociological Association.

BROWNHILL, S. and HALFORD, S. (1990) Understanding women's involvement in local politics: how useful is the formal/informal dichotomy? *Political Geography Quarterly* 9(4), 396–414.

BROWNMILLER, S. (1976) *Against Our Will: Men, Women and Rape*, Penguin, Harmondsworth.

BRUEGAL, I. (1979) Women as a reserve army of labour: a note on recent British experience, *Feminist Review* 3, 66–82.

BRUEGAL. I. (1986) The reserve army of labour 1974–1979. Feminist Review (ed.) *Waged Work: a Reader*, Virago, London.

BRYSON, V. (1992) *Feminist Political Theory: An Introduction*, Macmillan, Basingstoke.

BULL, M. and STONE, J. (1990) When the relationship breaks down, *Housing* April, 13–15.

BUTTON, S. (1984) *Women's Committees: A Study of Gender and Local Government Policy Formulation*, Occasional Paper, School for Advanced Urban Studies, University of Bristol.

Cambridge City Council (1991) Draft Local Plan. Cambridge City Council, Cambridge.

Campaign To Improve London's Transport (1987) *Free to Move: Women and Transport in Southwark*, CILT, London.

CAMPBELL, B. (1987) *The Iron Ladies: Why Do Women Vote Tory?* Virago, London.

CAVENDISH, R. (1982) *Women Workers On The Line*, Routledge, London.

CHARLES, N. (1983) Women and trade unions in the workplace, *Feminist Review*, 15, 3–22.

CHARLES, N. (1986) Women and the trade unions. Feminist Review (ed.) *Waged Work: a Reader*, Virago, London.

CLOKE, P. and LITTLE, J. (1990) *The Rural State? Limits to Planning in Rural Society*, Oxford University Press, Oxford.

COCKBURN, C. (1977) *The Local State*, Pluto, London.

COCKBURN, C. (1988) The gendering of jobs: workplace relations and the reproduction of sex segregation. In Walby, S. (ed.) *Gender Segregation at Work*, Open University Press, Milton Keynes.

COLENUTT, B. (1990) Politics not partnership. In Montgomery, J. and Thornley, A. (eds) *Radical Planning Initiatives*, Gower, Aldershot.

CONNELL, R. (1983) *Which Way is Up? Essays on Class, Sex and Culture*, Allen and Unwin, Sydney.

CONNELL, R. (1987) *Gender and Power*, Polity Press, Cambridge.

COOK, A. and KIRK, G. (1983) *Greenham Women Everywhere*, Pluto, London.

COOTE, A. and PATTULLO, P. (1990) *Power and Prejudice: Women and Politics*, Weidenfeld and Nicholson, London.

COVENEY, L., JACKSON, M., JEFFREYS, S., KAYE, L. and MAHONY, P. (1984) The sexuality Papers: Male Sexuality and the Control of Women, *Hutchinson Explorations in Feminism*, London.

DAVIDOFF, L. and HALL, C. (1987) Family fortunes: men and women of the English middle class 1780–1850. *Hutchinson Explorations in Feminism*, London.

DAVIDOFF, L., L'ESPERENCE, J. and NEWBY, H. (1976) Landscape with figures. In Mitchell, J. and Oakley, A. (eds) *The Rights and Wrongs of Women*, Penguin, Harmondsworth.

DELPHY, C. (1984) Close to home: A materialist analysis of women's oppression, *Hutchinson Explorations in Feminism*, London.

Department of Transport (1991) *Transport Statistics — Great Britain, 1991*, HMSO, London.

DI STEFANO, C. (1990) Dilemmas of difference: feminism modernity and post-modernism. In Nicholson, L. (ed.) *Feminism/postmodernism*, Routledge, London.

DOERINGER, P. and PIORE, M. (1971) *Internal Labour Markets and Manpower Analysis*, Lexington Books, Lexington, Mass.

DUNCAN, S. and GOODWIN, M. (1988) *The Local State and Uneven Development*, Polity Press, London.

DUNLEAVY, P. (1984) The limits to local government. In Boddy, M. and Fudge, C. (eds) *Local Socialism*, Macmillan, London.

DWORKIN, A. (1981) *Pornography: Men Possessing Women*, Women's Press, London.

EDWARDS, S. (1991) Policing 'domestic violence'. In Abbott, P. and Wallace, C. (eds) *Gender, Power and Sexuality*, Macmillan, Basingstoke.

EISENSTEIN, H. (1984) *Contemporary Feminist Thought*, Unwin, London.

EISENSTEIN, Z. (ed.) (1979) *Capitalist Patriarchy and the Case for Socialist Feminism*, Monthly Review Press, London.

ELLIS, V. (1988) Current trade union attempts to remove occupational segregation in the employment of women. In Walby, S. (ed.) *Gender Segregation at Work*, Open University Press, Milton Keynes.

Employment Gazette (1992) Women and the labour market: results from the 1991 labour force survey, *Employment Gazette* September, 433–442.

ERRINGTON, A., BENNETT, R. and MARSHALL, B. (1989) Employment and training in rural areas. *Rural Development Commission Research Report No. 3*, RDC, London.

Equal Opportunities Commission (1986) *Code of Practice: Equal Opportunity Policies, Procedures and Practices in Employment*, HMSO, London.

EVANS, B. (1992) Women in planning—letter to *The Planner* (4/9/92) p. 5.

FERGUSON, A. (1989) *Blood and the Root: Motherhood, Sexuality and Male Dominance*, Pandora, London.

FIRESTONE, S. (1979) *The Dialectic of Sex*, Women's Press, London.

FIRTH-COZENS, J. and WEST, M. (eds) (1991) *Women at Work*, Open University Press, Milton Keynes.

FOORD, J. and GREGSON, N. (1986) Patriarchy: towards a reconceptualisation, *Antipode* 18(2), 186–211.

FOORD, J. and LEWIS, J. (1984) New towns and new gender relations in old industrial regions: women's employment in Peterlee and East Kilbride, *Built Environment* 10(1) 42–52.

FOORD, J., McDOWELL, L. and BOWLBY, S. (1986) For love not money: Gender relations in local areas, *Discussion Paper* 76, Centre for Urban and Regional Development, University of Newcastle.

FORREST, R. and MURIE, A. (1988) *Selling the Welfare State: The Privatisation of Public Housing*, Routledge, London.

GAFFIN, J. and THOMS, D. (1983) *Caring and Sharing: The Centenary History of the Co-Operative Women's Guild*, Co-operative Union Ltd, Manchester.

Gateshead Metropolitan Borough Council (1991) *Draft Unitary Development Plan*, GMBC, Gateshead.

GORDON, M. and RIGER, S. (1989) *The Female Fear*, The Free Press, Macmillan, New York.

Greater London Council (1983) *Women and Transport Survey*, GLC, London.

GREED, C. (1992) Women in planning, *The Planner* 78(13) 11–13.

GREED, C. (1993) Forthcoming, *Women and Planning*, Routledge, London.

GREGORY, J. (1982) Equal pay and sex discrimination: Why women are giving up the fight, *Feminist Review* 10.

GREICO, M., PICKUP, L. and WHIPP, R. (eds) (1989) *Gender Transport and Employment*, Avebury, Aldershot.

GRIFFIN, S. (1991) *Pornography and Silence*, The Women's Press, London.

HALFORD, S. (1987) *Women's Initiatives in Local Government: Tokenism or Power?* Sussex University Working Paper in Urban and Regional Studies No. 58.

HALFORD, S. (1989) Spatial divisions and women's initiatives in British local government, *Geoforum*, 20(2), 161–174.

HALFORD, S. (1991) Spatial divisions, gender relations in local areas and local politics, *The Urban Change and Conflict Conference*, University of Lancaster, September 1991.

HALL, R. (1985) *Ask Any Women: A London Inquiry into Rape and Sexual Assault*, Falling Wall Press, Bristol.

HALSON, J. (1991) Young women, sexual harassment and heterosexuality: violence, power relations and mixed-sex schooling. In Abbott, P. and Wallace, C. (eds) *Gender, Power and Sexuality*. Macmillan, Basingstoke.

HAMILTON, K., JENKINS, L. and GREGORY, A. (1991) *Women and Transport: Bus Deregulation in West Yorkshire*, Transport Studies Unit, University of Bradford, Bradford.

HANMER, J. and SAUNDERS, S. (1984) Well founded fear: A community study of violence to women. *Hutchinson Explorations in Feminism*, London.

HANSON, S. and HANSON, P. (1976) *The Daily Activity Patterns of Working Women and Men. Are They Different?* paper presented to the Association of American Geographers, Milwaukee.

HARFORD, B. and HOPKINS, S. (eds) (1984) *Greenham Common: Women at the wire*, The Women's Press, London.

HARTMANN, H. (1979) The unhappy marriage of marxism and feminism: Towards a more progressive union. *Capital and Class* 8.

HAYDEN, D. (1980) What would a non-sexist city be like? Speculations on housing, urban design and human work. In Stimpson, G., Dixler, E., Nelson, M. and Yatrakis, K. (eds) *Women and the American City*, University of Chicago Press, Chicago.

HAYDEN, D. (1981) Two Utopian feminists and their campaigns for kitchenless houses. In Kelier, S. (ed.) *Building For Women*, Lexington Books, Lexington.

HAYDEN, D. (1981) *The Grand Domestic Revolution: A History of Feminist Designs for American Homes, Neighbourhoods and Cities*, The MIT Press, Cambridge, Mass.

HEARN, J. (1987) *The Gender of Oppression: Men, Masculinity and the Critique of Marxism*, Wheatsheaf, Sussex.

HEARN, J. and PARKIN, W. (1987) *'Sex' At 'Work': the Power and Paradox of Organisation Sexuality*, Wheatsheaf, Brighton.

HILLIER, J., DAVOUDI, S. and HEALEY, P. (1988) Unpublished RTPI document on gender balance of planning courses.

HILLMAN, M., HENDERSON, I. and WHALLEY, A. (1974) Mobility and accessibility in the outer metropolitan area. Political economy and economic planning, *Department of the Environment Report*, Policy Studies Institute, London.

HOLCOMB, B. (1984) Women in the rebuilt urban environment: The United States experience, *Built Environment* 10(1), 18–24.

Home Office (1975) *Sex Discrimination: A Guide to the Sex Discrimination Act 1975*, HMSO, London.

Islington Women's Equality Unit (1991) *Islington Women's News Women's Equality Unit*, Islington Borough Council, Islington.

JACKSON, P. (1991) The cultural politics of masculinity, *Transactions of the Institute of British Geographers* 16(2), 199–213.

JENSON, J., HAGEN, E. and REDDY, C. (eds) (1988) *The Feminization of the Labour Force: Paradoxes and Promises*, Polity Press, London.

KELLY, L. (1987) The continuum of sexual violence. In Hamner, J. and Maynard, M. (eds) *Women, Violence and Social Control*, Macmillan, London.

KIRBY, D. (1992) *Employment in Retailing: Unsociable Hours and Sunday Trading*, Paper presented at the annual conference of the Institute of British Geographers, University of Swansea, January 1992.

Lambeth Borough Council (1990) *Local Plan*, London Borough of Lambeth, Lambeth.

Leicester City Council (1991) *Local Plan*, Leicester City Council, Leicester.

LEONARD, A. (1991) Women in struggle: a case study in a Kent mining community. In Redclift, N. and Sinclair, M. (eds) *Working Women: International Perspectives on Labour and Gender Ideology*, Routledge, London.

LEVISON, D. and ATKINS, J. (1987) *The Key to Equality*: The 1986 Women and Housing Survey.

LISTER, M. (untitled article) *The Guardian* April 1991.

LITTLE, J., PEAKE, L. and RICHARDSON, P. (eds) (1988) *Women in Cities: Gender and the Urban Environment*, Macmillan, Basingstoke.

LITTLE, J., ROSS, K. and COLLINS, I. (1991) *Women and Employment in Rural Areas*, Rural Development Commission, London.

London and Women Planning Group (1991) *Shaping Our Borough; Women and the Unitary Development Process*, London and Women Planning Group, London.

LUCK, M. (1991) Gender and Library Work: the limitations of dual labour market theory. In Redclift, N. and Sinclair, M. (eds) *Working Women: International Perspectives on Labour and Gender Ideology*, Routledge, London.

MACKENZIE, S. (1988) Balancing our space and time: the impact of women's organisation on the British city 1920–1980. In Little, J., Peake, L. and Richardson, P. (eds) *Women In Cities: Gender and the Urban Environment*, Macmillan, Basingstoke.

MACKENZIE, S. (1988) Building women, building cities: towards gender sensitive theory in the environmental disciplines. In Andrew, C. and Moore Milroy, B. (eds) *Lifespaces*, University of British Colombia Press, Vancouver.

MACKENZIE, S. (1989) Women in the city. In Peet, R. and Thrift, N. (eds) *New Models in Geography*, 2, Unwin Hyman, London.

MADIGAN, R., MUNRO, M. and SMITH, S. (1990) Gender and the meaning of the home, *International Journal of Urban and Regional Research* 14(4), 625–647.

MALLIER, A. and ROSSER, M. (1987) *Women and the Economy: A Comparative Study of Britain and the USA*, Macmillan, London.

MALPASS, P. (1989) *Reshaping Housing Policy: Subsidies, Rents and Residualisation*, Routledge, London.

MALPASS, P. and MURIE, A. (1990) *Housing Policy and Practice*, Macmillan, Basingstoke.

Manchester City Council (1987) *Planning a Safer Environment for Women*, Manchester City Council, Manchester.

Manchester City Council (1991) *Draft Unitary Development Plan*, Manchester City Council, Manchester.

MARKUSEN, A. (1980) City spatial structure, women's household work and national urban policy. In Stimpson, C., Dixler, E., Nelson, M. and Yatrakis, K. (eds) *Women and the American City*, Chicago University Press, Chicago.

MARTIN, J. and ROBERTS, C. (1984) *Women and Employment: A Lifetime Perspective*, Department of Employment, OPCS, HMSO.

MASSEY, D. (1984) *Spatial Divisions of Labour*, Macmillan, London.

MASSEY, D. (1991) Flexible sexism, *Environment and Planning* D9, 31–57.

MATRIX (1984) *Making Space: Women and the Man-Made Environment*, Pluto, London.

McCARTHY, P. and SIMPSON, B. (1991) *Issues in Post-Divorce Housing*, Avebury, Aldershot.

McDOWELL, L. (1983) Towards an understanding of the gender division of urban space, *Environment and Planning* D1, 59–72.

McDOWELL, L. (1991) The baby and the bathwater: diversity, deconstruction and feminist theory in geography, *Geoforum* 22(2), 121–133.

McDOWELL, L. (1991a) Life without father and Ford: the new gender order of post-Fordism, *Transactions of the Institute of British Geographers* 16(4), 400–419.

Merton Borough Council (1991) *Draft Unitary Development Plan*, London Borough of Merton, Merton.

MILKMAN, R. (1976) Women's work and economic crisis, *Review of Radical Political Economy* 8(1).

MILLER, R. (1983) The hoover in the garden: middle class women and suburbanisation 1850–1920, *Environment and Planning* D1, 73–87.

MITCHELL, J. (1971) *Women's Estate*, Penguin, Harmondsworth.

MORGAN, G. and KNIGHTS, D. (1991) Gendering jobs: corporate strategy, managerial control and the dynamics of job segregation, *Work, Employment and Society* 5(2), 181–200.

MORRIS, R. (1992) Happy birthday opportunity 2000, *The Guardian* 27/10/92, p 11.

MORRIS, R. and WINN, X. (1990) *Housing and Social Inequality*.

MUNRO, M. and SMITH, S. (1989) Gender and housing: broadening the debate, *Housing Studies* 4, 3–17.

NICHOLSON, L. (ed.) (1990) *Feminism/Postmodernism*, Routledge, New York.

OC, T. and TRENCH, S. (1992) *Making Cities Safer for Women*, paper presented at the Anglo-German conference on Women and Cities, University of Hamburg, April 1992.

OLIVER, K. (1985) Women's public transport needs: a survey of local authority transport planners outside London, *GLC Women's Committee Bulletin* 25, 39–41.

OLIVER, K. (1988) Women's accessibility and transport policy in Britain. In Whatmore, S. and Little, J. (eds) *Gender and Geography. Contemporary Issues in Geography and Education*, 3(1)

PAHL, J. (1985) Refuges for battered women: ideology and action, *Feminist Review* 19, 25–43.

PAIN, R. (1991) Space, sexual violence and social control: integrating geographical and feminist analyses of women's fear of crime, *Progress In Human Geography* 15(4), 415–431.

PALM, R. and PRED, A. (1974) A time geographic perspective on problems of inequality for women, *Working Paper 236*, Institute of Urban and Regional Development, University of California.

PHILLIPS, A. (1987) *Divided Loyalties: Dilemmas of Sex and Class*, Virago, London.

PICKUP, L. (1983) Travel issues in women's job choice: an activity based approach. Unpublished Ph.D. thesis, University of Reading.

PICKUP, L. (1988) Hard to get around: a study of women's travel mobility. In Little, J., Peake, L. and Richardson, P. (eds) *Women In Cities: Gender and the Urban Environment*, Macmillan, Basingstoke.

PICKUP, L. and TOWN, S. (1983) *A European Study of Commuting and its Consequences*, Report to the European Foundation for the Improvement of Living and Working Conditions, Co. Durham.

POLLERT, A. (1981) *Girls, Wives, Factory Lives*, Macmillan, Basingstoke.

PUNTER, J. (1990) *Design Control in Bristol, 1940–1990*, Radcliffe, Bristol.

PUNTER, J. (1991) The long term conservation programme in central Bristol, *Town Planning Review* 62(3), 341–364.

RAVETZ, A. (1984) The home of woman: a view from the interior. In Attfield, J. and Kirkham, P. (eds) *A View from the Interior: Feminism, Women and Design*, The Women's Press, London.

REDCLIFT, N. and MINGIONE, E. (eds) (1985) *Beyond Employment: Household, Gender and Subsistence*, Blackwell, Oxford.

REDCLIFT, N. and SINCLAIR, M. (eds) (1991) *Working Women: International Perspectives on Labour and Gender Identity*, Routledge, London.

RHODES, D. and MCNEILL, S. (eds) (1986) *Violence Against Violence Against Women*, Onlywomen Press, London.

RICH, A. (1980) Compulsory heterosexuality and lesbian existence, *Signs* 5(4), 191.

RILEY, K. (1990) *Equality for Women: The Role of Local Authorities*, Local Government Studies, Jan/Feb, 49–68.

ROBERTS, M. (1991) *Living in a Man-Made World: Gender Assumptions in Modern Housing Design*, Routledge, London.

ROBINSON, O. (1988) The changing labour market: growth of part-time employment and labour market segmentation in Britain. In Walby, S. (ed.) *Gender Segregation at Work*, Open University Press, Milton Keynes.

ROWAN, C. (1982) 'Mothers Vote Labour!' the state, the Labour movement and working class mothers, 1900–1918. In Brunt, R. and Rowan, C. (eds) *Feminism, Culture and Politics*, Lawrence Wishart, London.

ROWBOTHAM, S. (1989) *The Past is Before Us: Feminism in Action Since the 1960s*, Pandora Press, London.

ROWBOTHAM, S., SEGAL. L. and WAINWRIGHT, H. (1979) *Beyond the Fragments*, Merlin Press, London.

Royal Town Planning Institute (1989) *Planning for Choice and Opportunity*, RTPI, London.

RUSSELL, B. (1991) *Silent Sisters: A Study of Homeless Women*, Hemisphere Publishing Co., New York.

RYDIN, Y. (1993) *The British Planning System: An Introduction*, Macmillan, Basingstoke.

SARSBY, J. (1985) Sexual segregation in the pottery industry, *Feminist Review* 21, 67–94.

SAUNDERS, P. (1982) *Why Study Central–Local Relations?* Local Government Studies, March/April, 55–66.

SCOTT, J. (1988) Deconstructing equality versus difference: or the use of post structuralist theory for feminism, *Feminist Studies* 14, 33–50.

SEARGENT, S. (1980) Masculine cities and feminine suburbs: polarised ideas, contradictory relations. In Stimpson, C., Dixler, E., Nelson, M. and Yatrakis, K. (eds) *Women and the American City*, Chicago University Press, Chicago.

SEGAL, L. (1987) *Is the Future Female? Troubled Thoughts on Contemporary Feminism*, Virago, London.

SEGAL, L. (1990) *Slow Motion: Changing Masculinities, Changing Men*, Virago, London.

SNELL, M. (1979) The Equal Pay and Sex Discrimination Acts: their impact in the workplace, *Feminist Review* 1.

SNELL, M. (1986) Equal pay and sex discrimination. In Feminist Review (ed.) *Waged Work: A Reader*, Virago, London.

SNITOW, A. (1990) A gender diary. In Hirsch, M. and Fox Keller, E. (eds) *Conflict in Feminism*, Routledge, New York.

Southampton City Council (1991) *Women and the Planned Environment: Design Guidelines*, Southampton City Council.

SPELMEN, E. (1990) *Inessential Woman: Problems of Exclusion in Feminist Thought*, The Women's Press.

SPENDER, D. (1984) *There's Always Been a Women's Movement This Century*, Routledge, London.

STANKO, E. (1988) Keeping women in and out of line: sexual harassment and occupational segregation. In Walby, S. (ed.) *Gender Segregation at Work*, Open University Press, Milton Keynes.

STEAD, J. (1987) *Never the Same Again: Women and the Miners' Strike*, Women's Press.

STIMPSON, C., DIXLER, E., NELSON, M and YATRAKIS, K. (eds) (1981) *Women and the American City*, University of Chicago Press, Chicago.

STONE, M. (1988) *Equal Opportunities in Local Authorities: Developing Effective Strategies for the Implementation of Policies for Women*, Equal Opportunities Commission, HMSO, London.

SUMMERFIELD, P. (1989) *Women Workers in the Second World War: Production and Patriarchy in Conflict*, Routledge, London.

SYMON, P. (ed.) (1990) Housing and divorce, *Studies in Housing No. 4*, Centre for Housing Research, University of Glasgow.

THORNLEY, A. (1991) *Urban Planning Under Thatcherism: The Challenge of the Market*, Routledge, London.

TIVERS, J. (1978) How the other half lives: an historical study of women, *AREA* 10(4) 302–306.

TRENCH, S. (1991) Reclaiming the night, *Town and Country Planning*, September 1991, 235–237.

TRENCH, S. and JONES, S. (1990) *Planning for the Safety of Women in Cities*, paper presented at the Association of European Schools of Planning, Reggio Calabria, Italy, November, 1990.

VALENTINE, G. (1992) *Towards a Geography of the Lesbian Community*, paper presented at the Anglo-German Conference, Women and the City, University of Hamburg, April 1992.

VALENTINE, G. (1992a) Images of danger: women's sources of information about the spatial distribution of male violence, *AREA* 24(1), 22–29.

VALENTINE, G. (1992b) *Coping With Fear of Male Violence: Women's Use of Precautionary Behaviour in Public Space*, paper presented at the Anglo-German Conference, Women and the City, University of Hamburg, April 1992.

WAGNER, P. (1984) Suburban landscapes for nuclear families: the case of green belt towns in the United States, *Built Environment* 10(1), 35–41.

WAJCMAN, J. (1983) *Women In Control*, Open University Press, Milton Keynes.

WALBY, S. (1986) *Patriarchy at Work*, Polity Press, Cambridge.

WALBY, S. (ed.) (1988) *Gender Segragation at Work*, Open University Press, Milton Keynes.

WALBY, S. (1990) *Theorizing Patriarchy*, Blackwell, Oxford.

WATSON, S. (1986) Women and Housing or Feminist Housing Analysis. *Housing Studies* 1, 1–10.

WATSON, S. (1988) *Accommodating Inequality: Gender and Housing*, Allen and Unwin, Sydney.

WATSON, S. and AUSTERBERRY, H. (1986) *Housing and Homelessness: a Feminist Perspective*, Routledge and Kegan Paul, London.

WEBSTER, J. (1990) *Office Automation: The Labour Process and Women's Work in Britain*, Harvester/Wheatsheaf, London.

WEKERLE, G. (1980) Women in the urban environment. In Stimpson, C., Dixler, E., Nelson, M. and Yatrakis, K. (eds) *Women in the American City*, Chicago University Press, Chicago.

WEKERLE, G. (1984) A women's place is in the city, *Antipode* 16(3), 145–153.

WEKERLE, G. (1988) Canadian women's housing co-operatives: case studies in physical and social innovation. In Andrew, C. and Milroy, B. (eds) *Lifespaces: Gender, household, employment*, University of British Colombia Press, B.C.

WEKERLE, G., PETERSON, R. and MORLEY, D. (eds) (1980) *New Space for Women*, Westview, Boulder, Colorado.

WHATMORE, S. (1991) *Farming Women: Gender, Work and Family Enterprise*, Macmillan, Basingstoke.

WILSON, E. (1983) *What's To Be Done About Violence Against Women?* Penguin, Harmondsworth.

WILSON, E. (1991) *The Sphinx in the City: Urban Life, the Control of Disorder and Women*, Virago, London.

WITZ, A. (1988) Patriarchal relations and the patterns of sex segregation in the medical division of labour. In Walby, S. (ed.) *Gender Segregation at Work*, Open University Press, Milton Keynes.

Women and Geography Study Group (1984) *Geography and Gender*, Hùtchinson, London.

Women and Transport Forum (1988) Women on the move: how public is public transport? In Kramarae, C. (ed.) *Technology and Women's Voices*, Routledge, London.

Women's Design Service (1988) *Women's Safety on Housing Estates*. Women's Design Service, London.

Author Index

Subject Index

while this theoretical concern with difference is not sustained